STREAMLINES

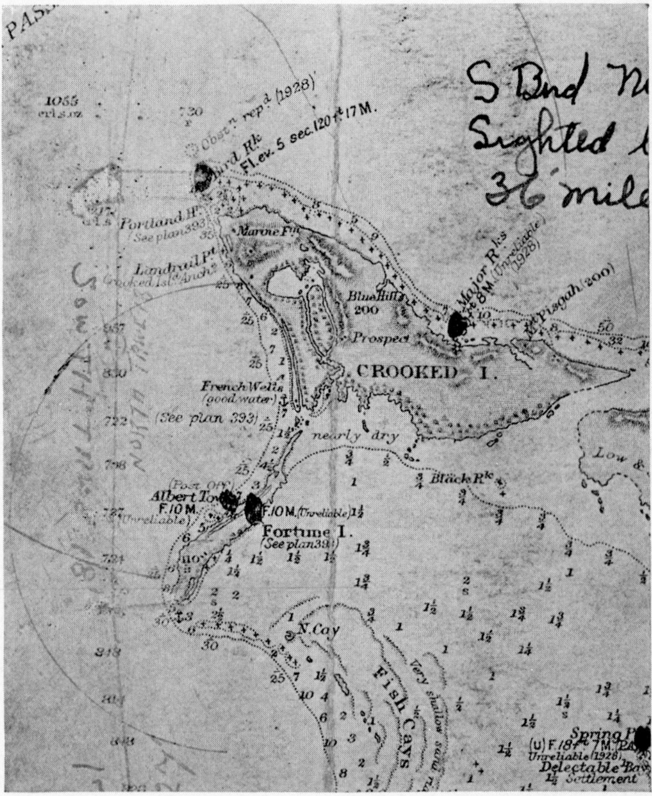

THE ORIGINAL OF "TREASURE ISLAND"?
(Admiralty Chart of the Bahamas. See p. 115)

Christopher Morley

STREAMLINES

MCMXXXVI

DOUBLEDAY, DORAN & CO., INC.

Garden City, New York

PRINTED AT THE *Country Life Press*, GARDEN CITY, N. Y., U. S. A.

FIRST EDITION

For BUCKMINSTER FULLER, scientific idealist . . .
["Whose innovations proceed not just from technical dexterity but from an organic vision of life."]

And EDMÉ ZIEGLER, Grand Vizier . . .
["Prime Minister or privy counsellor; from Arabic *wazir,* to counsel; *wazara,* to bear burdens."]

Almost all these testimonies were first printed in the *Saturday Review of Literature*. The note on *Tristram Shandy* was written as preface for the Limited Editions Club issue of Sterne's classic. The soliloquy here entitled *Mind Erosion* was broadcast by radio in a symposium under the auspices of the League for Political Education. The note on *Eumenides of Book Collecting* was written for *The Haverfordian*. The memorandum on *Style* is reprinted from *Designed for Reading*, an anthology published by The Macmillan Company. The courtesy of these various publishers is appreciatively acknowledged.

CONTENTS

CONTENTS

ILLUSTRATIONS

STREAMLINES

BROADWAY LIMITED

THE LONG WINDOWS were clear and luxurious above the shadowy platform (Union Station, Chicago). In the observation car and in armchairs and staterooms people were already at ease; comfortable people in the peace of Sunday afternoon; confiding people, who take things for granted. Secretly, even humbly, I felt my difference. Promoted for the moment from passenger to crew, I was putting on complicated overalls under the tuition of Mr Burchiel, road foreman of engines. Like a god, even my life was not my own. I had signed for the Pennsylvania Railroad an extensive document, renouncing for unwitting heirs, executors, assigns, publishers, attorneys and innkeepers, any peevishness they might feel if things went wrong.

5493 was waiting. I looked at her with the uncomprehending adoration one feels for locomotives; beside whom, since they have grown in the same scale as ourselves, every man is still a small boy. She was monstrous and cast a darkness about her in the dull November light. She had lately come from the rebuilding shops where they gave her an enormous new tender, a huge black shiny tank, smooth and flush. "Not a rivet in it," said Mr Burchiel proudly. Her driving-wheels stood as solid as foundations of a church. (I wish Euclid could have seen them.) It's not possible, the mind said, that such weights can be moved. Yet it is done, by the dynamics of hatred. Here are a tank of inert water, a box of angry fire. They damn each other by instinct, cat and dog. Of their indignation, hiss and growl and spit, those wheels make 90 miles an hour.

But there was no time for moralizing, even the most naïve. Mr Burchiel and I climbed into the cab where Mike Bruicks the engineer and Louis Koch the fireman were ready. It is Mr Burchiel's job to supervise the actual operation of locomotives on that division, but with two old-timers like Bruicks (43 years in service) and Koch (30 years) it is companionship rather than check-up. Mike was on his padded bench, with the forward gaze that an engineer never varies. You wonder, after watching for a couple of hours, if he *can* look sideways. He'll shout you an occasional remark, but his eyes don't leave the track. Louis was studying his fire. He trod a foot pedal which split the up-and-down doors. 5493 has automatic stoking. The coal, crushed small, feeds up into the furnace through a worm onto a flat plate, where jets of steam spray it to all parts of the fire. It looked pretty complete combustion to me, but Louis was not satisfied.

We all had a drink of very cold water from the spout of a can, and while I was still wondering where to stow myself we were off. *High Ball* (not like the drink, but both words accented equally) Louis shouted as each signal bridge came in view. Mike, on the other side of the cab, tallied it by repeating. There was just room for me to perch on the forward end of Louis's bench. The main steampipe which heats the whole train toasted my knee. Two lighted lanterns were at my feet, and I could see the track ahead. I'm afraid I tried to look as professional as possible, so as not to give anything away, but I was in a haze. A great black slope of dials, gauges, handles; a blur of hissing, piping and rumbling clatter;

a desire not to be in the way, is all I remember for the first few minutes.

"There's the Central flyer" said Louis as we pulled into Englewood (7 miles from Union Station). "She's due to leave just as we get in." It was our great rival, the Century, in whose cab I had ridden once. Yes, she was just pulling out: from the cab of 5318 her engineer waved me a gesture of admiration for our new tender, much bigger than his own. 25 tons of coal and 35000 gallons of water that tender carries, and 5318 was evidently envious. I waved back, conveying (I hope) that that's the sort of thing we're used to on the Pennsy. I saw *Van Twiller, Star Light* and other cars rumble by. Our own—*Herald Square, Craigie House, James Whitcomb Riley,* etc.—would get to Penn Station tomorrow morning at the same moment the others were slowing into Grand Central. "Water Level Route?" later said Mr Grady, the Train Secretary. "Sure, it's a good slogan—but they have to go 60 miles farther than we do."

After Englewood Louis began overhauling the fire. He was breaking up great clogs of soft gold with a long hook. He got the feed valve adjusted to his pleasure. *Clear* was now his shout instead of *High Ball.* He was courteous to yell in my ear everything he thought I ought to know; but as the noise increased I'm afraid I missed some of it. For, as she began to show what was in her, she opened a vast roaring undersong strangely like the yell of a thousand bagpipes. The long musical blast of the whistle was almost continuous; the traditional two longs, a short, a very long. Raving imperative in the first bellow (defiance, warning, blasphemy complete; the bearded damnation of a god in righteous fury) then dying away, in the final wail, to deep-chested sorrow for all the fools of the world. You saw them skipping across the track at suburban stations, or wondering whether they could make it at an unguarded country crossing. Mike let me take a hand at the cord. "The point is," he remarked crisply, "to keep blowing right up to the crossing."

"You'll see some of the things we have to worry about," said Mr Burchiel, who was keeping an eye on everything. "Some of these automobile trucks are getting big enough so you know it when you hit them." Almost at that moment Louis, who was on the other side of the cab, gave a yell. It was too late for me to see—we had gone 1000 feet before I could stumble over—but he told me that a car, trying to beat the train, had pulled up about three feet away from us. It was Sunday dusk; many cars on the roads, all pushing home for supper. I hope that unknown citizen of Indiana ate his with a thoughtful heart. As for me, I've stuck my nose into the gale as the Broadway roared over several hundred crossings. If they'd take my word for it, she can't dodge, and there 'd never be another Sunday night supper congealing uneaten.

Somewhere beyond Gary we got an Approach—three lights in diagonal instead of vertical (I hope I remember this right?)—which means reduce speed, with possible stop on the next two-mile block. I believe it was the Grand Trunk line which had to be crossed. The next signal was Clear and we picked up again, but it had cost us two or three minutes. In a schedule which allows 16½ hours for 908 miles every hour must count for over 55 miles; every minute lost puts one a mile behind. Now, as the brown prairie faded into dusk, Mike began to let her travel.

Leaning out beyond the narrow glass screen I could just glimpse the great knuckled cranks flying like horse's hoofs. Her huge black shape, stretching high before us, was too big to see in full. Louis's shout of *Clear* at every 2-mile signal had a note of exultation. The great pile of coal behind us sank visibly. In the vibration a good deal would jostle down onto the steel floor, and every now and then Louis would shovel it up, a long throw (higher than his head) back into the tender. "A hell of a way to fire an engine," he said jocularly—"backwards." A man who has fired an engine by hand speaks of the automatic method as a writer speaks of Kipling or Chaucer. You should hear Louis pay homage to the Standard Stoker. In his days of hand firing he "shovelled enough coal to cover the whole United States four feet deep." Now we were coming to the upgrade towards Valparaiso. "But it's all upgrade when you're firing by hand. Want to see some pink ice-cream?" he says, and opens the fire doors. The furnace, big as a bungalow, is a naked vault of flame, the brick lining seems actually soft and lathery with molten blaze, an absolute essence of fire, white below, and rose above. A terrifying sight, from which you recoil in dismay. "Pretty good," says Louis; and Mr Burchiel's comment is "That's perfection." In such a furnace there is no bed of coals, the fuel is deified before it ever touches bottom.

We roar through Valparaiso, a white island of snow in the dun twilight. That town, Louis tells me, gets snow earlier and keeps it longer than any other in the State, no one knows why. There's another upgrade towards Plymouth, we frolic it at 75. It's growing dark. A broad band of light spreads before us. A locomotive, like a motor-car, dims its lamp as it approaches another train, not to dazzle the engineer. Louis, squatting behind, takes just as good care of me as if I'd never signed that release. He knows every curve by heart (there are some, even though it looks so straight on the map) and if I happen to be standing up gazing stupidly about he warns me to hang on. When we meet another train he pulls me away from the window. Sometimes something sticks out or flies off. The grade near Plymouth is called Over the Hill to the Poorhouse. There actually *is* a poorhouse; Louis points it out as we yell by. "Where all the railroad men go when they get through."

Over the hill we really shove. I see Mike scooping out his watch. I find mine too, fumbling under flaps of overall. We're going to be a couple of minutes late? Louis denies it. "Mike and I are never late. We get there on time if we tear the wheels off her. She has what it takes."

She has indeed. Clear . . . Clear . . . even that routine cry, in Louis's Indiana tenor, sounds a tone of mystic fervor, orgiastic surrender. As far as I'm concerned, reason is gone; this is religion. Against the fan of light her great bulk looms monstrous, a raving meteor of sound and mass. "He's giving it to her," Louis screams. "How fast?" I yell. "About ninety." The sliding window creeps back in the wind pressure, the lighted lanterns dance over my feet . . . all the world's bagpipes sing, the airbrake valve chirps like a bird in a cage. . . . Mike's eyes are ahead, his hand forever on the brake. The mind can't think forward or back, is fulfilled with Now . . . I cannot analyze, this is mere ecstasy; madness under control (like writing *Moby Dick*) . . . Mr Burchiel, satisfied and watchful, pulls out the hose and wets down the coal in the tender. I even see him, over by the canvas curtain that flaps in hurricane, take the water can and swig a drink. There are lights of cars along the road. Through towns and stations we rip like—like tearing a strip of muslin; but there are no likes for this. Villages are torn open, blotted out by our frightful howl; they are wiped away, blown behind us. Louis turns the feed valve a trifle. Soot is gritting under my goggles. Clear . . . Clear . . . When the whistle yells we fly through a fog of steam, blinded for the moment by our own safety cry. *Keep —Out—ofmy—Wa-a-a-a-a-y.* I lean out as far as I dare. We take a curve that surprises me. It doesn't seem to bother her. Yes, says Louis, "she's an easy-riding engine."

The lights of Fort Wayne. This is the division town, home of Mike and Louis and many other railroad men. 5493 will go on to Crestline, but Mike and Louis stop here, and bring Number 5 back to Chicago at 4.55 tomorrow morning. And, incidentally, they don't speak of the "Broadway Limited." That's passenger and publicity talk. To them she's Number 28.

I think the only serious error I made was in saying "What's the population of Fort Wayne; about 50,000?" Louis was outraged. "My God, we've got 120,000; and one of the finest courthouses you ever set foot in."

Fort Wayne . . . 148 miles in 140 minutes; including a stop at Englewood and the first 20 miles through crowded tracks. Just time to shake hands, wriggle out of overalls. Better get on in front and walk through, said the conductor, we're pulling out. He suggested that I clean up at the first washroom, but I insisted on walking all the way back to *Herald Square*. I wanted Colatine to see my face.

Extraordinary how quiet it was back in that drawing room (the next-to-the-last car). Even though I knew 5493 was again doing comfortable 70, you'd think we were scarcely moving. Till we went forward to the diner, we couldn't even hear her whistle.

I woke, as I always do by instinct, just where I would have wished; at the Horseshoe Curve. The night had cleared, there was a wide lace of stars, and Orion watching the track of the Milky Way. At Altoona (3 A.M.) locomotives were standing in sociable groups in the dark; white aigrettes of steam rising into stillness; somehow like Queen Mary's hat. On the next track was a long string of silent cars, the maroon and gold of my first love, and a figure standing watchful with a lantern at the tail end, faithful as Orion. He was doing his job, and I rendered him a private unsuspected homage.

And again, a little after seven, I looked out as we flashed in sunrise, swiftly by familiar names. Strafford, Wayne, St Davids, Radnor, Villanova, Rosemont, Bryn Mawr, Haverford. Then I remembered. When I was a boy at college I lived three years in a dormitory not far from the Main Line. My bedroom window was toward the tracks, and twice a day a certain train caught my ear. About 7:15 in the morning it came rocketing down from the West, making a final sprint for Philadelphia. That was time to get up; just enough warning for the bath and the half-mile walk to breakfast. And about 7:15 in the evening, a strong difficult puffing upgrade, outward bound for names of mystery—incredibly remote—Harrisburg, Pittsburgh, Chicago. That was just after supper; it meant time to sit down under the green glass lampshade and get to work. Vaguely, as one turned to physics or French or Chaucer, that heavy rolling passage was both sedative and spur. It meant fidelity to task and yet also escape into fancy. Ohio, Indiana, Illinois; the Alleghanies, the Horseshoe Curve, the Johnstown Flood; all these were in that receding sound, with click and tremor of the rails narrowing in moonlight towards Bryn Mawr.

That train was, and still is, the Broadway Limited.

CHRISTMAS CARDS

I THINK (with a shooting pain of guilt and envy) of those remarkable people who have their Christmas all thought out a long way ahead; their greeting cards designed and printed; this very evening they are sitting down with an address list and a big sheet of stamps. They are addressing envelopes, and unless they have a highball handy their tongues are dry from licking.

I save Christmas cards, not in the scientific spirit of a collector but because I cannot bear to throw away such cheerful little symbols of kindness. One day last summer, moving a lot of papers out to the Knothole, I came across a box in which a mass of old cards had been stored. In curiosity I began to tabulate them according to their pictorial themes. Everything else in the world has been analyzed and index-numbered by sociologists, why not Christmas cards? —in which humanity surely expresses, without reserve, its most honorable yen. So I took 200 of them and here is how they broke down, classified by their dominant art-subjects:—

Snow Scenes (rustic)	15
Stage Coaches	10
Ships & Galleons	10
Waits & Carols	9
Scotties	9
Other Dogs	2
Crinolines & Top Hats	7
Monks & Medieval	6

Holly	6
Poinsettias	6
Victorian Scenes	5
Musical Staves	5
Churches	4
Xmas Tree Designs	4
Candles	4
Children	4
Reindeer	3
Drinking Scenes	3
Wise Men & Camels	3
Open Fireplaces	3
Hospitable Doorways	3
Star Designs	2
Mistletoe	2
Snow Men	2
Angels & Cherubs	2
Santa Claus	2
Rabbits	2
Mice	2
Birds	2
Sheep	1
Stables & Mangers	1
Clowns	1
Yule Logs	1

These (141) were all picture cards of public circulation, available to anyone. The rest of the 200 were individual and original: drawings or photos made by the senders, or private reproductions of art works, maps, reprinted poems, quotations, or what not. The fact that nearly one-third of the cards were original interests me; and perhaps the next comment the amateur Keyserling would make is the triumph of the Scottish terrier. He is abreast of Waits and Carols and will shortly overhaul even the stage-coach.

I was about to say that I had never yet seen an automobile on a Christmas card; then I remembered that the local oil company sent me one last year, showing a tank-truck faithfully delivering in a blizzard. But that was a commercial halloo and so not included in my study. It is evident that the Christmas card is becoming more secularized; some of the festival's most traditional symbols are now low on the list—the good old Yule log for instance. Observe how the sailing ship has risen as a figment of romance; and how poinsettia has caught up with holly. Among the original sketches I remember particularly a humorous one from good C. F. B. entitled "Bringing in the Yule Log in Scarsdale," and showing two plumbers carrying in a new radiator. Another friend's greeting, ingeniously expressive of Depression times, was printed in bright red ink on an ordinary brown-paper grocery bag. Among so many pretty tinsels and gay reminders nothing was somehow more touching to rediscover than a little folder in which a child had bound up her school exercises, with their grades and corrections, as homage for her mother.

Certainly in no merely statistical mood one looks over old Christmas cards. One finds the names of those from whom we shall never have greetings again. Some are lastingly associated in our minds with Christmas. I think of our good Oliver, hater of crowds and hurry. In the last years he was not able to do much shopping himself; it became a ritual for various friends to perform his errands for him on Christmas Eve while he waited at a 45th Street pub. His emissaries gathered there, one by one, with the parcels; unconstitutional old-fashioneds (themselves as bright as Christmas cards) were ranked deep on the board; very likely Oliver would feel the impulse to go through his unrivalled repertory of unseemly tricks with matchsticks (I wish I could remember them) and we would all get home late. More than one of that group collapsed his own tree that night as he trimmed it, but still holds both cause and occasion dear. One of my favorite Christmas cards was that on which Fred Van de Water reprinted his grand carol for sinners—

Ye drabs and wastrels, near and far,
Who pay propriety sore toll,
Our tavern portal hangs ajar
Our spits turn blithely o'er the coal.
Ho, tipplers! Loud your catches troll,
Ho, diners! Bravely crack your jest—
He loves good laughter, stout and whole
Who comes, each Yule, to be our Guest.

And I find, among these strangely varied reminders, a shabby little German Christmas card, postmarked in Hoboken years ago, from a young Dutch sailor who died in hospital not long afterward. A "casual of the sea" indeed was Tommy, simple and kind and helpless; he still lives in McFee's fine novel which was partly named for him.

There will be, this year as usual, the average quota of reprints of old Washington Irving's Yuletide passages; which are pleasant enough, but I have long hankered to see someone try a little Alexander Smith for a change. If I find myself getting unwarrantably cheerful I turn to *Dreamthorp* and read: "Is not the public air which European nations breathe at this moment, as it has been for several years back, charged with thunder? Despots are plotting, ships are building, man's ingenuity is bent, as it never was bent before, on the invention and improvement of instruments of death."—And this was written at Christmas 1862.

But, for myself, there's another piece—also actually written on Christmas Day—that I've long wanted to reprint. It's the preface to the great Constitutional History by old Bishop Stubbs (not Bishop when he wrote it). Stubbs succeeded Goldwin Smith as regius professor of history at Oxford when Smith went to the young wilderness of Cornell in 1866. He lived at Kettel Hall, which I dimly remember as an appanage of Trinity College. I presume that like most good churchmen and professors he had a large family, but even on Christmas Day (1873) while waiting for the goose and port wine he fled the uproar of the young Stubbses and took to his study. There he wrote words that students may well consider.

"The History of Institutions," wrote Professor Stubbs, "cannot be mastered,—can scarcely be approached,—without an effort. It affords little of the romantic incident or of the picturesque grouping which constitute the charm of History in general, and holds out small temptation to the mind that requires to be tempted to the study of Truth. But it has a deep value and an abiding interest to those who have courage to work upon it. It presents a regularly developed series of causes and consequences, and abounds in examples of that continuity of life, the realization of which is necessary to give the reader a personal hold on the past and a right judgment of the present. For the roots of the present lie deep in the past, and nothing in the past is dead to the man who would learn how the present comes to be what it is. Constitutional History has a point of view, an insight—and a language of its own; it reads the exploits and characters of men by a different light from that shed by the false glare of arms, and interprets positions and facts in words that are voiceless to those who have only listened to the trumpet of fame. The world's heroes are no heroes to it, and it has an equitable consideration to give to many whom the verdict of ignorant posterity and the condemning sentence of events have consigned to obscurity or reproach. Without some knowledge of Constitutional History it is absolutely impossible to do justice to the characters and positions of the actors in the great drama; absolutely impossible to understand the origin of parties, the development of principles, the growth of nations in spite of parties and in defiance of principles. It alone can teach why it is that in politics good men do not always think alike, that the worst cause has often been illustrated with the most heroic virtue, and that the world owes some of its greatest debts to men from whose very memory it recoils."

At the bottom of this fine statement the excellent man wrote "Kettel Hall, Christmas Day, 1873," and then repaired, I hope, to his dinner with strong appetite.

But we were speaking of Christmas cards. Mr Ogden Nash's witty plea for the old-time card instead of the modernist fantasia is worth reading aloud to your own particular group on the Day itself, "Epstein, Spare That Yule Log!" he calls it, it's in his volume *The Primrose Path.* Until some greeting card company is canny enough to offer us a composite design containing all the elements listed above (it should be a big selling number) I must confess a special affection for cards that suggest some kind of heat. To those who live in the country the primal problem of keeping warm still has much meaning. I often think of that superb little verse of John Crowe Ransom's, *Winter Remembered:*

Two evils, monstrous either one apart,
Possessed me, and were long and loath at going:
A cry of Absence, Absence, in the heart,
And in the wood the furious winter blowing.

But of all the prepared or printed sentiments for a Christmas salute, I have found none that seemed more graceful than a quotation from Stevenson on a little card from England. It is taken, if I remember, from one of his dedications: "This little paper traveler goes forth to your door charged with tender greetings. Pray you take him in." Perhaps, in the humility of one who seems too inefficient to prepare blazons of his own, that may stand as our Christmas homage.

And the procrastinator is always in good company. I smile at a leaflet among these I've been studying—the printer was reproaching Mr Bruce Rogers, on December 24, 1927, for not having his Christmas card laid out in type yet. "Why," said Mr Rogers, "I'm just starting on my card for 1925."

BIG MAILS GALORE

A YOUNG WOMAN (eleven years old at that time) was full of the lively curiosity which is so sweet and commendable in her nature. Also I think she felt that her small pocket-money was insufficient for her large and legitimately growing desiderations. In a corner of some magazine she saw a promise that if she would send her name she would receive Big Mails, Personal Big Mails, A Giant Mail, Big Mails Galore, Propositions Samples and Opportunities, Not Less Than $25 a Week, A Big Opportunity Package. Whether she also sent 10 cents I don't know: it would embarrass me to ask her. But the Big Mails Galore came along all right. I know because part of my job is to call at the post office.

Fortunately, by the time the Big Mails began coming the young woman's interest had gone on to something else. (Skis, or a bow and arrows.) So when I saw a mass of circulars lying around, my own curiosity, which extends to every kind of printed matter, began to operate. It might interest you to know what the Opportunities are that these Personal Big Mails offer. What would have happened if she had accepted the offer "A TEN POUND package of Big Mail for 25c if you will pay express charges" I dare not conjecture.

I'm not going to go into this in full detail because I still believe that print has valuable reticences. A complete study of these matters would perhaps be Mr Postmaster Farley's job if he weren't so busy sending out postage stamps. But here are some of the exciting possibilities the young woman might have considered if she hadn't been, fortunately, out skiing.

Pittsburgh, for 35c, would send her "one pound of old novels, foreign coins, war money, stamps, propositions." (How many old novels in a pound?) Revere, Mass., would print 1000 circulars for 40c. Chicago would guarantee her against loneliness with 30 names of gentlemen pen-pals and a Mystic Photo of future mate; also her own photo, size of a postage stamp, gummed to stick on letterheads, "will say much more about you than any wordy description when writing to pen-pals." Racine, Wis., wants her to show her loyalty to the President: "Beautiful silk banner shows a determined Roosevelt portrait and his signature." The director of the Association for the Development of Mind Power (Chicago) offers her (for $1) five long Letter-Lectures that will remove fear and ignorance and lead to a New Life. Does her life lack color? (How little he knows her!) These Miracle Working Letters will get her anything she wants. "Written in plain language. Nothing technical. Free from religious prejudices yet in perfect harmony with religious beliefs." Not all the goodly company of Envelope Stuffers are so free from sectarianism, though. Here's St Croix Falls, Wis., offering an 8-page pamphlet (10c) to prove that baptism does not necessarily mean complete immersion. But the fellow who is really savage is Hermansville, Mich. What has happened to make Hermansville so sore at the Catholic Church? I should not care to quote all his raving absurdities. He thinks the celibacy of the clergy is all hooey and breaks into verse:

Lives of all the priests remind us
They could lead much better lives
And departing leave behind them
Widows who have been their wives.

For 10c each he offers a list of books such as *Crimes of Priests; Priestly Celibacy Exposed; Vile Attacks Upon Women; The Priest and the Devil; The Sad Story of Mary Lily.* What happened to Mary Lily "within shouting distance of the palace of Cardinal Gibbons," he says, "chills one's heart and makes your blood run cold. Buy this book in quantity and circulate it." But *Behind Convent Bars,* which costs 25c, seems to be even more vigorous. I'm saving these obscene oddities until I meet Tom Daly, my favorite Papist, so we can have a good laugh together. Perhaps it's not just a laughing matter. *Priest & Women,* "a book for women only . . . for real red-blooded American women who do their own thinking" I suppose I (nor the Postmaster General) will never see. But this fellow in Hermansville is one of the boys who want us to know The Truth. He has some kind of a magazine, *The Yellow Jacket* (20c a year) "The best paper published to swat liars & leaches, hypocrits and humbugs, demigogs and dastards."

Let's get into more agreeable fields. Here's an optimist, in Akron, O., who wants my young woman to go into publishing. "Publish a Paper of your own. Only 50c Capitol needed." Braggs, Okla., wants her to start a hamburger stand, 25c full instructions; "for 10c extra I will give you a recipe of a Cidar without apples. Mix at night, ready to drink in the morning." Tampa confides that "Florida is the virgin mail-order field," will mail our circulars to his own sucker list for $2.50 a thousand. "Personal services of all sorts, private letters remailed, nontechnical information about Florida." Emmet, Nebr., offers us a 160-acre farm. Coral Ridge, Ky., says "Have your circulars mailed with mine to the Farmers." St Croix Falls, Wis., will tell us where to buy "$60 Monuments for less than half that price; geneological books if you are interested in your family history; Used Correspondence Courses, and Mexican Jumping Beans." Grandma's Herb Company, right here in New York City, wants to send us a bottle ($1.50) of tonic bursting with iodine, "phospherous," and all the mineral salts. Ambler, Pa., for $1 will teach us how to earn money writing for the papers. Erie, Pa., knows how to print photographs on handkerchiefs, scarfs or neckties. Williamsbridge, N. Y. C., will remove our superfluous hair. Oyster Bay, L. I., wants us to be Sane about Sex. Sarnia, Ontario, if we are lonely and blue, "will make you happy for the rest of your life if you will send only 10c for particulars." Goldsboro, N. C., will supply back issues of a Nudist Magazine, nothing left out.

Raritan, N. J., writes that he has heard of the young inquirer as "an experienced and capable salesman with a good following among the retail dealers." He would like her to represent him in a line of sundries and has a Foolproof Profit Sharing Plan. "To keep the curiosity seekers from receiving this plan, I am offering it to you for $2.00." An expert chemist of Evanstown, Ill., will send (for 35c) our choice of any one of several "monster formulas" from which we can make a Blood Cleaner Compound or medicines for Rheumatism, Heart, Kidneys, Asthma, Hay Fever, Female Tonic or "unpleasantness of entire nervous system" (which might happen to almost anyone). Los Angeles is more cheerful and sociable.

For only 3 cents they'll send us not only Big Mail but "a mouthpiece which fits roof of mouth, with it you can sing like a canary or squeal like a pig. Astonish and Mystify your friends." Deep Gap, N. C., an appropriate place, wants us to start a Pen Pals Correspondence Club. For 10c they will give "full instructions of this fascinating business."

You divine, shrewd as you are, that I'm only delicately turning over the more mentionable fragments of this mass of rubbish. The various appeals, on grounds of health and prophylaxis, to credulity or prurience, I pass by; though I admit a scholarly curiosity about Cincinnati's offer of "The Immortal Dante Trip Through Hell, 25 Different Cards, 25c." A fellow in Cleveland advertises "Better Printing for Less Money" but doesn't prove it in his list of wares, which include "$ Powder Compats for 2c, Toote paste 3c per tube, My 6 Nights in a Nudist Camp," and goes off the deep end with fine climax, "600,000 Articles." A "bookshop" in Fort Atkinson, Wis., will send "The Book of Forbidden Knowledge" for half price if you'll write down the names and addresses of five married friends ("your name not told to others"). Looking through this mess of tripe I thought at first that New England was not represented in the jackal industry, but here's Worcester, Mass., supplying (10c, sealed to adults) BIG VALUE HOTCHA BUDGET—"stories, poems, cartoons, also 100 Paris Type Pictures." Gloucester, Mass., has two pornograph peddlers who must be busy rivals. One has the Movie Card Picture Girl, "Just What You Been Looking For, Red Hot for Men Only"; the other the Red Hot Mae West Shimmie Dancer For Only 10c, and he adds with simple candor, "A Dirty Story, only 5c." And here, at the bottom of the pile, is Hermansville, Michigan, again. Perhaps the anti-Catholic stuff hasn't gone so well for now he's picking on Hollywood. *Harlotry of the Silver Screen* (12c postpaid) "unmasks the immorality of Hollywood and lifts the lid on the vilest ulcer in American life."

But whether ulcers have lids or not, I'm growing a little weary. I fall back with relief on the pleasant fellow in Buffalo who offers a First Aid Antiseptic Kit for 25c; the Novelty Jobber in Miami Beach who sells aspirin and opals; the excellent lad in Greensburg, Indiana, who (for $1) will give a chemical formula for saving furnace coal. Most of all, I think, I like the sportsman in Sudbury, Ontario, who says, "Surprise Your Friends by sending them Postal Views of Sudbury, the Nickel City." All you have to do is buy 5 picture cards of Sudbury for a quarter. Write your message, address them, and send them back to this gentleman with postage. He mails them for you, and all your friends think you've been staying in Sudbury. Naturally they're surprised.

I like, too, the honest merchant of Des Plaines, Ill., who says bluntly "What I am after is names. I represent a manufacturer who is willing to pay a good price for same."

But the name of that young woman isn't going to do you much good, old shark. Because I go to the P. O. myself, and after this Big Mails Galore and Opportunity Packages drop right in the basket.

MANDARIN AND MATHEMATICS

I FOUND the Old Mandarin at ease in his high penthouse apartment, which he has furnished somewhat in the likeness of an Eastern pagoda. On the table beside him were sheets of paper scribbled with figures and diagrams; he was shaking two dice in an ivory cup. One of his troupe of serving maids, pretty as a humming bird in bright silk jacket and trousers, brought us wine and sunflower seeds. Glass windbells tinkled on the terrace as we sat looking over the summits of Manhattan.

The old man's pleasure in mathematical diversions is well known, so I was not surprised when he handed me the ivory vase. "Throw the dice," he said, "without letting me see them. Remember the two numbers."

I did so, carefully concealing the result. It was the kind of throw I usually get; I am notoriously unlucky in anything to do with reckoning.

"Choose either of the numbers," he said, "and multiply it by five."

"O. K.," I said. "That's easy."

"Add seven, and then double the result."

"Wait a minute. . . . Yes, all right."

"Now add the other number."

"You mean the one on the other die?"

"Yes."

"O. K."

"What is the result?"

"46," I said.

"Then the numbers you threw were 3 and 2."

"Correct, but how do you know?"

"The formula is $10x + 14 + y$," he said, "x and y being the numbers you threw. I substracted 14 from the 46 you mentioned. That gave me 32; therefore 3 and 2 were your digits."

I adore that sort of thing, but I never can remember those ingenuities. One good night's sleep always wipes out all the arithmetic I've ever known.

"I'm glad to find you in a mathematical mood," I said, "because I've got a problem of my own. We want to give a big dinner party; big for us, that is. There are to be ten couples at a circular table. Our table is rather inconvenient, every other person has to sit with a leg between his knees; a table-leg, I mean. So we've fixed the positions of the ladies, each of them has a seat unimpeded by legs, the question is how to arrange their husbands with proper attention to social precedence and yet so that no husband adjoins his wife."

"When is the dinner?" he asked.

"Next Monday."

"You had better postpone it a year or so," he said, "until you can get some good book on the Theory of Numbers and study it. The problem involves what are called Discordant Permutations; even W. W. Rouse Ball, in his fascinating work on *Mathematical Recreations,* says the solution is far from easy. Offhand I should say there are something like 439,000 possible arrangements."

"That is the sort of thing that must make life in the White House very difficult," I suggested.

"Do you remember," said the Old Mandarin, "the classical story of the Chinamen and the American missionaries? A junk in the Yellow Sea, overwhelmed by a typhoon, had to lighten its burden. There were 15 Chinese and 15 missionaries; it was agreed that half of these 30 passengers must go overboard to save the lives of the rest. All 30 stood in a circle and every ninth person, beginning the tally with an old Manchu accountant who was the senior aboard, was to be thrown into the sea."

"It must have been a very slow-moving typhoon to allow for all that counting," I remarked.

"The true scientist," admitted the Old Mandarin, "prefers his experiments under exact laboratory conditions. However, the disturbance and confusion of the gale made it possible for the Manchu (an ancestor of mine, by the way) to place all the Chinamen in a certain order. Imagine the distress of the missionaries when they discovered that every ninth man was one of themselves. However, they were brave men and did not discover the trick until too late."

"I don't believe it's possible," I said.

"Try it for yourself," said the Old Mandarin. "The arrangement was as follows. C stands for Chinaman and M for Missionary." He drew a slip of paper from the inside of his skull cap; on it was written:—

CCCCMMMMMCCMCCCMCMMCC
MMMCMMCCM

"I always keep this memorandum with me," he added, "in case a similar emergency should arise in the subway. But Mr Rouse Ball (whose book should be in every prudent man's library) says it may be remembered by the sequence of the vowels in this jingle: *From numbers' aid and art, never will fame depart.* In that couplet the vowels *a, e, i, o, u,* represent 1, 2, 3, 4, 5. The arrangement therefore is *o* Chinamen, *u* Missionaries, *e* Chinamen, and so on."

"Wait for baby," I said. "Give me a minute to check on that."

"In times of political and economic disturbance," he continued, "it is pleasant to recline upon the bosom of mathematics, the nearest approach to Certainty obtainable in a life of illusion. The ancient problems of the Duplication of the Cube, the Trisection of an Angle, the Quadrature of a Circle, are innocent and heavenly employment. Is it not agreeable to know that your mind is going through precisely the same calculations which absorbed Euclid, Archimedes, Newton, Descartes? But I like my mathematics also tinctured with fancy. That is my Oriental bias, I suppose. The very phrase, a Chinese Puzzle, has become proverbial. There is a modern toy, you can buy it on Sixth Avenue, which unwittingly reproduces an Eastern legend. In this amusement you are given a wooden stand with three pegs; on one peg are placed a number of flat rings or disks of graded sizes, the biggest at the bottom. You are asked to shift these rings, singly, from one peg to another, never allowing a ring to rest on one smaller than itself, until the whole pile, in its proper order of sizes, is transferred to a different peg."

"Yes, I know those things," I said. "Horrible."

"The formula is $2^n—1$," he replied calmly, "^{n} being the number of rings or disks. Viz., if there are 8 rings on the peg it will require $2^8—1$, or 255, individual transfers to complete the shift. But all this is merely a childish recollection of an old Hindoo theology."

He rose ponderously from his chaise longue and took down a roll of parchment manuscript from a shelf. This was getting rather deep, I thought, and while his back was turned I swallowed a large hooker of the wine. I never dare do more than sip at it while he is watching. But it washed down some of the sunflower seeds (I've never learned how to crack them properly between my teeth) and I coughed violently. He looked gravely reproachful. He disapproves my rough Western manners.

"In the great temple at Benares," he read from his Chinese scroll, "beneath the dome which marks the center of the world, rests a brass plate in which are fixed three diamond needles, each a cubit high and as thick as the body of a bee. On one of these needles, at the creation, God placed sixty-four disks of pure gold, the largest disk resting on the brass plate, and the others getting smaller and smaller up to the top one. This is the Tower of Bramah. Day and night unceasingly the priests transfer the disks from one diamond needle to another according to the fixed and immutable laws of Bramah, which require that the priest on duty must not move more than one disk at a time and that he must place this disk on a needle so that there is no smaller disk below it. When the sixty-four disks shall have been thus transferred from the needle on which at the creation God placed them, to one of the other needles, Tower, temple and Brahmins alike will crumble into dust, and with a thunderclap the world will vanish."

There's always something about the Old Mandarin's solemnities that carries conviction, you feel that he very likely knows about things. And lulled by the odd tune of his voice, and the pungent wine, perhaps I had not closely attended the details of his reading. But I distinctly understood about the thunderclap and the end of the world.

"Gosh, O. M., that's serious."

He smiled. "I myself have not tarried over the computation," he said, "since Rouse Ball has figured it for us. He points out that the number of single transfers the Brahmin priests must make (that is, 2 to the 64th power minus 1) will take them quite a while yet." Again he drew a slip of paper from the scarlet silk lining of his cap. "The exact figure is 18,446,-744,073,709,551,615.—I like to keep a few data of that sort with me as consolation in moments of anxiety.

"So in the meantime," he said benignly, "we may still have leisure for amusement."

"Not with arithmetic," I pleaded; "all those digits give me fidgets."

"An approximate rhyme," he said. "I think I can use that. To reward you for being patient I'll show you figures of another sort. I've been doing some choreography. You'll be pleased to learn that by the theory of Numbers, 1934 ought to be a good year. I'll show you."

He rang a gong, and out onto the terrace ran a company of the little Chinese serving maids. There were sixteen of them and each carried a placard with a number. The Old Mandarin must have rehearsed this on purpose to surprise me, for they fell into position without command, gaily marking time to an insinuating music from a Chinese zither. They took their places in serial order, so that the numbers appeared thus:—

1	2	3	4
5	6	7	8
9	10	11	12
13	14	15	16

The Old Mandarin winked at me; when he condescends to so Western a gesture I know he must be feeling cheerful.

"Come on, digits, do your fidgets," he said. "Inner and outer squares, reverse diagonals!"

There was a gay shifting and twirling as the dancers, in tune to the music, performed a graceful evolution. On the stroke of a gong they came to rest in this order:—

16	2	3	13
5	11	10	8
9	7	6	12
4	14	15	1

"Now," said the Old Mandarin, "remark the gaieties of numerology. Take each row horizontally."

Little man, what now? I wondered.

"I mean, add up the numbers," he explained.

"This is certainly the way to teach arithmetic," I agreed. "They all add up to 34."

"Try them vertically."

The result was the same.

"Try the diagonals."

Still the same.

"The groups of four at each corner of the square."

Each of these quartets broke away in turn from the square, turning to music and grinning at me while I totalled their numbers. Still it was 34 each time.

"The four corners of the whole square."

Same result.

"The four in the middle of the square."

Same.

"The middle ones on opposite sides of the square."

Ditto.

While I was still marvelling at these figures the music struck up again and I found that the girls had taken a new order:

1	15	10	8
12	6	3	13
7	9	16	2
14	4	5	11

Moving prettily in time they broke the figure into various quartets each of which always gave the same total. Horizontals, verticals, diagonals, the four corners, the four in the center, the groups in each corner of the big square—in fact each component four in the whole arrangement, and even the middle pairs on opposite sides, always added to 34.

"It looks to me like sorcery," I muttered. "There must be an omen in it."

"Surely there is," said the Old Mandarin. "Every hundred years."

Of course it isn't everybody who has his own troupe of dancing girls to help him work out mathematical fantasies. With a wave of his hand the old sage dismissed them and they skipped away giggling and chattering. I left him leaning over the parapet studying the pattern of New York and sighing, I suppose, for more calculus to conquer.

For my own part, I was late getting back to the office; absent-mindedly I told the taxi-man 34th Street.

STREAMLINES

(*Thoughts in a Dymaxion Car*)

1

I'M INTERESTED in this not just as a car, which is relatively unimportant,

But as a symbol of what is forward in every phase of living.

Not only in locomotion, architecture, shipbuilding, but in morals and manners, clothes, religions, even in literature

We grope for the Streamline: to reduce unnecessary wind resistance.

2

The foreigner gazed with clear alien eyes on the subway advertising-cards.

Reading left to right they bespoke as follows the preoccupations of the American folk:—

Thinning hair, fluent nose, chapping skin, tussive throat, Parmesan breath,

The crumbling gum, the aching shoulder, the flattened foot, dandruff on the collar and every form of intestinal stoppage.

O God, he cried, rescue this people from ill health and self-abasement:

Dan Chaucer and Will Shakespeare took a little dandruff in their stride.

3

Don't be angry if you didn't hear from me.

Think, if you love me, how I revelled in my rare and precious silence.

"STRANGE SUGGESTIONS NATURE GIVES US"
(B. F. and Dymaxion)

4

Give me something to imitate, cried the American architect, planning Gothic cloisters and bell-towers for New England colleges.

Give me something to imitate and I'll make you the damnedest biggest finest most original imitation in the world.

5

I am appalled by the Yiddish Hurdler on the new terrace of Rockefeller City.

Under those glorious perpendiculars of building, under such strong simplicities of height, this gesticulating gigolo in gilt.

By the fountains of Babylon I sat down and roared with laughter.

Take him away, John, and carve instead Virgil's great motto for your City

Which you will find near the end of the VIth book of the *Aeneid*:—

DESCRIBENT RADIO ET SURGENTIA
SIDERA DICENT

6

Learn to play poker, said the Loch Ness Monster to the boys at a Quaker college;

It is closer to life than theories of economists.

And he was infinitely right.

7

I saw one man accidentally bumped by another in a crowd hurrying toward the subway; and he looked round quickly with a perfect gesture of anger; and then he saw how enormously large the other man was; suddenly he didn't look angry any more.

8

Here let me rest:
I will never again have to hunt for the phrase that would be best.
I am interred,
And need not search for the perfect word.
To be explicit,
If I did I'd probably miss it.
But write this on my tomb:
I knew the difference between Who and Whom.

9

Gasoline trucks had to learn the simple device of trailing a chain on the ground to carry off the static
So they wouldn't explode when they nozzled a filling station—
And this, like everything else, has its parable for poets.
Keep a few rusty links of prose in touch with earth, old son,
Or you'll carry one spark too many at the wayside pump.
Nothing ever happens anywhere that isn't a lesson to poets.

10

The Concise Oxford Dictionary speaks of the whale's *breach* as a "leap clear out of water"; I believe students of cetaceans still question this? But if lexicographers had to go out and hunt whales to be certain there would be no time to compile the dictionary. I am fond of obscure questions however; a man of joy delights in the unanswerable. If I were a typographer I would manufacture twice as many question-marks as any other symbol.

11

Long ago I learned the valuable habit of always putting my head under water in the bath-tub. I learned it as a child, aboard ship, because that was the best way to hear and relish the deep rhythm of the engines.

And when one becomes a man one must not put away childish things but continue them, for in an apartment house in New York I discovered that with my head under water in the tub, by some oddity of plumbing and simple physics I could hear what was being said in the apartment downstairs. This was of much service to me in a novel I was writing.

I overheard such odd things that I almost forgot to come up for air.

The student of sociology must learn to put his head below the surface and listen.

12

Wallowing in the tub, natural association of ideas brings me back to the breaching whale.

I see him rising, huge dark shadow, through the greengloom deeps. He comes to the surface, sighs and welters, rolls me his hopeless eye.

Like Melville, like the *Concise Oxford,* I thought sentimentally, romantically, of the whale. I supposed that when he thrashes the sea to silver with his mighty flukes he was moved by pride and power, pure *joie de baleine*. No, alas; my kinsman, L. N. M., who knows about whales, says it's the parasites that cause it. The whale has the itch. Whale-lice infest him, crab his huge suet, chew the soft gums of his mouth and his big speechless tongue and cause him furious grief. He thrashes the sea to silver with his mighty flukes in hope to rid this nuisance. His trouble is no more lovely than that of a hog under a rail fence.

Perhaps just so the great whales Shakespeare, Dante, Goethe, breached in the ocean of literature and thrashed dark seas of ink to silver foam. The parasites were at them: lice of dearth and anger, ambition and disease, laughter and desire. Hail parasites, collaborators!

13

I read in the newspaper
That a lady on a Singapore cruise
Was standing dreamily beside the vessel's rail
When a flying fish flew down the back of her dress
And she slapped the face of the gentleman next her.
So do we interpret the merriments of Nature
In terms of our trivial etiquette.

14

What strange suggestions Nature gives us, which we are too stupid to perceive.

Every 24 hours she abolishes consciousness and forgives us the impudence of thinking.

Might this mean we should begin every day with a new mind; draw the fires, clean out the clinkers, abolish memory, start afresh?

Yet we try to dilute the pure whiskey of Today with the gassy soda of Yesterday.

To make appointments for the future is spiritual suicide.

15

There is no end to the anomalies of human species. I know a man who split without flinching the most grievous intellectual dilemmas,

And accepted sociological paradoxes that would have frightened Pareto or Nick Butler,

But always thought something was going to jump out at him

From the burners of the gas-stove.

16

People who dress show-windows

Wear felt moccasins and tread softly.

This applies also to cabinet officers, bishops, head waiters, and magazine editors.

As the great philosopher Jules Verne said in his satire *Round the Moon:*—

"When a purely speculative discovery is announced to the public, it cannot be done with too much prudence."

"SKY CHIEF"

WHEN you know you're going to fly you watch the weather. The best place to get a look at it in our office building is from the washroom window. (That washroom has more influence on literature than you might suppose. There literary editors retire for occasional seclusion, to gaze off over one of Midtown's relatively open spaces, toward the steeps of Radio City, and make up their minds about some book they're reading.) It was a mild soft afternoon. As the bather feels the water with his hand before plunging in, I like to reach out and feel the air before flying. That air (I wished it could realize it) was going to carry considerable responsibility. I reached out and sifted a handful of it. It didn't seem thick enough. But walking through Times Square a few minutes later there was a tepid little breeze which felt more palpable; comfortingly supportive. The air of Times Square always comes thicker: densified by news, movies, gasoline vapor, showmanship and halitosis.

At the Air Desk, Penn Station: you study the folder. TWA's little picture of the pilot with a gyroscope inside his head is always comforting. You reflect that, in your own affairs, a little more gyroscopic control would be desirable.

In the limousine en route to Airport: the good old motto on the Main P. O. is an appropriate salute. *Not snow nor rain nor heat nor gloom of night stays these couriers on their appointed rounds.* Herodotus, isn't it? Why wouldn't *The Spirit of Herodotus* be a good name for a plane? Sometimes you almost wish something would stay those chauffeurs a little. On that amazing ramp that runs from Jersey City to Newark they touch 60, in plentiful traffic. The only part of flying that scares one is getting to the airport.

One of the passengers hadn't been in New York for thirty years, though he lived there as a young man. To leave N. Y. by air you Stoop to Conquer; I mean, you first go through the Holland Tunnel. This gave the 30-year absentee a great kick. Funny thing: as soon as I heard him speak about 30 years ago a thought of the old Haymarket (a rowdy resort) lit in my mind. And a moment later he asked about it, as oldtimers always do.

Airport: There she is, great silver Douglas, eagerly nosed up. NC13711, Skyliner *City of Chicago*. The 7 and the 11 should take the curse off the 13. (Air passengers are always superstitious.) Weight, please? (200) Weight of baggage (25). Wish I'd had time to get my hair cut when an air news reporter said *All you need is a fiddle-case*. The reason one postpones haircuts is probably because in the barber's chair one simply *has* to think; there's nothing else to do. And though we all pretend to hanker for "a chance to think," doesn't it rather scare us, really?

Air news reporters always assume that everyone boarding the Sky Chief is on the way to Hollywood on a contract. They are shocked when you let them down by saying you're only going to Columbus.

She turns her silver snoot toward sun. A roaring tryout of motors. Just this one moment I always keep my mind inboard. I try not to think anything heavy, or remember how the Peruvian pelicans used to struggle to get into the air. Those Newark marshes are unpleasantly near. This is the time to be busy with small concerns: fasten belt, accept gum from trim little hostess (did you know that they're not allowed to weigh more than 118, nor to marry within three years), admire one's own little stock of gadgets—air vent, reading lamp, ash tray with little convenient tab for stubbing out cigarette. Best of all, read one's favorite relaxation, Mrs Roosevelt's Day. How she can take it, you say to yourself; I guess I can carry on a while yet. Or something even more amusing: Congressman Fish seriously replying to some kidding by Heywood Broun. Mr Broun had stepped too far: had suggested that Fish wasn't a good football player at Harvard . . . careful: you'll almost find yourself saying It takes all kinds to make up a world . . . so look outside, (this is Seat 11, port side, just aft the wing) you're over Morristown, fields brown and pinkish in sinking light, dim wash of green in hollows.

Only 25 minutes out and over the Delaware already. On neatly striped roads below are cars creeping along; one passes another, both apparently crawling; this is faintly amusing to watch, probably because you are thinking that *they* are supposing they are going fast; and to see someone else thinking absolute what *you* (from taller purview) consider only relative, is always satisfying to the interior gyroscope.—You try not to say to yourself that the cars look "just like ants." But they do, exactly.

5.35 p.m. Pretty little points of light, red and green for port and starboard, brighten the ends of the broad silver wings. Approaching hills of Pennsylvania. Hostess lady (herself a delicious streamline figure) has also brightened herself with rouge, you observe. This is all part of the psychology of air traffic; but to be thoroughly nautical it should be rouge on left cheek and green on right. She is fastening the tray to your chair-arms for supper. Those marvellous cardboard picnic-boxes are the best fun of all; and shrewdly served to divert the mind from the bumpier bits of the Alleghanies. She yaws a bit (the plane, I mean), sways gently (myself I like it; feel of a yacht in a quarterly run of swell). She comes down the aisle (the hostess, I mean) with the big thermos flask, genuflects beside you like a priestess, carefully pours out hot coffee. We're crossing the Susquehanna, 6.05 p.m. Quite a little bump just then, as we skim over a solid chunk of air (it probably bounced up from the capitol at Harrisburg). Hope she won't spill that very hot coffee on her hand. There's a scar above the thumb. "Did you get that pouring coffee?" "No, that was long ago, when I was a little girl playing house."—Now she's playing house up here a mile high above the Juniata. (Which, by the way, the romantic TWA route-map misspells as *Juanita.*) The Juniata doesn't look blue from here, but muddy, somber, swollen with flood. You rummage that luxurious lunch-box (three joints of roast chicken, still warm from the Airport kitchen. Even the food has wings. Looking forward along the aisle you have a humorous vista of passengers gnawing away). Eating, you contemplate nasty parallel ridges of Alleghany, sharp wooded hogbacks fading into dusk. There are still some glints of snow in wrinkles of the hills.

6.30 p. m.—getting dark. *Sky Chief* skims (surprisingly close) over great brown folds of hill. Beacons glitter here and there, like lighthouses at sea.

These new luxury Douglases are extraordinarily quiet. To feel any vibration at all you have to put forehead against the window-pane, where it thrills like a cool hissing—sound rather than feeling. She floats with gentle sway in the gray gloom; no sense of speed or hurry; earth is fading away. A sprinkle of lights is probably Johnstown, but hard to identify; it's too dark to see, as I thought we might, trace of the recent floods. After the lunch-box and an extra serving of coffee the little lights snap on above the chairs; everyone smoking cigarettes but the ventilation is perfect; no fug. A comfortable little parlor in nowhere. There would be a notion of sleep if one were making the all-night flit. Odd to consider that several of your companions will be eating breakfast in Los Angeles.

7 p.m.—a sprinkle of lights below. Her great wing sinks softly, softly downward below you as she banks a wide turn. Loveliest of feelings, that slow eiderdown sinking, tilting. She drifts you down through the dark—the gray wing swims sideways and groping, reaching—oh, like a lazy shark in a green aquarium tank—you are coming back, almost with grief, to the heavy bond of earth—a little jolt, a softly rocking run with a few reluctant skips, a roar as the propellers change pitch—you taxi to a brilliant gangway. It's Pittsburgh. "Ten minutes on the ground" says your guardian angel, Miss Baker, madonna of the monoplane.

It was a little longer, as a matter of fact. Not Sky Chief's fault: we had to wait for some extra mail to be sorted. Chance for a brief glimpse of the control room (a clockmaker's paradise) which no one can enter while in flight. Mr Ashford and Mr Blaine, the pilots, sitting ready at those queer squashed-in wheels, with earphones and (I suppose) those gyroscopes inside their heads. My friendly cross-aisle neighbor, who has come from Boston, is trying to buy a box of candy for the madonna (it would be a gross breach to offer a tip) but Pittsburgh, just recovering from flood, is out of candy. Anyhow we have saved our lunch box peppermints for her as a small homage. (She doesn't eat until she goes off duty at Kansas City, at midnight.) Boston says there's a young journalism student sitting forward, wants to change places with him so he can interview writer during flight. I beg him not to; hope student doesn't think one churlish, but really I'm busy and happy interviewing myself. Does one interview the young curlew under its mother's wing?

Only about 75 minutes from Pittsburgh to Columbus, but what soft ones. Thinking vaguely of some line of Emily Dickinson's about the bumble bee moving like a train on rails of plush? The little lights click on and off as each passenger turns from reading to study the sky. Clear now, and more stars than one sees on the ground—Orion, for instance, has a lot more accoutrements in his hunting gear. The man in front of me gets out a star-map for March and verifies it. Across from him, a handsome lady smoking in a gentle slump of universal acceptance. Some are still reading the *World-Telegram* and must know Eleanor Roosevelt's Day by heart. Behind me is the tall attractive buff-haired girl who had been able to get a seat at the last moment: I overheard her say it was a matter of life and death for her to get to St Louis. Boston is gently going asleep as he watches the green light on the tip of the right wing. Another is putting himself to sleep by turning the air vent to shoot a gush of pure upward space on his scalp. Very good for thinning hair I dare say.

There is something diminutively domestic about the tiny looped-in window curtains. There is no sense of motion whatever: only occasional sparks from the exhaust, streaming under her wing, suggest the idea of speed—which is, I suppose, about 3 miles a minute. It seems a bit incredible to be checked in at the good old Deshler-Wallick by 9 p.m., where I look from my window and see the words blazing, LAUREL—HARDY. Yes, I say to myself, thinking of unknown pilots sitting among stars and radio beams—they're certainly hardy and they deserve laurel.

Only two days later, I had the pleasure of accompanying my friend the Vizier on his first flying experience. Columbus to Cleveland in a Condor; then (with one minute for the change) Cleveland to Chicago by Boeing. The first hop was bumpy and the Vizier chewed hard; I was worried for him when a lady up forward went into reverse. But in the smooth Chicago run he relaxed gaily; before long he was asking the hostess's special permission to smoke a cigar; and when he was told that he was dining at 9000 feet he was in an ecstasy. The new moon seemed to be hung just over his right ear, and he was pleased by her shimmer on the round snout of the Pratt & Whitney (where, flying against sunset light, you can just guess the dim haze or halo-circle of the roaring blades). City Slicker by habit, customer of big hotels and Pullman trains, perhaps this was the first time in 20 years he had been 9000 feet away from a Dry Martini—even in Prohibition.

Chicago at night is a pattern of jewels from above; but on the ground, it seems at first a city of cinders. That smoke-fouled and throat-stinging drive through dumps and gloom is too savage a paradox after a few hundred miles of sky. I love her too well to leave it so, unchidden. When will she use the old Fair Grounds for a lakeside airport, the most beautiful in the world?

MIND EROSION[1]

IT'S VERY VALUABLE, in the life of the mind, when we realize that we rarely know what we are really thinking about; under the casual exterior preoccupations of the day the deep current of our imaginative life moves subtle and often unsuspected. The conscious intelligence, which is the least important part of any artist, is often helpless and bewildered in its attempt to understand or utilize that interior flux of dream, intuition, fantasy—call it what you wish—which is the marrow of any distinguished creative excellence. I am tempted to call your attention to a series of three articles by Thomas Wolfe, called "The Story of a Novel." There with the engaging naïveté which is one of Mr Wolfe's highest qualities, and with a sense of tormented indignation and astonishment, he reveals something of the struggle of a young writer to put the whole feeling of life into literature, to break through to the inside of his mind. He is writing, of course, about his book *Of Time and the River,* and he describes how after several years' work and more than a million words written, he felt he was just getting started; when, to his chagrin, his editor told him that from the point of view of the publisher the book was finished. Perhaps Satan himself said that to the Creator on the evening of the Sixth Day. At any rate those articles by Mr Wolfe are not only of a quite touching frankness but also perhaps dangerous read-

[1] Radio talk, on the program of the League for Political Education, December 26, 1935.

ing for young writers. I fear lest some may draw from them the quite unwarranted conclusion that if you write a million words you can fatigue a publisher into accepting them.

Mr Wolfe's struggles in attempting to reduce his manuscript to tolerable proportion remind me of something that happened the other day to a scientific friend of mine. A distinguished artist in Mexico City was lately commissioned to do a symbolic mural for a government building. The Mexican ministry of art desired the painting to be modernist in style, and the artist decided to attempt in the central panel some graphic suggestion or representation of the Theory of Relativity. My mathematical friend received from the artist the following telegram: "Send by return wire intelligible statement of Einstein Formula." My friend with heroic patience condensed the necessary equations and assumptions into a Western Union Day Letter. Even under the most savage compression it cost him over $10. I rather suspect that the receiving office in Mexico City may have imagined it to be some sinister diplomatic or capitalistic code. I have a copy of that telegram and cherish it as a historic document.

I have lingered for a moment on Mr Wolfe because his confessions show—in an extreme, almost a morbid form—the struggle that confronts every artist in his task of catalyzing the emotional and sensory material of life into the soluble stuff of literature. These anxieties and horrors that he describes are not unique to himself, not even unique to the art of writing; they are a part of every imaginative frenzy from mathematics to manslaughter. In the case of Mr Wolfe they are especially severe, I gather, because he prefers to do his thinking on paper; apparently he does not edit in his mind before actually dipping the pen. Some others go through their struggle in the lonely cavern of thought, and the result does not come to ink until it has taken form and profile beforehand. The finest statement of this latter method was made by Mr Goudy, the great typographer, when he was asked how he designed a new font of type. He brooded a while and then said, "Why, you think of a letter and draw around it." But whatever method the writer adopts, or finds forced upon him, his first problem is to teach himself to think; and to find an audience which is hospitable to thought.

Now the concern that occupies my own mind is that probably never anywhere, at any time, was secluded or creative thinking so difficult to achieve as in America today. Every human being is endowed with a limited and infinitely precious stock of attention-power; and life today is such that—unless the individual is singularly obstinate and cunning—the native and tender innocence of the mind, the artist's birthright, is dissipated or conventionalized by endless, incessant, competitive demands. By newspapers, by electric lights, by telephone, by radio, by moving pictures, by airplane and motor car and church and school and State, by a thousand appeals, admonitions, and interruptions, the mind is assailed and distracted. When the time comes to throw the whole power of one's will into some superb task, too often we find our faculties grown brittle or callous by repeated overstimulus. We hear a good deal about the agricultural problem of soil erosion; hillsides denuded of fertile topsoil by the action of streams, or great regions of Middle Western richness scoured off by dust storms. Surely not less serious is the matter of mind erosion: the dust storms of daily excitement and of continual triviality can easily blow away the sensitive topsoil of the spirit. The result is a general barren and shallow nervous credulity. Think how many works of genius have been hysterically acclaimed in the past fifteen years and almost as quickly forgotten. As a practising critic I can include myself in the indictment.

Sometimes I read in the financial pages about what is called "Nuisance Money." Capital is notoriously timid, and when there are rumors of international trouble apparently a lot of money skips to and fro (by cable, I suppose) looking for a good, safe breeding place. I am no economist, but I always visualize capital as being not unlike a setting hen; she makes a great fuss when anyone gets near her nest.

In the same way there's an extraordinary lot of Nuisance Thinking evident nowadays: shoals or flocks of fashionable or momentary notions (economic or aesthetic) that rush to and fro; they hive suddenly in some magazine or clique; then as suddenly buzz away. I often think of the old fellow described by Hazlitt as having been "frightened to death by a ventriloquist." Whole slabs and sections of the American public are in constant danger, it sometimes seems, of that same fate. We have many ventriloquists in our public life: in literature, in religion, in politics. By ventriloquists, I mean people who talk in a deep menacing tone from the emotional entrails rather than from the rational skull. One great ventriloquist was tragically removed by assassination some months ago; but there will always be plenty more. Particularly in the months to come, with political issues paramount, we may expect to hear the deep stomach tones of the professional terrorizer.

All this is a part of life and has its influence on literature. The books of our time have borne the birthmarks of our own era; it is not to be blamed upon the Muse if in an age of hysteria, cynicism, and fright some of her offerings show the stigmata of the general alarm. The magnificent achievements of science have also raised up devils to plague us, principalities and powers we have not learned how to control. I mention only one, of such terrific scope that it reaches from zenith to pit and is efficient in both regions: the great life-giving and destroying angel, Publicity. People can be killed with photographs as surely as with guns.

The arts are encouraged by reasonable publicity but they need privacy too. Sudden convulsions of excitement, waves of fashionable acclaim, are not always salutary. May I recall the humorous interlude of Gertrude Stein? The Muse herself is wary of little groups, intellectual totems and fetiches, fashionable sensationalisms. The dreams, powers, tendencies which forward great creation move silently and very far underneath the surface. I remember a scientific report I read in the newspaper some time ago, about a rancher in the State of Washington. By some oddity of his molecular constitution he was painfully sensitive to the radio waves which pass through most of us unnoticed. His body acted as a kind of storage battery, and whenever anyone in the neighborhood turned on the radio he suffered severely. If it was only a local station the effect was not much worse than neuralgia, but when a really powerful national hookup was coming through, his condition was deplorable. When the White House was on the air he turned pale, his eyes bulged, the veins of his neck stood out like cords, and he usually fell down in convulsions. He experimented with a homemade remedy, which was to carry a cane wound with copper wire to act as a lightning conductor. Finally an engineer in Tacoma was able to help him—he invented a kind of condenser which goes up the victim's sleeves and down his trouser legs and discharges the coagulated electricity through his boots.

That homely illustration has its application to the arts. Not by sudden spasms of bandar-log excitement or novelty does literature win new ground; but by subtle continuous sensibility, by patient and laborious choices, by the onward flow and increase of a nation's awareness. The creative sympathies that will help to beget the next great novel are now moving unguessed and unperceived in thousands of us who will be its readers. Perhaps one sound advice for a writer is a line I found in the instruction booklet for the Ford car. It says—"Don't ride the clutch." In other words, keep the narrative moving steadily and without sudden shifts of tempo. It must have continuity—the mind of the reader must be able to flow concurrently, and without apprehensions of abrupt change of technique. It's a good motto for governments too. How many business men have been worried because they could feel the heavy federal foot hovering on the pedal?

As a final provocative for argument or personal testimony, I suggest one more thought. Literature is not separate from life but is one of many evidences of living. We can think of it as a form of companionship, or of communication; or as an attempt, heroic and impossible, to make life stand still long enough to be looked at. But however you describe it, it is subject to the general conditions and humors of the life around it. And when you see a phenomenon which is very evident in one department of living you are likely to find its analogues elsewhere. The outstanding physical phenomenon of our time is an actual change of shape in the mechanics of civilization. The so-called streamline principle, already familiar in all forms of transport, is evident in intellectual activity also. As well as houses and clothes and furnitures, so have the arts and even perhaps the religions shown some tendency to simplify, to reduce unnecessary friction, to adopt an outline that will pass with diminished resistance through the opposing medium (whatever that may be). Now the opposing medium, in the case of a writer, is the mind of the reader. If he can so shape and mold his story that the reader, instead of resisting, collaborates with him, actually does part of the work (even unconsciously) the writer has achieved a high artistic triumph. And I seem sometimes to discern, in the work of some writers who are intuitively ahead of their generation, what I like to think of as a kind of streamline dynamics. Virginia Woolf once said that "The novelist of the future will take reality for granted." By that I suppose she meant he won't waste time and energy on describing details of furniture or scenery that the reader can well supply—would even prefer to supply—from his own mind. Willa Cather said the same thing in a brilliant essay years ago, *The Novel Démeublé*—that is, unfurnished. This introduces a topic too large, and perhaps too professional, to enter into now in detail. I am suggesting merely that one neglected consideration in the art of writing is this: not how much can you do *for* the reader, but how much can you cajole him into doing for you. How much of your book can the reader write for you, in his own mind? I coined an aphorism once—coined is too precise a word; I mean I laboriously chopped it out—that one test of any form of expression is the area of silence it covers. I don't believe I can exactly restate what I meant by that, but I *feel* its meaning. There can never be any precise testing-blocks or efficiency tables for the success of a work of literature, because it is published new and different in the mind of every reader, but I can't help thinking that when it attempts to say or show everything, an art is on the wrong track.

Finally let me say that two lines of a poem by the late Sir William Watson are good medicine to remember—

> *"Momentous to himself as I to me*
> *Hath each man been that woman ever bore."*

WAS SHERLOCK HOLMES AN AMERICAN?

"I think the fellow is really an American, but he has worn his accent smooth with years of London."

—*The Three Garridebs*

A CAPRICIOUS SECRECY was always characteristic of Holmes. He concealed from Watson his American connection. And though Watson must finally have divined it, he also was uncandid with us. The Doctor was a sturdy British patriot: the fact of Holmes's French grandmother was disconcerting, and to add to this his friend's American association and sympathy would have been painful. But the theory is too tempting to be lightly dismissed. Not less than fifteen of the published cases (including three of the four chosen for full-length treatment) involve American characters or scenes. Watson earnestly strove to minimize the appeal of United States landscapes of which Holmes must have told him. The great plains of the West were "an arid and repulsive desert."[1] Vermissa Valley (in Pennsylvania, I suppose?) was "a gloomy land of black crag and tangled forest . . . not a cheering prospect."[2] Watson's quotation from the child Lucy,[1]—"Say, did God make this country?"—was a humorous riposte to Holmes, spoofing the familiar phrase Watson had heard too often in their fireside talks. There is even

[1]*A Study in Scarlet.*

[2]*The Valley of Fear.*

a possible suggestion of Yankee timbre in the Doctor's occasional descriptions of the "well-remembered voice." The argument of rival patriotisms was a favorite topic between them. Watson never quite forgave Holmes's ironical jape when after some specially naïve Victorian imperialism by the Doctor (perhaps at the time of the '87 Jubilee) Sherlock decorated the wall with the royal V. R. in bullet-pocks. (Or did the Doctor misread as V. R. what was jocularly meant to be V. H.—because Watson too insistently suggested a sentimental interest in Miss Violet Hunter of the Copper Beeches? An H. in bullet-pocks, if the marksman's aim was shaken by a heavy dray in the street, or by the neighboring Underground Railway, might well look like an R.)

Why, again, does Watson write "It was upon the 4th of March, as I have good reason to remember," that the adventure of the Study in Scarlet began? And why was Holmes still at the breakfast table? It was the 4th of March, 1881, and Holmes was absorbed in reading the news dispatches about the inauguration, to take place that day, of President Garfield.

Was Holmes actually of American birth? It would explain much. The jealousy of Scotland Yard, the refusal of knighthood, the expert use of Western argot, the offhand behavior to aristocratic clients, the easy camaraderie with working people of all sorts, the always traveling First Class in trains. How significant is Holmes's "Hum!" when he notes that Irene was born in New Jersey.[3] And Watson's careful insertion of "U.S.A." after every American address, which always irritates us, was probably a twit to tease his principal. True, as Inspector MacDon-

[3] *A Scandal in Bohemia.*

ald once said,[4] "You don't need to import an American from outside in order to account for American doings." But let us light the cherry-wood pipe and examine the data more systematically.

Holmes's grandmother was "the sister of Vernet, the French artist."[5] This of course was Horace Vernet (1789–1863), the third of the famous line of painters in that family. Horace Vernet's father (who had been decorated by Napoleon for his *Battle of Marengo* and *Morning of Austerlitz*) came from Bordeaux and Horace's grandfather, the marine painter, from Avignon. Here we have an association with the South of France which Holmes acknowledges by his interest in Montpellier[6] where he probably had French kindred. Like Sir Kenelm Digby, who delivered there the famous discourse on the Powder of Sympathy,[7] Holmes knew Montpellier as an important center of scientific studies. (See *The Empty House.*) It is deplorable that our Holmes researchers have done so little to trace his French relationship. It is significant that though he declined a knighthood in Britain he was willing to accept the Legion of Honor in France.[8]

Much might be said of Sherlock's presumable artistic and political inheritance from the Vernets. His great-uncle's studio in Paris was "a rendezvous of Liberals."[9] Surely the untidiness which bothered Watson at 221B is akin to the description of Horace

[4]*The Valley of Fear.*

[5]*The Greek Interpreter.*

[6]*The Empty House.* Cf. also *The Disappearance of Lady Frances Carfax.*

[7]Ann Macdonell: *The Closet of Sir Kenelm Digby* (1910), p. xxxi.

[8]*The Golden Pince-Nez.*

[9]Encyclopaedia Britannica, article *Vernet.*

Vernet "painting tranquilly, whilst boxing, fencing, drum and horn playing were going on, in the midst of a medley of visitors, horses, dogs and models."[10] Holmes's grandmother, one of this radical and bohemian and wide-travelling family, brought up among the harrowing scenes of the French Revolution and the Napoleonic wars, may quite possibly have emigrated to America.[11] It is not inconceivable then that at least one of Holmes's parents was an American. My own conjecture is that there was some distant connection with the famous Holmes household of Cambridge (Mass.). Every reader has noticed Holmes's passionate interest in breakfasts: does this not suggest the Autocrat of the Breakfast Table?

I will not cloud the issue with futile speculation, though certainly it is of more importance than many of the controversies (such as, was Holmes's dressing gown blue, purple, or mouse-colored?).[12] But before proceeding to recount some specific passages which prove our hero's exceptional interest in America let me add one more suggestion. The hopeless muddle of any chronology based on the *Gloria Scott* and Musgrave Ritual is familiar to all students; Miss Dorothy Sayers has done her brilliant best to harmonize the anomalies. But all have wondered just

[10]Ibid. Perhaps Sherlock as a child got his first interest in boxing and fencing from great-uncle Horace.

[11]Turning to the telephone book, as Dr Watson did for Garrideb, I find that several of the Vernet (Verner) family came to the U. S. There are 2 Vernets in Brooklyn, 3 Verners in Manhattan, 1 Verner in Floral Park, L. I.

[12]Elementary. This particular gown was blue when new. (*The Twisted Lip.*) It had gone purple by the time of the *Blue Carbuncle.* During the long absence, 1891–94, when Mrs Hudson faithfully aired and sunned it in the back yard, it faded to mouse (*The Empty House*).

what Holmes was doing between the time he left the university and his taking rooms in Montague Street. My own thought is that the opening of the Johns Hopkins University in Baltimore in 1876, and the extraordinary and informal opportunities offered there for graduate study, tempted him across the water. He was certainly familiar with papers in the chemical journals written by Ira Remsen, the brilliant young professor who took charge of the new laboratories in Baltimore. Probably in Baltimore he acquired his taste for oysters[13] and on a hot summer day noted the depth to which the parsley had sunk into the butter.[14] In that devoted group of young scholars and scientists, and in the musical circles of that hospitable city, he must have been supremely happy. His American-born mother (or father) had often told him of the untrammeled possibilities of American life. The great Centennial Exposition in Philadelphia (1876) was surely worth visit; there he observed the mark of the Pennsylvania Small Arms Company.[15] During his year or so in the States he travelled widely. He met Wilson Hargreave (who later became important in the New York Police Department[16]) perhaps in connection with the case of *Vanderbilt and the Yeggman*, a record of which he kept in his scrapbook.[17] He went to Chicago, where he made his first acquaintance with organized gangsterism.[18] I suggest that he perhaps visited his kins-

[13]*The Sign of Four.*

[14]*The Adventure of the Six Napoleons.* Holmes's interest in the butter-dish is also shown in *The Musgrave Ritual.*

[15]*The Valley of Fear.*

[16]*The Dancing Men.*

[17]*The Sussex Vampire.*

[18]"My knowledge of the crooks of Chicago," v. *The Dancing Men.* Cf. also allusions in *The Valley of Fear* and *The Three Garridebs.*

men the Sherlocks in Iowa—e.g. in Des Moines, where a younger member of that family, Mr C. C. Sherlock, has since written so ably on rural topics.[19] He must have gone to Topeka;[20] and of course he made pilgrimage to Cambridge, Mass., to pay respect to the great doctor, poet and essayist. From Oliver Wendell Holmes, Jr., then a rising lawyer in Boston, he heard first-hand stories of the Civil War, which fired his interest in "that gallant struggle." Indeed he spoke to Watson so often about the Civil War that Watson repeated in the story of *The Resident Patient* the episode of the Henry Ward Beecher portrait which he had already told in *The Cardboard Box*.[21] It is interesting to note, in passing, that when Holmes spoke in that episode of having written two monographs on Ears in the *Anthropological Journal,* the alert editor of The Strand at once took the hint. A few months later, in October and November 1893, the Strand printed "A Chapter on Ears," with photos of the ears of famous people—including an ear

[19]C. C. Sherlock: *Care and Management of Rabbits* (1920); *The Modern Hen* (1922); *Bulb Gardening* (1922), etc.; v. *Who's Who in America.* Iowa is a great apiarian State; undoubtedly from the Sherlock side came the interest in roses, bee-keeping, etc.

[20]Otherwise how could he know that there was no such person as Dr Lysander Starr? (*The Three Garridebs.*)

[21]There was no duplication in the stories as first printed: *The Cardboard Box* in The Strand Magazine of January 1893, *The Resident Patient* in August of the same year. In the latter story as it absurdly appears in the collected editions the description of the "blazing hot day in August" is repeated for "a close rainy day in October." The explanation is that Dr Watson withheld *The Cardboard Box* from book publication for 24 years; perhaps because it revealed some anti-American bias in his never having had the portrait of Beecher framed. But the Beecher incident showed Holmes's keen observation, and in compiling the *Memoirs* Watson carelessly spliced or trepanned it into *The Resident Patient.* Then, when he republished *The Cardboard Box* in *His Last Bow* (1917), he forgot this.

of Dr Oliver Wendell Holmes. Surely, from so retiring a philosopher, then 84 years old, this intimate permission could not have been had without the privileged intervention of Sherlock.

Speaking of the Strand Magazine, it is odd that our researchers do not more often turn back to those original issues which solve many problems. The much belabored matter of Holmes's university, for instance. There was never any question about it, for in Sidney Paget's illustrations Holmes is clearly shown sitting in Trevor's garden wearing a straw hat with a *Light Blue* ribbon[22] (He was, of course, a boxing Blue.) Why has such inadequate honor been paid to those admirable drawings by Paget?—Oxford was unthinkable to Holmes; with what pleasure he noted that Colonel Moran[23] and John Clay[24] were both "Eton and Oxford."

In the *Bruce-Partington Plans* one of our most suggestive passages occurs. "You have never had so great a chance of serving your country," cries Mycroft. But is Holmes moved by this appeal? "Well, well!" he said, "shrugging his shoulders." All emotions, we know, were abhorrent to that cold, precise mind,[25] and certainly militant patriotism among them; at any rate until many years later when bees, flowers, Sussex, and long association with the more sentimental Watson had softened him to the strange

[22]*Strand Magazine,* Vol. V, p. 398. While speaking of the *Gloria Scott,* has it been pointed out that Holmes never admitted to Watson why he chose Mrs Hudson's lodgings? She was the widow of the ruffian Hudson who blackmailed old Mr Trevor—and so more than ever "a long-suffering woman." And of course the rapid disappearance of Watson's bull-pup was because Holmes had been bitten by one in college days.

[23]*The Empty House.*

[24]*The Red-Headed League.*

[25]*A Scandal in Bohemia.*

SHERLOCK HOLMES WEARING
CAMBRIDGE RIBBON
(Drawing by Sidney Paget in *The Strand Magazine*.)

outburst about "God's own wind" on the terrible night of August 2nd, 1914.[26]—Plainly he resented Mycroft's assumption that England was his only country. Mycroft, seven years older, had earlier outgrown the Franco-American tradition of the family. If Mycroft had ever been in the States he had striven to forget it; indeed no one can think of Mycroft without being reminded (in more respects than one) of the great expatriate Henry James.[27]

That Holmes had a very special affection and interest in regard to the United States is beyond question. He had much reason to be grateful to American criminals, who often relieved him from the ennui of London's dearth of outrage. The very first case recorded by Watson was the murder of Enoch J. Drebber, the ex-Mormon from Cleveland. Irene Adler, *the* woman, was a native of New Jersey. In the Red-Headed League the ingenious John Clay represented the League as having been founded by the eccentric millionaire Ezekiah Hopkins of Lebanon, Pa., "U.S.A." In the Orange Pips, Elias Openshaw emigrated to Florida, rose to be a Colonel in the C.S.A. and made a fortune. Although Watson tries to prejudice the reader by painful allusions to the habits of these people, there is plentiful evidence that Holmes considered America the land of opportunity. (Watson preferred Australia.) Both Aloysius Doran[28] and John Douglas [29] had struck it rich in California. Senator Neil Gibson,[30] "iron of nerve and leathery of

[26]*His Last Bow.*

[27]It is possible that Mycroft's experience had been in Canada, not the U. S.—Sherlock says Mycroft was known at the Foreign Office as an expert on Canada (*The Bruce-Partington Plans*).

[28]*The Noble Bachelor.*

[29]*The Valley of Fear.*

[30]*Thor Bridge.*

conscience," had also made his pile in gold mines. Hilton Cubitt, the Norfolk squire, had married a lovely American woman;[31] and Holmes was glad to be able to save Miss Hatty Doran from Lord St Simon who was not worthy of her.[32] He yawns sardonically at the *Morning Post's* social item which implies that Miss Doran will gain by becoming the wife of a peer. That case is a high point in Holmes's transatlantic sympathy. He praises American slang, quotes Thoreau, shows his knowledge of the price of cocktails, and utters the famous sentiment:—

> "It is always a joy to meet an American, for I am one of those who believe that the folly of a monarch and the blundering of a minister in far-gone years will not prevent our children from being some day citizens of the same world-wide country under a flag which shall be a quartering of the Union Jack with the Stars and Stripes."

Which reminds one obviously of the fact that when Holmes disguised himself as Mr Altamont of Chicago, the Irish-American agitator, to deceive Von Bork, he greatly resembled the familiar cartoons of Uncle Sam.[33] He visited Chicago again in 1912–13 to prepare himself for this role; I wish Mr Vincent Starrett would look up the details.

Holmes's fondness for America did not prevent him from seeing the comic side of a nation that lends itself to broad satiric treatment. In *The Man with the Watches*, one of the two stories outside the canon,[34] Holmes remarks of the victim "He was

[31] *The Dancing Men.*

[32] *The Noble Bachelor.*

[33] *His Last Bow.*

[34] The other is *The Lost Special;* both are to be found in *The Conan Doyle Stories,* London (John Murray), 1929. Holmes appears in both these stories by obvious allusion, but Watson suppressed them, probably because Holmes's deductions were wrong. See p. 259.

probably an American, and also probably a man of weak intellect." (This rhetorical device for humorous purposes was a family trait: we find it in Mycroft's description of the senior clerk at the Woolwich Arsenal—"He is a man of forty, married, with five children. He is a silent, morose man.")[35] After his long use of American cant for Von Bork's benefit Sherlock says "My well of English seems to be permanently defiled."[36] But these japes are plainly on the principle "On se moque de ce qu'on aime." He kept informed of American manners and events: when he met Mr Leverton of Pinkerton's he said "Pleased to meet you" and alluded to "the Long Island cave mystery."[37] He knew "the American business principle" of paying well for brains.[38] He did not hesitate to outwit a rascal by inventing an imaginary mayor of Topeka—recalling for the purpose the name of the counterfeiter of Reading years before.[39] (Those who escaped him were not forgotten.) But nothing shows more convincingly his passionate interest in all cases concerning Americans than his letter about the matter of *The Man with the Watches,* alluded to above. Even in Tibet, where he was then travelling as "a Norwegian named Sigerson,"[40] he had kept up with the news. This was in the spring of '92; how Watson, after reading the letter in the newspaper, can have supposed his friend was really dead passes belief. There are frequent humor-

[35]*The Bruce-Partington Plans.*

[36]*His Last Bow.*

[37]*The Red Circle.* The mystery, on true Sherlockian principles, is that there are no caves on Long Island.

[38]*The Valley of Fear.*

[39]*The Three Garridebs, The Engineer's Thumb.*

[40]*The Empty House.*

ous allusions to American accent,[41] the shape of American shoes,[42] American spelling.[43] I suspect that Holmes's travels in these States never took him to the South or Southwest;[44] for he shows a curious ignorance of Southern susceptibilities in the matter of race,[45] and in spite of his American Encyclopaedia[46] he did not know which was the Lone Star State. Let it be noted that the part of London where he first took rooms (Montague Street, alongside the British Museum) is the region frequented more than any other by American students and tourists.

That Holmes was reared in the States, or had some schooling here before going up to Cambridge, seems then at least arguable. His complete silence (or Watson's) on the subject of his parents suggests that they were deceased or not in England. A foreign schooling, added to his own individual temperament, would easily explain his solitary habits at college.[47] If he had gone to almost any English school the rugger jargon of Cyril Overton would have been comprehensible to him[48] or he might have picked it up from Watson, who played for Blackheath.[49] Watson, moreover, if he knew more about Holmes's family, may have been moved by jealousy to keep silent. Already he had suffered by the contrast be-

[41] *The Hound of the Baskervilles.*

[42] *The Dancing Men, The Valley of Fear.*

[43] *The Three Garridebs.*

[44] The "remarkable case" of the venomous gila lizard (v. *The Sussex Vampire*) need not suggest Arizona. It probably came from Number 3, Pinchin Lane (*The Sign of Four*).

[45] *The Yellow Face.*

[46] *The Five Orange Pips.*

[47] *The Gloria Scott.*

[48] *The Missing Three Quarter.*

[49] *The Sussex Vampire.*

tween the corpulent Mycroft and his own older brother, the crapulent H. W.[50] Or his neglect to inform us may just have been the absent-mindedness and inaccuracy which we have learned to expect from good old Watson—and which were even acquired by his wife, who went so far as to forget her husband's first name and call him "James" in front of a visitor.[51] The Doctor has hopelessly confused us on even more important matters—that both Moriarty brothers were called James, for instance. Considering the evidence without prejudice, the idea that Holmes was at any rate partly American is enticing.

As Jefferson Hope said,[52] "I guessed what puzzled the New Yorkers would puzzle the Londoners." So I leave it as a puzzle, not as a proven case, for more accomplished students to re-examine. But the master's own dictum[53] is apposite:—"When once your point of view is changed, the very thing which was so damning becomes a clue to the truth."

[50]*The Sign of Four.*

[51]*The Man with the Twisted Lip.* This was probably the cause of the first rupture between Dr and Mrs Watson. Has it been pointed out, by the way, that there is premonitory allusion to a second Mrs Watson in *The Disappearance of Lady Frances Carfax,* where Watson evades Holmes's question as to who was his companion in the hansom? Also the Doctor had been bucking himself up with a Turkish bath.

[52]*A Study in Scarlet.*

[53]*Thor Bridge.*

DOCTOR WATSON'S SECRET

I SPOKE some time ago of the secret in Sherlock Holmes's life, his American connection. Perhaps it is permissible now to remark upon an even more carefully hidden arcanum, Dr Watson's clandestine marriage.

The infuriating inconsistencies of Watsonian chronology have cost scholars many a megrim. The more carefully we examine them the more deeply confused they seem. Some authorities (*e. g.* Miss Dorothy Sayers) have attempted to account for slips on the theory that Watson misread his own handwriting in his notes. Others (*e. g.* Mr S. C. Roberts) have fallen back upon the regrettable hypothesis that occasionally the Doctor was not "in his normal, business-like condition." Still others (*e. g.* Mr R. E. Balfour) reject from the canon stories that appear incompatible. It is true that *The Sign of Four* begins with neither Holmes nor Watson in completely rational state. Watson had had Beaune for lunch, which affected him so that he thought it was his leg that pained him (instead of his shoulder). Holmes had taken a 7% solution of cocaine. Holmes's addiction to the drug was (at that period) habitual; but why had Watson taken the Beaune on that particular day? We shall see. It was to screw up his courage for an imminent ordeal.

Let me digress a moment, at the risk of repeating matter familiar to all genuine Holmesians, to note a few of the outstanding anomalies which must be reconciled. The case of the *Noble Bachelor* is dated (by the hotel bill, the high autumnal winds, and the age of Lord St Simon) as October 1887. This, Watson says, was "a few weeks before my own marriage." And the somewhat elastic time-allusions in the *Stockbroker's Clerk* also imply that the wedding took place late in the year. On the other hand both *The Crooked Man* and *The Naval Treaty* distinctly suggest that the marriage was in the spring or early summer.

How may these contradictions be reconciled? Surely not by the assumption that good old methodical Watson ("the one fixed point in a changing age") was simply careless or muddled. Watson wove a tangled web in his chronology because he was deliberately trying to deceive. Why not adopt the reiterated thesis of the master himself: when you have excluded the impossible, whatever remains, *however improbable,* must be the truth. The truth must be that Watson had contracted a secret marriage with Mary Morstan, some time before the adventure of *The Sign of Four.* His allusions are perfectly comprehensible if we realize that he is sometimes referring to the actual date of that union; and sometimes to the purely fictitious occasion (late in the autumn) which he and his wife agreed to represent to their friends as the time of the nuptial.

The extraordinary year 1887 is crucial in any study of Holmes-Watson history. All scholars have noted the exceptional number of important cases assigned to this year. Particularly, beginning early in February, there was the business of the Netherland-Sumatra Company which took Holmes abroad. Watson, now in full health and vigor, did not spend his entire life sitting in Baker Street, or even at his club playing billiards with Thurston. How and when he first met Mary Morstan we do not know; probably in connection with the earlier case when Holmes was "of some slight service" to her employer, Mrs Cecil Forrester. (I like to think, incidentally, that Mrs Forrester's "tranquil English home," with the stained glass in the front door, the barometer and the bright stair-rods, was in Knatchbull Road, Camberwell, for which Boucicault named the villain in *After Dark.*) At any rate, both Watson and Miss Morstan were lonely and financially insecure. Their romance was immediate, but both were afraid to admit it to their associates. Miss Morstan would lose her position; Watson would incur the annoyance of the misogynist Sherlock.

I will be as brief as possible, for once this hypothesis is grasped, all experienced Watsonians will observe the wealth of corroborating circumstances. Let us re-examine the chronology of the year 1887.

First of all, we cannot accept Mr Roberts's conclusion that *The Sign of Four* belongs to 1886. The facts are positive: Mary Morstan had received six pearls, one every year, beginning in May '82. She calls that "about six years ago"; in reality it was only just over five years, but she thought of it as six because she had that number of pearls. Also she says her father disappeared in "December 1878—nearly ten years ago." From the beginning of the year '87 her grieving heart would naturally think of the bereavement as in its tenth year. Even in her sorrow her precise mind could not reckon it so until the calendar year '87. I accept July 1887 as the date of the *Sign of Four* adventure—preferring to follow the postmark on Sholto's letter rather than Watson's subsequent reference to a "September evening." As for the yellow fog (rare in July, surely?) seen by Holmes, it was at least 7% cocaine. But mark well:

we now have for the first time an explanation of Watson's mysterious telegram that morning. He and Mary Morstan Watson, weary of meeting by stealth, had at last decided to break their news to Holmes. The mystery of the pearls, which they had often discussed, was an additional motive. Watson had gone to the Wigmore Street Post Office (as a matter of fact isn't it just around the corner in Wimpole Street?) not primarily to *send* a wire but to receive one. Addressed *Poste Restante* was a message from Mary. She had received the puzzling letter from Thaddeus Sholto and appealed to her husband for advice. He wired back telling her to come to Baker Street. And the Beaune for lunch was his attempt to fortify himself for the revelation to come. Observe, throughout the narrative, how slyly old Watson concealed from Sherlock the fact that he and Mary were already intimate.

Recapitulate, then, the events of 1887. Early in the year, probably February or March, while Holmes was absent in the Netherland-Sumatra business, Watson and Mary Morstan were secretly married. They met as and when they could, but told no one. Their anxious and surreptitious bliss was interrupted by the news (April 14) that Holmes was ill in Lyons. Watson hurried to France, he and Sherlock returned together, and spent April 25–27 at Reigate (*The Reigate Puzzle*—originally published as *The Reigate Squire*). Perhaps this was followed by the matter of the Grice Patersons in the island of Uffa—where *is* Uffa, by the way? But if it is (as it sounds) in the Hebrides, Shetlands or Orkneys, the Grice Patersons would have sense enough not to go there until midsummer.

Holmes was in aggressive spirits after the Reigate

visit; Watson was gloomy. His secret preyed on his mind; he wrote many letters to Mary. (He had in his desk "a sheet of stamps and a thick bundle of postcards.") At the time of the Jubilee (June 21) it was the shooting of the V. R. into the wall that finally convinced Watson he must make a break. "With me there is a limit," he said in *The Musgrave Ritual.* He made up his mind to take charge of his own check-book, find a home, and resume practice. *The Sign of Four,* coming just when it did (July 8) was a happy coincidence. His anxieties about Miss Morstan becoming heiress of the Agra treasure were just as sincere as if he had really been only a suitor. Since their marriage had been concealed, everyone would be sure to think him a fortune-hunter.

After the excitement was over, the pair went through the appearance of a formal engagement for the benefit of Holmes and Mrs Forrester (not to say Mrs Hudson). May it not have been Watson's now frequent visits to Knatchbull Road that brought the Camberwell Poisoning to Holmes's attention? No doubt soon after *The Sign of Four* Mary had her summer vacation, and she and the Doctor used this for a furtive honeymoon—perhaps in "the glades of the New Forest"; Southsea would have been a little too public. So when the elated husband, narrating the *Five Orange Pips,* speaks of his wife he forgets that she was not at that time known as such. It was not until November that he found a home of his own, left Baker Street and set up housekeeping in Paddington. The *Noble Bachelor* affair in October preceded by a few weeks what they agreed to call their "marriage." They simply told their friends, about Guy Fawkes Day, that they were going to slip off quietly to a registry office. Probably the medical practice was bought as of January 1, 1888.

Sitting on a pile of cushions with plenty of shag tobacco, and following the master's cardinal principle, the preceding seems to me the only possible solution. This chronology harmonizes many apparently conflicting statements. It makes intelligible the allusions at the beginning of *A Scandal in Bohemia* (March 20–22, 1888). It gives sense to Watson's eagerness that Sherlock should become interested in Violet Hunter; how delightful, the Doctor thought naïvely, if he and Holmes should both marry governesses—and alumnæ of the same agency, for undoubtedly Mary, too, had been a client of Westaway's. When the case of *The Stockbroker's Clerk* came along in June '88, Watson jumped at the chance to go to Birmingham with Holmes. He thought he might be able to persuade Sherlock to run out to Walsall (only 8 miles away) to see Miss Hunter at the school where she was headmistress.

I must not weary you in the matter of Dr Watson's private affairs; but there is just one more point which is essential to mention. We were arguing that the correct date of *The Sign of Four* is July (1887) rather than September. The most apparently damning evidence against July has been ingeniously pointed out by Mr H. W. Bell in that indispensable little volume *Baker Street Studies* (London: Constable & Co.). Holmes insisted on Athelney Jones staying for dinner—for which he had ordered "oysters and a brace of grouse." Neither of these are in season in July. But is not this precisely what Holmes meant by his following remark to Watson: "You have never yet recognized my merits as a housekeeper." Surely he was calling attention to his cunning in being able to procure these luxuries when they were impossible for most people.

If my suggestion is acceptable that Dr Watson and Miss Morstan had been secretly married in the spring but agreed to pretend that it didn't happen until autumn, other chronological reconciliations are possible. We now see that the *Naval Treaty* (in "the July which immediately succeeded my marriage"—viz., the next July after their collusive wedding-date in November) must have been in July '88. The treaty had been drawn up in May of that year, obviously in view of the illness of Frederick III of Germany and the probable succession of the young Kaiser—whose temperament was only too likely to necessitate readjustments of the European balance of power. There were two other cases in that month, you remember: *The Second Stain* and *The Tired Captain.* Watson's ingrained mixture of duplicity and naïveté in regard to the date of the Morstan marriage is delightfully shown when years later he sets down the story of the *Second Stain.* It happened, he says, "in a year, and even in a decade, that shall be nameless"—quite oblivious that in his earlier reference he had unmistakably dated and identified the episode.

From here on the succession of events is fairly plain. *A Case of Identity* is evidently late spring of '88. *The Crooked Man* is the summer of '88. Myself I should prefer to place *The Engineer's Thumb* in '88 ("not long after my marriage," he says), but Watson positively assigns it to summer '89. *The Valley of Fear* must have been in January '89;[1] fol-

[1]See, however, Mr A. G. Macdonell's disturbing suggestion that it was ten years later. In *Baker Street Studies,* edited by H. W. Bell, London, 1934.

lowed in June by *The Man with the Twisted Lip* and that autumn by the great *Hound of the Baskervilles.* Watson's long absence from home and practice while visiting Baskerville Hall may well have been another trial of Mrs Watson's disposition; but we find her in June 1890 generously urging the Doctor to accompany Holmes to Boscombe Valley. Immediately after returning from Boscombe Valley Holmes became interested in *The Lost Special* (one of the cases outside the legitimate canon, never recorded by Watson). 1890 closes with the *Red-Headed League* and the *Blue Carbuncle;* it is pleasant to think of Holmes and Watson sitting down cheerfully to the post-Christmas goose: their last intimacy before the tragic events of April and May 1891.

It is also possible to believe that Watson's innocent and timid subterfuge of the secret marriage quite escaped Holmes's attention. Sherlock had grown into the habit of regarding Watson as a lay figure who would never do the unexpected; the great detective was intensely absorbed in his own ideas and except on those mischievous occasions when he turned the full focus of his observation upon his companion he was not likely to speculate much on Watson's private thoughts. And a man of Watson's upright, simple and candid nature, once driven in upon himself, can develop surprising foxiness. It pleases me to think that the self-sacrificing Doctor was dashing enough to seize the romance that came his way. His pangs, his honorable yearnings, his necessities for concealment, gave him (every student has noticed) a special tenderness for women in distress. In brooding the problem of his later marriage one could be tempted to wish that the superb Grace Dunbar of *Thor Bridge* might have been the second

Mrs Watson. (She also had been a governess.) But knowing Senator Neil Gibson, it is unlikely.

Having caused endless embarrassment by his transparent attempts to disguise the facts of his first marriage, no wonder Watson said nothing whatever about the second. And apropos the second matrimony (which all scholars agree to place about the end of 1902) it is interesting to note that Watson chose to establish his renewed menage in Queen Anne Street. It crosses Harley Street, is only a stroll from 221 B, and still very near the Wigmore Street Post Office. The other most famous resident of that immediate neighborhood is *The Young Man with the Cream Tarts.*

EPISTLE TO THE COLOSSIANS

(March, 1934)

LETTERS dropped in the mail chutes at the top of the Empire State Building fall so far and so fast that they must be slowed down to prevent scorching. At the 65th and 38th floors (so I once read in a newspaper article) there are devices to retard the drop. When I think about New York, and the grotesquely accelerated behavior some of us show, that seems symbolic. Surely we need occasional slow-down devices or zones of pause, to avoid burning up. The Three Hours for Lunch Club was founded for that purpose, but I fear its influence is not very wide.

An expert English observer of political doings, who was in charge of urgent relief works during the War, remarked the other day that in Washington lately she had seen the affairs of peace proceeding at a war-time pace, and men exhausting themselves in fatigue and pressure.

My own recourse when I find excitements too intense is riding in the subway. It is the most interesting cloister in New York, for it is there that one is most alone. Only two or three times, in twenty years of subway travel, have I ever met anyone I knew. One is completely and blissfully anonymous; and what a gallery of portraiture. What a school, also, of good manners. Physically the conditions are not ideal, but mentally the subway passengers are well bred. No one dreams of forcing his ideas upon you, of interrupting your meditation or trying to get you to sign books or read manuscripts. The subway is perfect spiritual privacy.

I am reminded, irrelevantly, of the grand saying attributed to Mrs Patrick Campbell by Alexander Woollcott in his mischievously witty book *While Rome Burns*. Mrs Campbell, congratulated on her marriage, said how pleasant it is to sink back "into the deep, deep peace of the double-bed after the hurly-burly of the chaise longue."—And now I see in the paper that the young Emperor of Manchukuo began his reign with three days of purification and thought. (He'd better take it while he can, for the destiny of a buffer state is not always easy.) It suggested to me also to stay away from the office today and meditate these things. But so subtly infectious is the damned tohu-bohu it becomes as alluring as tipple. One wants to begin telephoning around and find out what's going on. Nothing is so admirable as to see our own G., sweet-natured mistress of the switchboard, when calls begin to rise to the forenoon peak and perhaps she has also a lap full of correspondence to deal with at the same time and some Visiting Fireman is looking through the little hatchway (like Shere Khan at the mouth of the cave in the grand old *Jungle Book* picture) and the whole excitement and *brio* of the publishing season seems to be coruscating around her small corner. I myself am very likely a bit haywire at that moment, maybe it's the day when the Book of the Month Committee meets, but I catch G's eye and we both burst out laughing. "Well, Gittel, life gets a bit complicated," I remark, and she replies, "Yes, but we have fun." The world of books and magazines may be small potatoes in turnover but it is enormous in comedy.

It seems to be much the same in most offices; and

not only in offices but in domestic and social life too. Perhaps *thought,* in any strong intuitive sense, is gradually being eliminated. Often a whole day will go by without anything that can properly be described as cerebration. And certainly there are many writers who have mistaken for thought what was only bad temper. Perhaps purposeful and intentional thinking is overestimated. I wonder if economic processes can be reduced to simple diagrams of physics as a recent book pictorially suggests. I wonder about "planned economy." (I'm just wondering, not concluding.) I find that many believe Franklin D. Roosevelt to be a great leader not for any far-reaching schemes of rehabilitation but because he seems to be flexibly opportunist. Perhaps the Great Man is not so much he who imposes his will on the Time, but the one who divines the destiny of the Time and lets it impose on him. The danger of such a course is in too sudden and impulsive decisions where the event is subject to hazard.

Perhaps bookstores are not sufficiently appreciated as slow-down devices or zones of pause. They are rarely crowded; even the humblest of them always has something one hasn't read and which may well startle the mind. Publishers and editors and reviewers have mostly too little time to think; booksellers perhaps too much. It seems odd to me that the bookseller doesn't try to do more of the publisher's thinking for him.

Last night a group of men were discussing the general hysteria of the present age; the great rapidity with which all means of communication have outrun the value of whatever we have to communicate. (I must re-read Kipling's Bandar-log, one of the greatest of satires.) It is even significant that News was once called Intelligence; but not so often nowadays. In our anxiety to talk constantly with all parts of the world, by cable, radio, telephone, and newsprint, we almost forget the best kind of talk there is, with one's self. The bookseller has that chance; I wish we heard more of his musings.

By chance I discovered another place of pause. On Sixth Avenue near 47th Street, unspoiled and uninfluenced by the eccentricities of that neighborhood (the Bowery of uptown), is a demure little bazaar of notions and dressmaking materials. A bookseller friend was leaving, in snowy weather, for vacation in Mexico, and I thought to buy her a handkerchief in case of rheum. I went into this delightful elderly place where you recognize the muslin and linen smells of shops you visited in childhood with your mother. There are dress patterns, scissors, ribbons, spools of thread, Victorian underwear, all sorts of feminine falbalas and fixtures. Gentlewomen of established mien serve you with an air of soft surprise; and best of all, there are the antique cash-carriers that sing on overhead wires back to the cashier's cage. I begged permission to pull the handle and ejaculate the money myself. I hadn't worked one of those air-line carriers since I was a young clerk in the original Old Corner Book Store in Boston. The haberdash ladies said they would let me do it again, so I shall solicit my family for small millinery commissions.

A thought in my mind lately has been, if I were going away from New York and might not return, what would I most wish to remember? The motto for such a memorandum would be appropriately, in the Epistle to the Colossians: "Yet am I with you in the spirit, joying and beholding your order . . . the head of all principality and power." I think of a photograph printed in the *Herald-Tribune* in October 1932 showing a line of workmen, in a warm autumn lunchtime, sitting at ease on an awful girder over 800 feet of space at the top of the RCA building. I think of those superb photographs of the city taken by Samuel Gottscho, which specially show the strange light-effects of our Babylon and make one see our heights and distances with new eyes. The camera with its art to hold the moment in spell, to drench it in crystalline streams of stillness, suggests the sadness that is inherent in every glimpse of beauty. The lens of the eye can also summon up those visions of millennium when we have seen (gazing aside hastily at the wheel of a hurrying car) the East River from the Queensborough Bridge, in a pinkish dusk; or pigeons near the City Hall and people strolling in the noonday pause; or lights reflected in Central Park reservoir on a night of fog. Or would it be the strange silence of Riverside Drive in a summer dawn, broken only by the chirp of crickets and the ambling hoof-clops of milk and roll deliveries? Sometimes in middle darkness, below Riverside, one is startled to hear the shrill heroism of cock-crow. Even in the fatal coops of the poultry-train, waiting on the New York Central freight-track, bruised and weary chanticleer has heart to salute the turning planet. Nor would I forget the glimpse of Manhattan's peaks seen from far out on the Northern Boulevard of Long Island. From twenty miles away, as the car comes over the rise between Roslyn and Manhasset, you see them glitter toward the morning, and wonder what the Colossians are doing today. Strange Etruscan and Babylonian touches in her design are part of her oddity; humorous ingenuities too: once on the Manhattan Bridge I applauded an advertiser who had rigged a huge electric coffee-cup sign so that the exhaust rising from someone else's chimney behind it made the imaginary coffee steam with savor. *Verweile doch, du bist so schön,* I have said to her a thousand times in pauses of amazement; but I would not idealize her in memory.

BOUNDARY LINES

ONE of the things I'd like to do this summer would be to have another look at the Canadian border. I've never forgotten the glimpse of it we had two years ago in a vehicle called the Little Goat. I call her that not only because she's nimble on hills; it's the translation of the French name of her well-known make.

I've got a particular reason for wanting to re-examine the Canadian boundary line. Like Thoreau, I also have been putting up a hut in the woods, out on Long Island. I'm a collector, and I need a place to collect my thoughts. I met a delightful French Canadian carpenter and woodsman from the State of Maine, who had been out of work and said he'd build it for me.

In the old days, in our rustic suburb, there were no rules and regulations of any kind. You could stick up anything, from a henhouse to a landlord, and no one would be surprised. But while we were living in town, a couple of years ago, the Salamis Estates secretly turned themselves into an Incorporated Village. That means we have a zoning law and building ordinances of our own. Fred the carpenter and I had got our shack pretty well along before we discovered that we had transgressed all the rules and were well over an imaginary latitude known as the Building Line. And my neighbor Mr Larry Nielsen, building inspector of the Salamis Estates, out for a stroll one evening, was shocked and embarrassed to see a half-finished building for which he had issued no permit.

Embarrassment was universal. Fred and I quit work pending a meeting of the Board of Appeals. The Italian mason from another (and probably more venal) village was heartbroken to discontinue in the middle of building the chimney, of which he is justly proud. "Beelding inspec?" he exclaimed. "You feex. He just wanta da greft."

Fortunately the Village Clerk, Mr Phil Hodge, is a book publisher; I explained to him that I had innocently chosen that particular spot because it was as secluded as possible; that I planned to plant poison ivy all around it to exempt it from public haunt; and I needed that exemption in order to do my reading for the Book of the Month Club. As he is the sales manager of *Anthony Adverse* I hoped this would move him.

Mr Hodge sympathized, but said of course it must go to the Board.

So the first thing to do was to find out exactly how badly we had erred. Fred, the carpenter, is one of those fellows who can do anything. He said he had an old transit, and we would run a line along the boundary of my wood-lot to see exactly how close to the edge we were. And Larry Nielsen, whose honor was involved in this error of mine, came along to see fair play.

I always supposed, in my simplicity, that to run a straight line was a simple thing to do. Well, you look up the title deeds and this is the sort of help they give you. I'm quoting exactly from the documents. "Beginning at a point in the westerly line of a highway soandso, distant 94.54 feet southerly from a monument at soandso, running thence on a curve to the left having a radius of 2436.20 feet and the chord of which curve bears south 26 degrees 4 minutes 10 seconds east and has a length of 89.30 feet a distance of 89.03 feet along the westerly side of said highway to a point; thence south 46 degrees 53 minutes 50 seconds west . . ."

There's plenty more of it, but I spare you. First, even supposing you find the monument—which is too imposing a name for a little concrete stub that's been buried in jungle for thirty years. Did you ever try to measure exactly 94.54 feet? And on a curve, too. Or to carry a string 2436.20 feet long on a straight line through all the neighbors' properties? It can't be done, at least not without their suspecting something is wrong. That string, if we had been too accurate with it, would have gone right through the bathroom of a neighbor's house. It was a hot day, and the lady was taking a bath. Chivalry comes before surveying. It looked sufficiently brazen the way we had the little telescope trained on her window. Fred kept trying to get a better focus, but finally said he thought the instrument really ought to go back to the maker for correction.

But shooting a straight line down the edge of the wood-lot was the real job. A lot of trees grow up in 30 years or so, and even a transit can't see through them. Fred said he thought he could get a clear shot if we rooted out some of the wild grapes; but I pleaded to save them; they were to be the privacy screen for the shack. In the matter of calculating angles Larry Nielsen believed the scale should be read clockwise, but Fred thought the other way. Since the whole boundary was only 202 feet (but quite bumpy) I thought we could do it well enough by pacing; and I privately decided to call perpendicular an angle they measured as 95° 10′.

Then we discovered another monument, under

some more poison ivy, and decided to complete the survey with our piece of string. The string was pretty straight except where it went round the grape tree. I think we may have wobbled a little with the plumb line.

Before taking the results of our survey to the Board of Appeals we were having a cooling drink. How come, I asked Fred, that you happen to have a transit? Gee, boss, he said, "I was one of the gang that surveyed the Canadian boundary, all the way from the State of Washington to New Brunswick."

I've been looking again at the Canadian boundary on the map. It looks pretty simple, just a straight line and the Great Lakes, until you get near the State of Maine. When Fred got that near home, after his long trip all the way across, his hand certainly shook with emotion. If Canada has a few thousand square miles that really belong to us, or the other way round, I know just how it happened.

DIARY FOR DAUGHTERS

THE YOUNG MAN and the Old Man were left to keep house while the Family went away for a brief holiday. The Old Man promised a faithful report on the good-will, stock, and fixtures. This is it.

The Knothole, August 15

Everything under control. I'll take the simpler elements first. The Y. M. went off to work at 7.45, on the hoof. He knew it would be futile to try to rouse the O. M. to drive him to the train. However the O. M. was up and around not much later. This was Thursday, the maid's day off, and the O. M., in sole command, fortified himself for responsibility. By which I mean he had an egg to his breakfast, and made sure there was hootch in the cupboard against any buckling of spirits.

First, the turtle. I can't call him Oswald, as your instructions suggest: it seems taking a liberty (he is very reserved) and I don't feel Oswaldish about him. I think of him, if at all, as Oggie, for Ogden Nash, who wrote gaily about turtles. You said there must be enough water in the tank so he can approach his food from below, yet not so much as to fatigue him with constant swimming. I measured with the sewing tape; mean depth 2¾ inches. It seems to be all right, for he's snapping busily at floating ant-eggs. What happens if he eats them all: do I have to plunder the big anthill in the garden?

Confidential: I forgot to put away the jam last

night and the ants got into the kitchen cupboard. Don't tell anyone: but how about letting Oggie have the run of the grocery shelf? I don't like to keep mashing the ants and leaving them there—or does he only eat ants in egg form? Let me know about this.

Now the white mouse. She's wonderful, no trouble at all. I brought her cage outdoors into the fresh air. It seemed to me that she was a bit moody: too much publicity, I think: the cream bottle you put for her to sleep in doesn't give her much privacy, and it's rather hard and slippery. I know myself that if the room gets light I wake up terribly early. I thought at first she was a little bloodshot, but I guess her eyes are always red? (Let me know.) I found some green crepe paper in the garage, wrapped around an old flower-pot. Just the thing. I crumpled it up into a nice complicated mass and put it in the cage. She was delighted: she's been spending the whole day rummaging around inside it.

Let me answer your next question before you ask it. I went to the post office and there wasn't any mail for you.

The Baby—I almost forgot the Baby! She's fine. She played around the floor while I was having breakfast, and I shut her up in her pen this morning while I was working. She doesn't like a pen any better than I do my own kind, and she cried a little, but I gave her a ball to play with. At eleven o'clock she had lunch, per your schedule, and I put her to bed for her nap.

I intended then to look up William Watson's poems about Wordsworth and Tennyson; Watson was a very fine English poet who died the other day. As I get homesick for little Helen playing the piano (especially *The Isle of Capri* and *I'll Never Say Never Again, Again*) I was thinking of Watson's pretty verses about the keyboard.

Five-and-thirty black slaves,
Half-a-hundred white,
All their duty but to sing
For their Queen's delight—
Now with throats of thunder,
Now with dulcet lips,
While she rules them royally
With her finger-tips!

When she quits her palace,
All the slaves are dumb—
Dumb with dolor till the Queen
Back to Court is come. . . .

But about that time Smudge, the terrier, came back very wet and muddy from the neighbor's goldfish pool. It's extraordinary, Paddy Cassidy (who gets Smudge into those wild games) always looks clean and demure while Smudge gets so trampish. As Blythe truly said, dogs usually take after their owners and Mr C. looks neater than I do.

One of the grand things about living in the country, always so much to do around the place there's really no need for any thinking; so instead of going back to William Watson I hunted out my old gloves, dug up some fine big poison ivy roots and planted them carefully alongside the chimney of my cabin. The ivy was astonished: the first time in all these years that it has been treated with such kindness. But it will grow faster than anything else I know, to take the newness off the chimney. Just as I was watering and fertilizing the roots, arrived a load of gravel for the roadway; the driver was surprised to see poison ivy so pampered.

I reopened William Watson. This is fine, isn't it—he was writing about Poetry in an age of witty triviality:—

Thenceforth she but festooned the porch of things;
Apt at life's lore, incurious what life meant.
Dextrous of hand, she struck her lute's few strings;
Ignobly perfect, barrenly content. . . .

The porch . . . festooned the porch of things . . . I hadn't put those cushions out to dry (they got wet in the thunderstorm last night). While I was doing so, two little colored boys wanted to sell tickets for something—I didn't bother to find out what. No one sells me tickets without a struggle.

Now I knew it was time for lunch. You don't need a clock for that: promptly at 1 o'clock and 7 o'clock Mittens the cat appears from nowhere and looks expectant at the back steps. If a writer could hide himself, between meals, the way a cat does, what a good writer he might get to be.

No one feels like working immediately after lunch. As you know, there's a very comfortable bunk in the Knothole. The question is, what is the absolutely perfect reading to go to sleep on? I vote for Santayana. The woods drowse and rustle in the warm summer siesta; and Señor Don Santayana's comfortable prose (never dull, never ornate; always melodious, lucid, inconspicuously urbane) gently abolishes the mind. You lay down the page to think it over . . . as gently as the tide rising at Lloyds Neck something mists, softens, blurs . . . while you are trying to think of the right word . . . annihilates? . . . obliterates? . . .

It's almost 3 o'clock. According to instructions, time for Smudge's lunch. (Smudge has been tied up since her frolic with Paddy.) As usual she has wound her chain three times round a tree. It's no use to try to coax her to walk round in reverse and unwind it herself. She lies down on her back with paws upward, feeling that this mysterious shortening of scope is guilt of some sort. You may as well pick her up and totter thrice round the tree yourself, like a witch in Macbeth. The Baby, upstairs, hears the rattle of the chain and begins to make appeal. Smudge gets her lunch, strictly according to the formula you posted over the kitchen sink. Then she goes to examine the new gravel-pile in the backyard. This is evidently (she thinks) an ingenious playground specially arranged for her. Paddy Cassidy thinks so too. The word has gone round: Yay, dogs! Smudge has a gravel-pile over at her house! They begin digging, snouting, barking. Chow Snyder trots over, in his dignified way, to have a look. I tie Smudge up again, order Chow and Paddy home, put the Baby in the pen with a toy to keep her quiet, have another look at the white mouse (such a comfort she is, the most unexacting of pets) and return to the Knothole to work.

William Watson was at his best, perhaps, in those lovely verse epigrams. I wish I could exactly remember that one that goes something like this—

Momentous to himself as I to me
Is every man that ever woman bore:
Once, in a flash, this truth appeared to me—
And then no more.

I know that isn't exact; I think I have it in a book up at the house; but if I go across the garden the

Baby will see me and it may rouse her to a holler. But here's one of Watson's delightful things, his little poem about the queer feeling we sometimes have, World-Strangeness, the sensation that this marvellous earth is too mysterious for us ever to get really used to it—worldbroken, we might say:—

In this house with starry dome,
Floored with gemlike plains and seas,
Shall I never feel at home,
Never wholly be at ease. . . .

The Baby's crying! I've taken her out of the pen, and brought her down here to the Knothole. I've carried out a jug of iced tea from the house, for me, and a couple of biscuits for her. She's never been in the Knothole before; she won't settle down until she has explored it thoroughly. . . . I wonder how she got that gob of chewing gum on her coat? Not my fault, I swear it. . . . I'm drinking the tea very carefully, trying not to jangle the ice to arouse her curiosity. . . . She's climbing into the bunk, she's lying on her stomach with her legs flattened out behind like a frog (you know how comic she looks) . . . I think maybe she'll take a nap. I turn carefully and catch her bright dark gaze. That was a mistake; she perks up at once and looks ready for comedy of some sort. I'll pretend I was looking at something else. I'm reading Watson, *Wordsworth's Grave:*—

Afar though nation be on nation hurled,
And life with toil and ancient pain depressed,
Here one may scarce believe the whole wide world
Is not at peace, and all man's heart at rest. . . .

She's eating a charred stick she got out of the fireplace. The little bitch, I never heard her slip down off the bunk. I take it away from her. She goes and gets it again. What about it, I think. Perhaps instinct knows better than I. You didn't say anything about charcoal in your instructions. It's supposed to be very good for indigestion, isn't it? Perhaps she feels a colic coming on and is antidoting beforehand? I let her munch a little of it and then hoick her back on the bunk. Lie down! Go to sleep!

Poetry! Marvellous, on a summer afternoon to read the noble verses of that proud, sad, difficult heart; lines that now suddenly seem cut in stone, as no poet's ever can until he is gone forever—and learns the answer to his own question:

Whether 'tis ampler day divinelier lit
Or homeless night without.

Reading his strong lines makes one crave a deeper nobler voice in the music of our own puzzled age—

Where is the singer whose large notes and clear
Can heal, and arm, and plenish, and sustain?

. . . . There he is, indeed; I hear him, and so does the Baby. The Good Humor van goes jingling down the road. She seems to recognize that merry little gong. She was lying so quietly too, with one soft ear crumpled under her. Perhaps I oughtn't to let her sleep like that, it'll give her a cauliflower? But I mustn't expect too much of her. After all, she's only a cocker spaniel, 4 months old.

She's been asleep for an hour! But I think I hear Mittens yowling. I'll bet Smudge has got off the chain and drunk Mittens's milk. (The snap on the chain doesn't catch properly.) I better go and see.

The instant I leave, the Baby springs up from perfect sleep. She thinks she is deserted for ever.

Anguish! She's standing wildly against the screen-door, paws high to beseech. She looks like Helen Jacobs serving tennis.

Smudge has been in the goldfish pool again.

I'm going to give Mittens the can of kippered herring I've been saving for my Sunday breakfast. Will that be all right?

I really *will* be careful with the strawberry jam. But if you see any anteaters in Quebec, better bring them back with you.

Goodbye, darlings: I must drive down to the station to meet Y. M.

THE OLD MAN, P. D. Q.

P.S. P. D. Q. means *Père de Quatre.*

Another P.S.—Do you remember this of Watson's, about a dog:—

His friends he loved. His fellest earthly foes—
Cats—I believe he did but feign to hate.
My hand will miss the insinuated nose,
Mine eyes the tail that wagged contempt at Fate.

MANDARIN ON THE ROAD

Editor's Note: *We translate excerpts—carefully chosen—from a letter of the Old Mandarin to one of his cronies in China. We have had to abbreviate: Oriental philosophers like to expound their thoughts in full, with many divarications.*

The "Idlers of the Bamboo Grove" (sometimes translated "Tipplers") are the direct descendants of the group of poets founded by Li Po 1200 years ago. It is the oldest literary club in the world. See Herbert Giles's fascinating History of Chinese Literature, *p.* 152.

I

EXCELLENCY, *Thinker of Long Thoughts!*—I shall not return to China this summer. This Hegemony of Haste, passing (on the whole, with enviable tranquillity) through deep social change, is too interesting. Particularly at this season, when the Sons of Speed are on the road in swarms, the time is valuable for observation. Even after all these years there is much I do not understand, and probably misinterpret. But I tell you plainly what I see. You say that when the Idlers of the Bamboo Grove retire to the pagoda for wine and contemplation they read aloud my letters. Salute them from the ancient expatriate who has learned from these delightful "folks" (their name of affection for themselves) to exonerate himself from the burden of thought. (Yet there are sad symptoms that this most persistent of human maladies may eventually infect the Americans also.) . . . Give my love to the comeliest of the serving maids. I am not sure of her name—I think it was Po Lil Chile—but I remember her pretty ankles.

A few notes on a trip, by gasoline-litter (motor

palanquin) in the great province of New York. . . . Many signposts along the way commemorate events in the history of this nation; particularly where something happened to the detriment of the British or Red Indians, whom these people seem to have disliked with equal fervor. I should have been pleased to pause and study some of these notices, feeling they were certain to arouse conjecture; but they usually come where the palanquin is travelling 40 and another vehicle just behind is impatient to pass. Besides, as my host casually remarked (on a steep slope of the Mountains that Kill Cats) his brakes were loose and it was difficult to stop. Sufflamination, I said, is not an American specialty; to which he made no answer. So our halts were only at replenishing stations, which my friend chooses by some occult principle, based on plumbing and the necessities of his family. . . . Consideration for the female is a fundamental doctrine in this country; undoubtedly for that reason the British and Red Indians fared so badly here.

. . . . From the Island of Length we crossed into the Island of Height by the upper roadway of the Bridge of Queens, and saw the magnificent sweep of their extraordinary buildings. One of the finest of these is a huge hospital (the design of which, I am told, was suggested by the Palace of the Popes at Avignon) where the patients have a salutary view of the hastening vehicles over the bridge; thus those already injured in traffic are encouraged by watching those who are about to be. At a pause in a crowded street a peddler urged us to buy a toy called "Joe Penner's Duck." This, I vaguely gathered, was an instance of the native passion for catchwords, fetiches and jocose effigies which are suddenly popularized by voices in air or print and flood the country in recurring spasms. Another example would be the frequency of legend about a well-formed actress, Miss West, who has become their mythical Venus Callipyge or Venus Genetrix. It would be difficult to imagine in a civilization of more age and lassitude, such delightful enthusiasm aroused by familiar mammalian fact. Perhaps it shows how deeply (even if subconsciously) the American male resented the epicene tendency of his women a few years ago. Or perhaps it shows a return (after the Era of Fiscal Effusion) to the simpler pleasures; as they used to say in Chicago during the Great Deficit, Wine, Women and Song turned to Beer, Momma, and the Radio. Or perhaps (most likely of all) it shows nothing except that the enjoyment of stupid old men (like Keyserling, Spengler, Pareto, and myself) is attempting to account for things. Some of the folklore about Miss West is difficult for the foreigner to understand: for instance the riddle about the Province of Montana. . . .

Going up the Drive Beside the River that bright Monday morning I noticed two unexpected things. One, a neat little horse-drawn green wagon trotting uptown. *Spick & Span Laundry,* it said. If my dividends continue to fail I shall probably have to take to the laundry business myself (surely there is no occupation more genuinely serviceable) so I was interested. Messrs. Spick and Span, I assume, are two alert Jewish fellows: I have seen in the Book of Telephones (the best reference work on sociology) that they also own a dairy, a window-cleaning business, and a hosiery. Other memorable glimpse was an old ship of sails, *Tusitala,* still at her long mooring on that barren shore. When salty tide sweeps up the Henry Hudson River it must itch at her keel. She lies there, under the high cliffs of apartment houses, like a poem that got stranded in an anthology of prose.

Across the Bridge of George Washington we were now out and away, in the clear. Young men beside the road embarrassed me by a fixed glance and gestures of the thumb seeming derogatory; but these (my host explained) intend no disdain; on the contrary they are Desiderators of Hitch. Disregard them, said my friend: the litter is full; besides, the driver's responsible for any injury to a non-paying guest. (Which I also was, I reflected.)

It was the first of the month of Julius, the beginning of the great holiday season, and most vehicles were loaded with camping and æstivating gear; some families were packed into bright-colored tax-palanquins which sped along as though demented by escape from the city.

You will remember, O Lover of Detailed Information, that I sent you several large-scale maps to identify my inquiring excursions in this remarkable country. To these I pray you refer. We crossed a small corner of the Province of Innovated Jersey; what my host describes as the Scottie Country, for indeed that section is greatly given to the breed and sale of Scottish terriers. In dogs—as in wine, sporting gear, dress clothes, literature, steamships, head-waiters, perfumery, lecturers, and all other luxuries—the Americans are distrustful of their own products. See on the map Hohokus, Saddle River, and Ramsey, all of which I thought attractive; and Ramsey placards itself as "the 3rd healthiest place in the U.S." I was eager to stop and inquire about the other two, and why, but my host was urging his car forward, anxious for more truly savage scenes. When near Sloatsburg, in the Hills of Ramapo, he saw a sign advertising overalls, he announced that we were really in the country. Where the Blue Jeans Begin, he added; a remark not worth repetition save that it reminds me of an interesting philology: the word *jean* (coarse blue cotton cloth, worn by the American coolies) is corrupted from the name Genoa. Now at a roadside counter we halted for Beer and Hamburgers; the latter are fried patties of triturated beef, augmented (unless you expressly veto) with onion. My host, who falls readily into casual conversation, asked Mrs Wanamaker (who manages the stand) if she were related to the renowned mandarin of that name. "No," she said; "if we were maybe we wouldn't have to work so hard." . . . My own acquaintance with the late Mr Wanamaker was limited to the literary form invented by him, the Department Store Essay. These homiletic maxims (or minims), respectfully known as The Writings of The Founder, were in praise of piety, patriotism, and other encouragements of the bland, benign, and beautiful. Considered as opuscules of prose they were opaque in style but mercifully brief. . . . A study of our Chinese epigram-form known as the *stop-short* would be of great value to American writers. But it is amusing that every nation considers the others so unnecessarily verbose. . . .

Sentimentalists often deplore advertising along the highways. Not I. Often these notices are valuable glimpses of the national psychology. Admirable lyrics, and much in the sly humor of our own race, are those in honor of a shaving unguent; they are cunningly spaced on succeeding posts so that they may be comfortably read at about 50 miles per hour. They inculcate the virtues of prudence or æsthetics. I hoped my host would notice:—*Keep well to the right—Of the oncoming car—Get your close shaves —from the* 1-*pound jar;* and this, again indicative of the national delicacy toward women:—*If you think—She likes your bristles—Walk barefooted— through some thistles.* As this shaving cream comes from Burma it naturally has some of our Oriental subtlety.

I had supposed that the County of the Sullivans, of whose beauty I had heard, was chiefly Irish or Celtic. This however was not so, at any rate along Road Number 17. From the town of Goshen onward the instruction of Genesis 45, 10, has been taken seriously. Surely characteristic of American paradox was to find, in the heart of this inland region (in the town of Monticello), eating houses proclaiming "Chinese and Sea Food." So does this heteropathic nation always hanker for that which is difficult, different, or far-away. To be indigenous, here, is to be indigent . . . in Chicago, I remember, the most prosperous cafés are those which represent themselves to be London chop-houses or Heidelberg beer-halls. . . . Of course the most creative artists are usually hybrid; our Chinese lethargy is probably due to inbreeding? The great advantage of America, from the point of view of humor and eventual artistic achievement, is the strong infusion of Irish and Jewish, whose nimble wit and excessive volatility prevent the dull Saxon temperament from subsiding into its customary stupor.

A slightly ferocious feeling is imparted to this pretty upland region by the frequent repetition of the word Kill in their names of place. The early settlers must have been a bloodthirsty lot: not only are cats killed in those mountains but beaver, deer, bear, and I dare say an occasional pedestrian. Thither also prizefighters usually retire for strengthening before their combats. Among the vacationists it is often difficult to distinguish sex, except where a Miss Western contour is unmistakable; for all wear stop-short breeches of extreme truncation, and are grilled roast-fowl-color by sun. This is well: to be incessantly reminded of the disparities of gender is stimulating for poets but it is incompatible with philosophy. . . .

We lunched at a clean little eating-house in the pleasant town of Roscoe, served by a lady called Kathryn who makes good pie. The menu said "An American Restaurant with Scotch Prices," which alarmed me as I had no Scotch money with me. . . .

Now we began to see country of sweet charm. We followed young waters of the Delaware and Susquehanna Rivers, those magnificent streams of which the Province of Penn has made so much talk it is forgotten that their beauty begins in the Province of New York. (So is the true origin of reality often unremembered.) My host showed himself an imperfect citizen in that he turned off from the main ways and followed the lovely and unfrequented Road 79. This was at the bifurcation of Windsor where we paused at a replenishing station. These pumps of plenty, where Distance and Locomotion are miraculously distilled from tall bright-painted standpipes, are (as I have told you before) the true wayside shrines of the American folk; chapels of ease in their great religion of Let's Itinerate. In spite of modern mechanism and sanitation these places preserve some of the old kindliness of the livery stable, the inn, the crossroads store. On a chair in this gasoline sanctuary at Windsor the checker-board was laid out, ready for play when a pause should occur in service. Checkers (my host explained), like the overalls noted earlier, is a sign of the real country.

Road 79, beautiful and sparse, brought us all the way to Ithaca. I will write more later.

This, O Student of Truth, from him whose inward notions are ever at thy command.

II

(*Further Translations*)

I PROMISED further notes on my explorations. This time my host determined on an enormous detour to avoid driving through New York City. He showed me a note printed on the map of Socony (one of these people's chief cartographers). Of the region including New York, Newark, Jersey City, Montclair, Morristown, etc. the map said warningly "This area is distorted." I was glad therefore that we went another way. Besides, a direct route would have taken us through Parsippany, which I do not know how to pronounce.

On a peaceful Sunday afternoon we set out. My friend had his engine filled with some new kind of lubricant said to contain Castor Oil. The local garage commended it, and my friend, long experienced in domestic matters, liked the idea. Castor Oil had been good for the children, why not for the vehicle?

It is instructive for me to travel with M., for though in many ways a typical American, operose and credulous, he has (when away from work) occasional flashes of irony or doubt. For instance his method of finding his way through the reticulated road system of Westchester County. The only thing to do, he says, is pretend you're going to DANBURY; then, when no one is looking, you can turn off and head somewhere else. This is symbolic of much in American life.

We took the Oyster Bay–Stamford ferry. M. is always hungry as soon as he starts on a trip, so aboard the *Sankaty* we had crackers and pop. He said he realized now that he was Grown Up, for he could not finish a bottle of cream soda. "Thirty years ago I thought this stuff was better than champagne."—In American literature, however, both cream soda and champagne are more esteemed than the still wines of deep vintage.

In Stamford a policeman with peremptory gesture forbade us turning left on the Boston Post Road, so we were carried some way eastward by the polyphloisboian Sunday traffic; Bostonians, I suppose, frantic to get home. This highway is rated Number 1 of the United States; avoid it. What would Cotton Mather and other of its early travelers think of it now? Particularly I am always shocked by the long platform-trucks on which new motor-cars are piled up. . . . Eventually we were able to find our way to delightful Road 137. This passes through the pretty country behind Stamford much favored by the people of arts and letters. As Mr Heywood Broun (one of their philosophic mandarins) has said, in that neighborhood you cannot throw a stone in any direction without hitting a writer; he added this would not be a bad idea.

The obliquity of the inhabitants is imitated by the roads themselves. "As crooked as number 22" is an old folk-saying in the region of Katonah. I have heard that more poets live along Road 22 than any other highway (of whom Miss Edna Millay is probably my favorite; she has something of our Chinese melancholy and brevity). Another interesting habit of Road 22 is the way it skirts the edge of New England all the way up but warily avoids ever crossing the frontier. M. tells me that you can follow it to Lake Champlain and the Canadian border; and that a great deal of poetry came down that way in bottles during the consulship of Volstead.

We were overcome by dark near Pawling. My host, who has a good eye for a wayside inn of the right sort, spotted Broadmeadows, a spacious old house where we lay in comfort. A huge barn adjoining is used in summer as a theatre. Young actors seek to improve themselves in their profession by playing in vacant barns and wharves during the vacation. This gives entertainment to the summer colonists and spares the New York theatre many superfluous versions of the favorite American play; which invariably proves that the husband and wife really did like each other after all, but that the husband is the juice of a tree. (I have forgotten the exact word, and my dictionary is not at hand.) As the inn kitchen was not working we ate at a Log Cabin down the road. Log Cabins are placed frequently by the American wayside, to remind these people of their primitive beginnings; as the cooking would also do. My host's usual order is 2 oldfashioned cocktails and the Western sandwich (which, like the civilization for which it is named, is sown with nuggets of enduring onion). I was wondering if it was the latter which kept him awake a while. No; conscientious motorist that he is, he was brooding that he had parked the car, inside the stable of the inn, in such position that it would be difficult to back out. If you find an American lying awake at night you may be sure it is some practical problem that besets him. . . .

There is no more excellent feeling than the early morning start, after coffee and eggs, in a willing car and unknown road ahead. My goodnatured host and his charming lady, seeing my eye brighten upon that landscape, my nostril expand to the sweet air of late summer, rallied me on my exhilaration. The Old Mandarin's perfectly happy they said; slept, fed, and transported, now he gazes about to see what he can find wrong with our civilization. To which I offered my usual reply, that one makes fun of that which one loves. We diverted from argument to congratulate Road 22 on its narrow escape. A sharp curve led us to a signpost which said BOSTON CORNERS, and added "The geographic remoteness of this district of 1040 acres led Massachusetts to cede it to New York in 1855." As a bumper against Massachusetts the State of New York has here put one of its magnificent State Parks, the Taconic Reservation. There are 70 of these in all; for 50 years now this State has been working to preserve its forests, waterfalls and choice areas of natural beauty for the unspoiled enjoyment of the public. This indeed is a social achievement which I heartily applaud. Mr Keating, who runs the general store and P. O. at Copake Falls (at the entrance to Taconic Park) gave me a booklet describing all the New York State Parks; it is well worth study. (EDITOR'S NOTE: published gratis by the State Council of Parks, Albany, N. Y.)

We drove up into the beautiful forests of the Taconic range, along a brook oddly named *Bash*

Bish—perhaps the Indians' imitation of the sound of tumbling water. High in those mountain solitudes we visited a true philosopher, M.'s friend Professor W., a mathematician from McGill University, who had rented a cottage for the summer. In that keen air and wide sunshine he was meditating on the Dynamics of a Rigid Particle; and exemplifying it also, for his household, disregarding both Standard and Daylight times, lived by some special horology of their own which they had brought from Montreal. Consequently though ourselves had only lately breakfasted it was their time for lunch. In the sunshine outside the cottage sat another scientist from Montreal, basking comfortably in shorts and devotedly studying a huge book. This can be nothing less than Astronomical Tables, we thought, but it proved to be some technical encyclopedia of Stocks and Bonds. "What a grand way to spoil a perfect vacation," M. exclaimed; the scientist replied (a little sadly, I thought), "It's a case of trying to protect some investments."

Such full blessing of highland air and sunshine, I thought, would protect an even more valuable investment.

Our next big event was crossing the new Rip Van Winkle Bridge, one of the many "Gateways" to the Catskill Mountains. The pontiff at the Rip Van Winkle toll-gate was so courteously pleased to see us that I got the impression (wrong, perhaps) that this noble structure is not doing as much business as they had hoped. Thence we plunged into the hills. Lunch at a Log Cabin was ill chosen, for after roasted chicken-thigh, beer, pie, and ice cream, my host became very sleepy at the wheel. A glazed stupor in his eye, an occasional swerve on a winding road, were not reassuring. His mental associations are mostly of a simple kind and what really brought him to was finding Grand Gorge. From this place, it appears, came his household milk (it seems a long way) when he was living in a New York apartment. Every night, visiting the ice-box, he would observe bottle caps printed GRAND GORGE. This, he said, always seemed an appropriate name for his midnight gluttony. This topic woke him up. Also, when we turned off at Stamford (a different Stamford) and down towards Delhi and Walton, we saw Bear Spring Mountain on the map. Was this the Bear Spring that supplies water to so many offices in the city? How many beautiful stenographers and young clerks have drunk from those big bubbling green carboys (he said); and have made the office cooler an occasion for appointing subsequent rendezvous. If this were the authentic Bear Spring, every office manager should make pilgrimage to it.

. . . Upstate New York, not only in its place names but also in its urban architecture, evidently underwent a strong palladian or demirep-classic influence about a hundred years ago. The balconied portico of the custard-colored Clinton House in Ithaca is a charming example. It is a comfortable hotel; perhaps its pretty waitresses (who are keen about books) can persuade the management to put reading lamps by the beds. It is amusing to see somewhere on the main street a building of the colonnaded Greek type fitted out with a new practical front for shop-window purposes; and this too is not unsymbolic in the field of education. M., who likes to make early start, observed a car with license-plate *U. S. Geological Survey 3040* setting out from the hotel at 7.30 A. M. "If the government's on the road, we ought to be too" was his comment. Nor would he pause, even to buy gasoline, until we reached the attractive little filling station of Mary Clark in Dundee. This is midway the marvellous concrete road that curls over the highlands between Lake Seneca and Lake Keuka. My host was depressed when Mrs Clark and her assistant Ray Vaughn did not seem to think much of his castor oil lubricant. They thumbed it with care and said firmly they did not think it had enough body.

. . . On the way back from Lake Keuka my host, perhaps a little jealous of the admiration we had shown for New York, wished to take us through a corner of his native Pennsylvania. Seeking the right turn he was scanning all signs hastily as we passed. In the town of Waverly is a board which says *Lunchen 50*. "Fifty miles to Lunchen," he pondered innocently. "Where is that town, I don't see it on the map." We pointed out the rest of the legend to him: *Dinner 85, Overnight 1.00*.—As we hastened along the Susquehanna Valley a furious honking just behind alarmed us. Some secret guilt in M.'s bosom caused him to suppose it the police. He pulled over and slowed. A car rushed by, a large face thrust out of it, almost maniac with cordiality, and yelled "Hello, Nassau County!" Our license number bore the same key-letters as the other's; and Livingston meeting Stanley in the bush could not have been better pleased. This, too, I felt was America.

REASONS OF MY OWN

I

Washington, D. C.

THIS has been a wonderful season for reading. After three winters spent in town, where I had only an iron ration of books at hand, I've been back in the country and in the shelf-crammed room where I have spent more time than anywhere else on earth. For fifteen years books have been accumulating around me in that small chamber, and the pleasure this winter has been exploring among the things I had almost forgotten were there. Hidden behind sea-chests of manuscript, piles of magazines, masses of galley-proof from the Book of the Month Club, I have rediscovered many ancient favorites and excitements. And I promised to write you some notes on books that have meant most to me, and why. So much nonsense has been uttered about book collecting, so many people been terrorized into pursuing first editions or limited issues, I wanted to utter a word of devil's advocacy. The only "association copies" that I cherish are those that have personal associations for me. The only reasons for valuing a certain book are reasons of my own. No dealer could possibly appraise my library in dollars and cents. The only purpose of these letters is to encourage you to make your own choices. A first edition of the *Rubaiyat* bought at auction could not possibly mean more to me than the hideous little copy—bound in Guernsey-cow-colored suède and loathsomely illustrated by Gilbert James—which was given me by old John Loder the Woodbridge bookseller who actually knew FitzGerald and remembered discussing with him the impossibility of selling the famous first pamphlet. *Reasons of My Own* would be an accurate subtitle for these offhand comments, for they can have no worth unless I speak my own candor.

For a good many weeks now, so excited about the idea that I could hardly wait to begin, I've been imagining myself setting down these notes for you in the familiar surroundings of that room. I would go along the shelves, choosing by my own occult principle of selection, reviewing some of the books which (as John Donne said, in the poems I have vainly tried to make you read) "make one little room an Everywhere." Then (why is life so fertile in paradox?) I find myself by chance writing this first letter in the once familiar setting of a newspaper office. It is a very quiet and orderly editorial room, much more pleasantly furnished than those I once worked in, but with the good old professional air of intense concentration. In the far corner, by the window, the young cartoonist with his large blank sheet tacked on the drawing board is brooding over today's paper in quest of an idea. Three or four other editorial writers are sitting at their flat-topped desks making notes or skirmishing inwardly for a good lead. A young woman in a black and white check suit has actually made a start on her piece, whatever it is; a minute ago she was pattering swiftly on the typewriter but now she seems to be stuck. I see her unconsciously snap her fingers with annoyance; she pauses, twirls sideways in the revolving chair, sits with her hands interlaced in an attitude of grievous consideration, and ponders a red book. On the revolving bookcase a big Webster lies open. On the desk I have borrowed for the moment is a big pile of bound volumes of the *Congressional Record*—rarely sought by collectors: yet I am quite sure that if there were time to go hunting in it I could find much trove.—Incidentally I still think the old pigeon-holed rolltop desks of my newspaper days were better to write at than these modern flat planes. In the dust and stuffing of the good old pigeon holes a vacant mind could always find some surprising suggestion; and bending forward into the cavern of the desk gave one a comforting sense of privacy.

So, away from the books I wanted to consult, and under the grievance of time, this cannot be more than a preface to our little series. But it pleases me that it is written on that good coarse stuff known to every newspaper man as Copy Paper. I had not handled a pile of those loose sheets in a long time; and straightening them into alignment I cut the tendon between thumb and forefinger just as I so often used to do. Newspaper writers must always remember that copy paper has very sharp edges; in more ways than one.

But a brief visit to Washington, even for only a few hours, has its suggestions. All over the city and suburbs the little pink signs have appeared which say *To Cherry Blossoms*. They point the way toward the famous Japanese cherry trees which line the lagoon and are now just coming into flower. At a time when there is so much international irritability a remembrance of that charming gesture from one government to another is surely in order. Some travelers say that the imaginative Japanese consider the plum blossom a more subtle and significant beauty than the cherry; they would have liked to pay us the supreme compliment of sending plum trees rather than cherries, but they had heard so much about George Washington and the cherry tree they believed it to have some deep American symbolism. At any rate the original cherry that was cut down has been replaced by thousands that have become a national delight.—The innumerable cars parked around the lake, however, are not those of the pilgrims of beauty; they belong to government workers who have to leave them there and proceed on foot to their huge office buildings a mile or so away. I see no solution for the capital's parking problem unless they might use the interior of Washington Monument for vertical parking.

It is not before me here, but in any list of Books That Have Influenced Me (you'll not forget, by the way, to look up R. L. Stevenson's essay with that title) it is fair to give first place to the little primer in which I first learned to read. Without that no other books would have meant anything. The title page is gone, so I can't tell the date of issue, but it was called *Monroe's Chart Primer,* published by E. H. Butler and Co., Philadelphia. As I remember, each of its pages was also used, greatly enlarged, as a classroom chart. The pictures, when seen again, must come back in vivid recognition to many kindergarten pupils of the 90's. I reproduce one here—which I think must have had a profound effect upon my whole life. For, though theoretically indolent and easy of pace how much of my life has been spent in catching trains. I'm sorry you can't see that the young student had colored the picture lusciously with a purple pencil.

Monroe's Chart Primer did not only instil the

Lesson 3. Sound of r.

r a n

ran

an ran

ran man

man A man

A man ran.

A man ran.

(11)

"MONROE'S CHART PRIMER"

rudiments of legibility but had its æsthetic messages too. "In these exercises," says the preface, "the pupils should be led, by the example of the teacher, to use a sweet and loving tone. . . . The teacher requires the pupil to repeat such expressions as *Good Morning, How do you do,* etc., until they learn to speak them in a sweet, agreeable tone." My clearest recollection of the little kindergarten in which the Monroe Primer and Charts were used is of the day when the teacher, keeping us in suspense before unrolling the sheet that carried the new lesson, warned us it was going to be difficult. "Now children," she said, "this is going to be a hard word and you may have trouble with it." We were all agog, and I can feel again the flash of ecstasy as the chart unrolled and I saw a combination of letters which, however preposterous, I easily recognized—I think I must have been doing some extra-curricular reading. The word was *Through*—and as I examine it on the paper before me it looks just as irrational now as it did then. Only yesterday a twelve-year-old niece of mine here in Washington told me a story that she had met in her reading, which is apropos. It appealed to her because she lived several years in Switzerland and is familiar with problems of foreign pronunciation. A Frenchman, she told me, visiting over here for the first time, had been having the usual difficulties in learning to say such anomalous words as *through, plough, though, rough,* and had grown to expect almost any absurdity in the English language. But the last straw, she said, was when he saw a sign on a moving picture theatre: *Cavalcade, Pronounced Success.* At this he fell in a swoon and decided it was impossible to learn how to speak English.

One disturbing feature of these rediscoveries on

the shelves is the number of old favorites I can no longer find. In those sudden flushes of enthusiasm which are creditable to the heart but cause melancholy later, one lends most precious old copies and never remembers to whom they went. My grand old *Happy Thoughts* by F. C. Burnand, for instance: who has it? I have a subsequent copy—a reissue brought out in London a few years ago with preface by Robert Lynd, but not at all a substitute for the vanished red copy imprinted by Roberts Brothers of Boston. I bought it at Leary's nearly thirty years ago because it was an exact duplicate of the copy that had been read to pieces in the family in my childhood. And the only other book perhaps that can compare with *Happy Thoughts* as the autobiography of a complete simpleton, *The Diary of a Nobody* by George and Weedon Grossmith—I had a copy of the little reprint edition which included Hilaire Belloc's superb preface. I wonder where that went? I've recently been able to replace it by a copy of the original edition (1892) but in this case it was the reprint which was precious to me; it was introduced to me by a reader of the original Bowling Green.—My copy of *The Way of All Flesh,* read with such delight in 1916 when Billy Phelps reintroduced it to the world; what became of that? And now that Enid Bagnold is soon to become famous for her superb *National Velvet* I wish I could find again the little anonymous *Diary without Dates* which first apprised the watchful of her exceptional talent.

II

I SPOKE of Stevenson's *Books Which Have Influenced Me;* it did not occur to me until later that you might have some trouble in finding it. It was written in 1887 for the *British Weekly,* and the editor whom Stevenson chaffs in the first paragraph was (I suppose) his Scottish contemporary William Robertson Nicoll. I don't remember in which of the regular trade volumes it is reprinted; Scribners', if they remember their R. L. S., can probably tell you. I was rather aghast to see the Scribner imprint on a recent book which spelled Lloyd Osbourne as *Osborne,* but I grant that the sheets were imported from England.

(Lloyd Osbourne, bless his heart, has been much in my mind lately, and I wish he would tell us how he fares. It would specially interest me to know whether he found Wallace Beery and Jackie Cooper, in the movie of *Treasure Island,* in accordance with his classic taste.)

Perhaps the easiest place to run down that essay is in an excellent little book called *Learning to Write,* edited for Scribners' in 1920 by J. W. Rogers. Oddly enough it was not until then that anyone had the sensible idea of putting together in one convenient volume all Stevenson's brilliant and scattered comments (not only in the essays but in his letters, too) on the arts of composition. This, with C. E. Montague's *A Writer's Notes on His Trade,* is among the very few books about writing worth a student's frugal budget. In Mr Rogers' book you will also find Stevenson's exciting analysis *On Some Technical Elements of Style in Literature,* an essay which now celebrates its 50th anniversary; it was published in April 1885. It is specially odd in that Stevenson, after crabbing Macaulay for a "barbaric love of repeating the same sound," in the succeeding paragraphs falls—unconsciously, I assume—into the same trick. Take the final pages and note the extraordinary and wearisome repetition of the sounds P, B, D. But this lively essay, which will set you to examining the melodies of prose more closely than ever you did before, is by no means old at fifty. You will find in it some interesting arguments for disregarding the laborious mumblings of Gertrude Stein.

I think I mentioned *Books Which Have Influenced Me* largely for its fine tribute to Walt Whitman. Stevenson very justly says that no one can talk truth about the reading that has moved him without becoming warmly autobiographical, for which the *British Weekly* of 1887 (edited by a Scottish dominie) was not the place. After naming Shakespeare, Dumas, Bunyan, Montaigne, and the Gospel according to Matthew, he comes to *Leaves of Grass*. I wish his comment might still be printed upon the wrapper of that great library of living. "A book of singular service," he says; "a book which tumbled the world upside down for me, blew into space a thousand cobwebs of genteel and ethical illusion and, having thus shaken my tabernacle of lies, set me back again upon a strong foundation." He adds the shrewd proviso: "But it is only a book for those who have the gift of reading." How rare those are is very little guessed; least of all by the professional cheerleaders. Stevenson comes back to this thought at the close of his testimony:

> For, after all, we are vessels of a very limited content. Not all men can read all books; it is only in a chosen few that any man will find his appointed food.

I have dallied a while on these now unfashionable essays of R. L. S. not only because almost any day he is likely to be rediscovered as the ideal companion for youth but also because it gave me pleasure to re-read them in volume 4 of the great Vailima Edition. One remembers Max Beerbohm's vivacious protest at the idea of putting Stevenson, so informal and temperamental a writer, into the rigid tombstone uniformity of 26 tall grenadier volumes. As in all such interments, the slab remains, the spirit vanishes. They are uneasy to handle; the book is too gross for comfort; as soon as you begin to enjoy yourself, crack go the paper labels. But that set is dear to me just the same, for it was a generous gift from Frank Doubleday. It was published (in this country) by Scribner; but in memory of the fact that it was F. N. D., as a young man at Scribner's, who first went about getting all Stevenson's books under one publisher, the printing of this final and all-inclusive edition was done at his Country Life Press on Long Island. So this adds other associations to that pleasant place when I drive by its grounds, and brings both Scotland and Samoa to the level parterres of Garden City.

And perhaps President Roosevelt is a Stevensonian, too. The thought occurred to me yesterday when I read his dispatch in the paper. On a fishing vacation in the Bahamas, he reported "Spent most of day exploring narrow river leading to lagoon on Crooked Island. Party caught several varieties of sunburn." You may remember that not long ago I suggested Crooked Island as a likely original for Treasure Island. With its neighbor Fortune Island it is not altogether unlike the shape on Billy Bones's map. As the newspapers have been a bit vague about its location I reproduce it here from an Admiralty chart; if you look carefully you can see the narrow river explored by the President and his sunburned buccaneers. I wish we might hear more details.[1]

Just as I am slipping that volume of the Vailima Edition back into its place I notice that one of its flyleaves was signed for me, under date "March 1922," by dear old Will H. Low, whose *Chronicle of Friendships* (1908) gives so charming a picture of R. L. S. in the student days at Barbizon and in the Forest of Fontainebleau. I must have carried it out to Bronxville with me on one of those happy visits to Mr Low's studio where he delighted to recall memories of Louis. On my long shelvage of Stevenson miscellanies one of the pleasantest things is the little essay Will Low wrote for the old Bowling Green in

[1]F. D. R., who owns a First Edition of *Treasure Island,* wrote me as follows describing his observation of Crooked Island in 1935:—

"We went in a very light draft launch through the narrow inlet between Crooked Island and Fortune Island. From then on, in going northeasterly toward the river, we had great difficulty in getting over two or three miles of shallow water. Finally we reached the river and from there all the way up to the lagoon we found an average depth of about twenty feet and an average width of not more than two hundred feet. A little way up the river was divided in two by the Island, the north end of which is in the lagoon. We took the right-hand or easterly branch and during the last mile, before reaching the lagoon, we passed magnificent steep coral cliffs with caves in them. That is the westerly side of what the chart calls Blue Hill. On top of the Hill is an extraordinarily interesting looking ruin—the foundations and lower part of what must have been quite large, stone buildings. We passed a number of small boats filled with rather poverty-stricken but perfectly happy Negroes, and we tried in vain to find out something of the Island and the ruins.

"It is wholly possible that in the old days the outer entrance contained a fairly deep channel, because many similar entrances in these Islands have been closed up in the past hundred years by hurricanes. If there ever was a deep water entrance to the river it would have provided the most ideal spot for a pirate or buccaneer lair that you could possibly imagine. The masts of even a tall ship in the lagoon would be completely invisible from the sea; the hill where the ruins are is a Gibraltar."

the *Evening Post,* called *Stevenson and Margarita.* "Margarita" was a brand of tobacco, now vanished from the earth, to which R. L. S. was addicted; and Mr Low's reminiscence was prompted by a ballade written by C. B. Gilbert with the refrain *What kind of tobacco did Stevenson smoke?* The ballade came in as a contribution in the mail: I withheld it from print until I had elicited Mr Low's reply and could publish both question and answer together. Mr Arthur N. Hosking afterward put them into a little privately printed book (Mayflower Press, New Rochelle, 1922), adding as frontispiece his own etching of Tusitala.

It was not my intention to spend this evening taking you along the Stevenson shelf, which would almost need a book of its own. I will add, however, that Margarita's neighbor is, appropriately, Stephen Chalmers's *Enchanted Cigarettes.* That was Balzac's phrase for artistic projects that never came to actuality; and Mr Chalmers pleasantly sketches "the novels and tales of Robert Louis Stevenson which he never wrote, with the approximate time and place when and where he did not write them." This little book was published by Houghton Mifflin at a time when the whole world seemed thundering into the abyss, September 1917; it is interesting to note that publishers would even then take pains with a venture so tenuous and so innocent. I myself, today, not devoid of anxieties public and private, wondered whether I had better write grievance on large affairs; and concluded that harmless ploiter among the shelves could do no possible mischief. And even if our whole economy is bound for the pit I should like to be able to leave some record of what has given me so much pleasure.

Seeing that signature of Will H. Low's has given me a twinge: for I cannot lay hand on a first edition of *The Wrecker* in which I once got Mr Low to autograph the Epilogue for me (which was dedicated to him). I think I can honestly say that I have never, since reaching maturity, been forward to ask for an autograph unless there were some very special sentiment involved. To ask a signature where there are private ligatures of association is piety and symbol; but the habit of requesting signatures of mere complaisance, wholesale and haphazard, involves an affront to delicacies that some people can never understand. To attempt to explain them would be more difficult than to comply. I remember with shame that once in my teens I wrote what I supposed was an amusing letter to Mark Twain, hoping to cajole an autograph out of him. I asked if he were descended from Aurelius Prudentius Clemens, an ancient hymn writer whom I found mentioned in my reading. I have often thought since of that childish impertinence, and honored him the more for ignoring it.

But I don't see my first of *The Wrecker;* haven't seen it, I suddenly realize, for a long while. But I well remember buying it from James F. Drake one time when I was feeling flush; and what a grand sensation that is, as well as I can recall. I have here another copy, one of the little Heinemann pocket editions which I asked Mr S. S. McClure to sign for me one day when he was lunching at Garden City. Why ask him? Well, he was the germ of suggestion for the character of Jim Pinkerton in the story. That will give you a clue as to my feeling about autographs. I would much rather have a signature, con amore, from someone I actually know who has some connection (even if only in my mind) with the book, than a merely formal disinterested scrawl from the unknown author. I am happier in personal inscriptions from Lloyd Osbourne, written for me, than I could possibly be in the purchased handwriting of Tusitala himself. For the ultimately fastidious collector the *auto* in autograph needs to be double or reflexive—written by himself for myself. For that reason I don't gravely miss the book signed by Thomas Hardy which seems to have gone from my shelves. It was given me by a good friend, and I was proud to have it; but it was one of several which Hardy just casually signed for a passing caller, and had no close association for me.

I mentioned *The Diary of a Nobody* by George and Weedon Grossmith, a trifle of most endearing humor—certainly not merely "satiric" as booksellers sometimes describe it, for it enters with understanding pathos into the small joys and struggling gentilities of a middle-aged cockney clerk. I name it again because to my pleasure I see that Edgar Wells lists it in his current catalogue as "a very much neglected book." It belongs on the shelf beside the *Happy Thoughts* of F. C. Burnand, to whom it was dedicated. Weedon Grossmith's delightful illustrations are a large part of the book's charm; its mood is that of which the best present exemplar is Mr Webster's Timid Soul cartoons.

Apropos catalogues, the sagacious John Winterich spoke of the author of a recent rather scatterbrained book as "a catalogue-built collector." It is a perilous way of accumulating the data and divinations of print. I know of no better example of the errors it begets than this: the author of that volume, misled by something he saw in some catalogue or circular, mentions as a desirable collectors' item a work that never was published at all. It was abandoned in galley proof. I know, because I was one of the authors; and shall not tell you what the writing was. But never, my dear, base your bibliographic data upon anything but an actual examination of the book itself. Catalogues have their most valuable merits, but the bookseller's passionate will to believe must always be ratified against personal knowledge.

A salient instance of the temperamental zigzag of book "values" comes under my eye as I write. Here are two catalogues that arrive simultaneously from two highly responsible dealers. One lists *The Innocents Abroad* of 1869 at $75, the other at $2. Both are first editions; one is "a fine copy," the other "has been somewhat trimmed in rebinding."

I was also pleased to see in Edgar Wells's catalogue Edmund Gosse's two volumes of the poems of T. L. Beddoes. A later edition (which I think of privately as my Twin Beddoes) came to my desk lately, the gift of a generous Beddoesian from Honolulu who was shocked to learn that I know nothing more of him than the few songs usually printed in anthologies. It seems to me pleasant that my own copy, which Linda Castle found in a bookshop in San Francisco, comes bringing association of the Pacific—an ocean whose shores and islands would have brought happiness to that tragic poet. If Beddoes is only a name to you, look him up in the Oxford Book of English Verse—

If there were dreams to sell,
Merry and sad to tell,
And the crier rang the bell,
What would you buy?

Which, incidentally, would be a tentacular motto for a bookshop.

Beddoes committed suicide. I have often thought that an interesting study could be written of the conditions and temperament of poets' lives that have led many of them to seize the abhorred shears. That title—*On the Suicide of Poets*—was one of a list of possible books I was compiling the other day. I projected the first announcement of an imaginary publishing house (Foresight and Company). It would begin by saying that they believed there was a great deal more fun in the book business than most publishers or booksellers are actually having. To avoid overhead they would employ no travelers; to avoid bores the address of their office would never be divulged. All business would be conducted by telephone, or by correspondence to a Post Office Box. Every publisher has fairy-tale freaks of this sort that amuse his leisure.

TRISTRAM SHANDY

NOTHING NEW is likely to be said at this date in a note on *Tristram Shandy*. I always like to think of the astonished mirth of its very earliest readers. Zounds! they must have said to themselves. It did not concern them (nor does it us) that much of manner and matter was lifted from Rabelais and Burton. As Professor Saintsbury said in his essay on Sterne (which I wish might be reprinted in every edition; so manly, temperate and wise) "Where he is best he does not steal at all, and that is the only point of real importance."

Reading *Tristram Shandy* for the first time is one of those initiations that should not be deferred too late. I suppose it most often happens in college. I've never forgotten the bewildered excitement of my volatile classmate Mifflin McGill (at Haverford) when during our sophomore year he went about for months on end bursting into sudden cackles, repeating passages that had seized his fancy, and still scarcely believing it possible that so much of human absurdity had really been put into print. I suppose that same discovery is made perennially by several hundred or thousand young readers. There is too much snigger in Sterne's laughter, sometimes; but those who would read the book only for love of smut are always defeated by its difficulty.

Much of the wealth of Sterne's wisdom (and lubricity) will escape the prentice reader. Lorry was a mature man (aged forty-five) when he began to write *Tristram,* and some of his japing (and tenderness) requires a fairly long perspective of grievance and folly. But when the reader is fit, he will probably agree that the random, idiotic and grotesquely physical paradoxes of carnal clay have nowhere else been so brilliantly suggested. One of Sterne's subtle remarks is that—

> "Attitudes are nothing, ma'am—'tis the transition from one attitude to another—like the preparation and resolution of the discord into harmony—which is all in all."

As an axiom of literary virtuosity, this shrewd saying is exquisitely illustrated in Sterne's writing. He modulates from one key to another with superb address. And perhaps no writer has ever lingered with more tender and malicious effect upon the momentary postures which betray our human oddity. It is a profound instinct, for the highest art of fiction is to seem to make life stand still, unconscious of itself, long enough to be looked at. Consider (as he bids us) the occasion of Corporal Trim dropping his hat, to illustrate the finality of death. Consider My Father pausing on the stairs; My Mother listening at the door (the door with the imperfect hinge). There are plenty more instances, and more mischievous ones that show Sterne's cunning at setting the scene. The famous episodes of Trim's knee, or the "concupiscible" widow in the sentry box, are familiar enough. The Fly, the Oath, have become stock examples in every textbook. But we prefer sometimes to look for marks of genius in less intentional show passages. So don't miss that scene in the kitchen, and the "fat foolish scullion."

Perhaps *Tristram Shandy* should be read first at not over twenty years, and again at not less than forty. After that, or even between those ages, you may use your judgment. Few, except the proofreader and Professor Saintsbury and Governor Cross, read every word. I would not for anything be the proofreader, as *Tristram* contradicts every rule on which the printer forms his rigid cosmos. Every detail of punctuation and typography is absolutely Sterne's own, studied to convey the effect he had in mind. The biographers sometimes comment on the fact that Sterne always went up to London to be on hand for the publication of successive batches of volumes. Surely it was to have a last precautionary look at those difficult proofs. The stereotyped reader, unaccustomed to tricks, is often taken aback by these typographical freaks. Many booksellers have had the experience of copies returned by innocent customers, complaining that the book is defective because some pages are blank, or blacked out, or some chapters transposed. That is not really a very subtle form of mirth, though it always seems so to the green reader. Sterne's finest touches are less obvious.

It is said that *Tristram* was begun in the hope of recouping Sterne's losses in farming. If so, no agricultural depression was ever better justified. Great books make great demands on their readers. In essence you can regard it as a soliloquy of some two hundred thousand words (only a guess, I haven't counted them) for the purpose of introducing one very gross episode. The final remark of Tristram's guileless mother—"L—d! said my mother, what is all this story about?"—might well have been made the motto of the whole work. Or you can think of it as a treatise on midwifery, on education, on "the construction and come-at-ability of that animal called Woman," or on the endearing simplicity of two delightful old men. Myself I sometimes grow weary of Sterne's more deliberate bids for laughter: the asterisks and aposiopeses, the typographic vaudeville, the ancient after-dinner-speaker's device of insisting that the bawdy thought he has suggested isn't at all what he meant. Our parson does all these better than anyone else; but there's a whoreson lot of it. To me the greatest thing in the book is its echo of a vanished soldiery. Sterne was an army child and his earliest memories were of Marlborough's veterans. Like Shakespeare before him, and Kipling after, he saw that certain unique qualities and savors of English character came to their highest pitch, both comic and pathetic, in the art of war. They went to war in kindness, in a very special mood of simplicity and rude mirth. The moving absurdity and seriousness of Uncle Toby and Corporal Trim are what, above all, list this book among the superior few. It is all very well for Sterne to tell us that *Tristram* was written "against the spleen,"—viz., to cause laughter. Yes, much of it was, but it had also larger intentions. Great captain of innuendo and the double entendre, he also knew how to achieve his purpose by saying nothing. You might meditate on the genius with which My Mother is conveyed to us, though she is almost always offstage (abed, usually). How well we know her. "She never asked the meaning of what she didn't understand."

It's very human that poor Lorry, who seems to have made rather an unhappy mess of his own marriage, should set out to compose so confident an essay on conjugal dynamics. More than once it almost seems as though he had said the last word on the topic—but that will never be said. The joint and

diverse ejaculation of Uncle Toby and My Father—
——God bless } 'em all said my uncle Toby and
——Deuce take } my father, each to himself—
comes as near it as we are likely to get on the masculine side. But how about the distaff? Do women read *Tristram?* I doubt it. I wish some intrepid scholiast would compile me a list of the great books of the world which are, by the peculiar astringence of their humor, less likely to appeal to ladies. That is a roundabout way of saying, more bluntly, the books Women Don't Care For. The only purpose of so silly a list would be to set them on to reading them.

As to the much palavered theme of Sterne's lewdness, let's at least be frank. You will find none of his lubricities, no not one, which most of us have not grinned at (however ruefully or secretly) in our own thought. He plunged home to perennial springs of shameful human glee. Condemn him, we condemn ourselves. It's a pity, we have already admitted, that there's too much snigger in his woodpile. He goes far beyond good taste. But laughter often does. It is godlike, knowing not good nor evil.

We say to ourselves, let's not be too solemn about the masterpieces of comedy. The grisly legend of poor Yorick is that his corpse was taken by body-snatchers and dissected by the anatomists at Cambridge. That legend has been enacted more than once in too pickthank comment on his book. But great things, however light their tone, compel us to take them respectfully. Digressions are the sunshine of reading, Sterne says somewhere. This book, which is all digression, is also all sunshine. It is impossible to imagine that any writer ever had more fun than our deplorable vicar dipping his wicked quill. He had that singularly rich fun that can only be had by one writing for highly intelligent readers.

And if you suppose that the much advertised "stream of consciousness" method is anything new, where will you find it more accurately employed than in *Tristram Shandy?* When the very newest shock-merchant is too wildly acclaimed for qualities supposed unprecedented, I am sometimes tempted to whistle "Lillabulero"—and pace a few toises with Uncle Toby. As I write this note I see a new novel reviewed thus: "defies classification . . . a cock-eyed book; mad, repellant, weird and perverse, provocative, sometimes brilliant, many times beautiful, always exciting." If *Tristram Shandy* were published today for the first time I wonder what adjectives we would have left for it?

EUMENIDES OF BOOK COLLECTING

SOMETIMES I'm almost sorry that the Caliph Newton called his famous book *The Amenities*. It has added to the pious and wrongheaded notion that book-collecting is just a pleasant sentimental pastime carried on by a lot of wealthy and warm-hearted *aficionados*. This misconception reminds one of the shallow legend that grew up for so many years about the name of Charles Lamb, considering that pain-haunted soul as just a gentle blatherer. There are amenities, of course, in book-collecting; but acerbities also. Perhaps the gods of the true collector are eumenides; we call them by a gracious name to placate their cruel character. For the collector in whom I am interested is not just the dilettante of title-pages and states, editions and errata. He collects books that make him think—loathsome and unwilling preoccupation.

It seems almost a pity to write about the true passion of book-love; it would be unseemly if that became fashionable which should proceed from private vital instinct. But I cannot resist a word of applause in honor of the Pearsall Smith Prize, named for one of the most agreeable misanthropologists of our time and certainly one of the most delicate nerve-systems of literary appreciation with which the name of Haverford has been connected. To quote Pearsall Smith's own favorite John Donne, we may say of Smith himself as Donne said of the Holy Ghost, "he is an eloquent Author, but yet not luxuriant; he is far from a penurious, but as far from a superfluous style too."

But this is not an essay on the quiddities of Pearsall Smith In His Humor. It is a few remarks by request, on the pleasure and value of beginning young as a book collector. I've never forgotten the good advice F. B. Gummere gave us at the beginning of our freshman year, twenty-eight years ago this autumn. "Find your way to Leary's," he said; and even on the thick ears of the class of 1910 that suggestion had its penetrating power. You are luckier now than we were then; you don't even have to go as far as Leary's (though still worth going to) for Mr McCawley, a true paramour of print, is close by. I'm even hoping that some day he'll add an annex of second-hand books so that we may have our own Paul's Churchyard and Paternoster Row. In my time there was a reprehended haunt of erring spirits, the Red Lion in Ardmore; since, I believe, amalgamated into the Autocar factory. How much better intoxicant does a bookstore offer. "Sweet God," cried Cobden Sanderson, "souse me in literature." It is the ebriety without crastine grief.

As I understand it the Pearsall Smith Prize offers no premium for rich bindings, rare editions or any Persian apparatus of collecting. It is to be awarded for evidence of genuine personal taste, ingenuity of search, or perhaps completeness of purview in any particular field. It is to encourage what is one of the most subtle and enduring pleasures of the intelligent man, the habit of owning books—and of discriminating between those desirable to own, those preferably borrowable. I imagine that the winning assortment might be either a general gathering of the books a student thought of as an ideal collection for college years, or it might be a closely knit referendum upon some special theme—a study of some bibliographic problem, the complete works of some minor favorite, or a tracing out of a consecutive topic through several generations. When I say a "minor favorite" I do so deliberately; some of the most exquisite pleasures of print are to be found in pursuit of the smaller names. In the great autumn forest of literature there are innumerable leaves; the scrub and underbrush often reward us with the most brilliant colors. In such a competition every entrant has his own sure reward. One or two, by happy chance, may develop the first twinges of that highly specialized sense for books that is so exciting and so rare. You have all had an opportunity to see, in the adventures of Professor Hotson, what thrilling escapades of detective science are possible in the world of print.

The book collector, I intimated, has his sombre phases; it is a melancholy of his own, proud and fantastical. (What a delicious theme for a collection of books would be the idea of Literary Melancholy; and how, at the chance thought, one hankers to turn back to *As You Like It* and read again, instantly and with new clarity of eye, the sullen fits of Jacques; finding, as one does ever in Shakespeare, new and astounding immediacies of purport.) And just now, thinking of Pearsall Smith, I reached out for a volume of John Donne—the writer upon whom, though often unconsciously, so many of today's poets have fed their hearts. Opening at hazard I find this:

Whoe'er thou beest that read'st this sullen writ
Which just so much courts thee, as thou dost it . . .

The point is worth note. The great books, the deep thoughts of great men, grant us no more than the effort we make. Literature is no easy emulsion. It requires, and opens itself only upon evidence of, the most brilliant and practised attention. The extenuated subtleties of its skill are incomparably diverse. If we knew precisely why a skilful writer uses one word rather than another (and he always does) we would know much more about the history of literature.

So the man who collects books not merely for the sentimental accident of edition, but for the quality of thought they bring him, has something more than amenity to consider. Perhaps part of the time his mind will dwell upon the darker sorrows and absurdities of men. But there is enormous laughter, too. You may have noticed the enigmatic paroxysms of applause issuing from the privileged alcove where the *Private Papers of James Boswell* were lately published. For the mature lover of books, who knows how much more frankly men talk in ink than *viva voce,* experiences more howling mirth than any other. *Nulla dies sine risu* is his motto. I was thinking, at this moment, of the other of the two great Elizabethan Dons—Don Marquis. In his *Chapters for the Orthodox* there is some deep rolling thunder of belly-laughs that come from the very cellar and coalbin of human nature. His burlesque of Faust in hell—which, among a vigorous crepitation of slapstick, also emits pungent philosophic and theologic truth—would provide a life-long memory for any college dramatic club that produced it. And where will you find a more tender flash of literary grace than the description (elsewhere in the same book) of Mark Twain in Heaven, with his own private river to play with, nigger stevedores and steamboat races and cursing and everything. These races were so hilarious, and Mark's cursing gave the archangels so much pleasure, that Satan grows jealous and wants Mark to bring his river down to Hell. But Susie Clemens and William Dean Howells won't let him go.

The Susies and the William Dean Howellses of this world will always be a little grieved about some of the private thoughts of the book collector, who faces (with Hardy, with Anatole France, with Whitman or Montaigne or whom you will) the ultimate candors of the inquisitive mind. But no one, no one on earth, can come between the reader and his book. It's best of all when you have your own copy in which you can record your own side of the argument. Wherever you touch the web of literature you'll find ramifying filaments that lead on and on. If you were to begin by collecting Don Marquis (not a bad idea) you would soon find yourself led back to Mark Twain and Voltaire.

O. HENRY, 1898

OLD QUERCUS, my eccentric colleague, sometimes uses in his discourse homely parables which require apology. Recently he found himself in Cleveland on a Trade Survey, accompanied by Eddie Ziegler, traveler for a large publishing house. When Quercus, desiring to make mannerly impression on the customers, put on his new ropecoes he found them too slack about the midriff. They had been bought in haste, without careful alteration. Evidently a pair of suspenders was going to be necessary—something which Old Quercus, by meridian increase, has not used for many years. Mr Ziegler courteously offered his own; but explained that he himself would need them that night for his evening breeks. "Oh, that 'll be all right," said the old trouper. "I won't need them then; when I squeeze into my dinner jacket I'm absolutely rigid." So they arranged it, and Quercus wore the hoist by day and Mr Ziegler at night. But Mr Ziegler, a man of delicate sensibility, was embarrassed when Old Quercus in his public appearances insisted on using the episode as a starting-point for his talk, maintaining that it was a symbol of the oneness and mutual support of author and publisher. Such intimate reciprocation, he declared, was vital for both Business Man and Artist. It was idle for one to chide the other for differences in purpose and temperament. Sometimes the artist reproaches the business man for not having created a stable and prosperous world in which the writer need worry about nothing but his writing. Sometimes the business man deplores the artist's unpractical truancy from obvious fact. Both these expostulations, cried Old Quercus, are vain. Let publisher and author remember they are both wearing the same suspenders. "Yes," replied Charley Jackson, Cleveland's delightful Scotch bibliophile, "and both draped on the shoulders of the bookseller." Meanwhile Mr Ziegler, looking very handsome in his dinner clothes, was blushing gently.

Every day, Old Quercus was wont to declare, should be (if we are alert for its suggestions) an artistic whole; it should have its unity of plot; its rise, climax and denouement; should supply just the analogies we need. The ambiguity of the suspenders was at once confirmed by two succeeding glimpses which emphasized the endless paradox of living. Passing through a maze of rearward alleys on the way to the Hermit Club in Cleveland, the visitors were struck by a sign that seemed significant. It said simply, SHORT CUT TO EUCLID. How helpful that would have been in the days of schoolboy geometry, Old Quercus thought. But in Cleveland, by constant habit, Euclid is thought of only as a street, not as a mathematician. Perhaps as much as anyone he was the founder of our modern world, but he is the Forgotten Man. (There are two reasons for forgetting anything: one, because you never see it; two, and more usual, because you see it everywhere.) Was it some old surveyor, triangulating the Western Reserve, who named his base line for the patron saint of exactitude? There's another philosophical term that Old Quercus always notices in Cleveland, it has something to do with real estate or hereditaments, the *Cuyahoga Abstract*. There is something rich and strange about that phrase. A whole school of contemplation could be founded upon it.

The thought of Euclid, the exquisite logic and rationality of his demonstrations, his temerarious axioms and postulates—magnificent in the pure world of thought but how difficult among the compromises of fact—"Let it be granted," he cries, "that a straight line may be drawn from any one point to another point"; well, try to draw a straight line from Al Smith to Father Coughlin—caused pondering Old Quercus to think that perhaps what we need are more Euclids; more direct and logical thinkers; more sensibility to the pleasures of severe deduction. He remembered Edna Millay's fine sonnet: "Euclid alone has looked on beauty bare." He imagined the old geometer ravished by the beauty of the circle; stupefied by the anxiety as to what happens to parallel lines. He became, for the moment, a very Puritan of thought; thinking the gross world well lost for an orderly analysis of plane figures.

At that moment (he was in Gordon Bingham's office at Burrows Brothers on Euclid Avenue) there were siren and shout in the street; looking outward, he saw an enormous motor bus, preceded by police escort, go swiftly by. A huge thing, long as a Pullman car, all gray enamel and silvery trimmings. He only saw it in one instant flash, but the legend painted on it, incredible enough, was DAMASCUS TO BAGHDAD. Can these be towns in Ohio, he wondered? But no; the next day an item in the *Plain Dealer* (another fine name, by the way) reported that the vehicle was on its way to Hoboken to be shipped to Beirut, then to begin regular service across the Syrian Desert. And a whole vision of the Arabian Nights rose in his mind: fishermen and brass bottles and jinni (spelling doubtful, but you don't have to spell a thing when you just think it) and kalendars and kaliphs and viziers, dark alleys and whispers and veiled figures exhaling musk, white hands plucking at sleeves, stairways in soft Eastern shadow, come up and see me some time, and his (Old Quercus's) wavering spirit forgot the austerities of plane geometry and the Cuyahoga Abstract. There are other curves besides the circle, and Caliphs as well as Euclid have looked on beauty bare. He might have "moaned" (like Reggie Fortune) to co-ordinate two notions of life so confusingly and suddenly opposite. He went about his affairs, resolving secretly to have another look at the poems of James Elroy Flecker.

In another middle-Western city he greatly enjoyed a certain hotel: a gorgeous pile of misdirected zeal. It's hard, he told me, to convey his impression without seeming stupidly satiric. He loved the place. It was what it was, riotously and unashamed. Only architects and decorators of enormous vitality could have accomplished anything so splendidly wrong. From the tiny fat bellhop in scarlet uniform (tight as Quercus's own dinner jacket) to the bedrooms crowded with purple and green chairs, antimacassars, lace curtains, parchment lamp-shades, French prints, walnut wardrobes, dressing-tables, mirrors, salutations and gadgets, everything was ornate, wholesale, exuberant. It was the emblem of an epoch when America went cul de sac: bursting with back-pounding cheer, heaping physical on physical, color on color, gravy on potato, Astoria on Waldorf. There were too many Spanish grills, oil paintings, vases, plush settees, potted ferns, panelled lobbies. There was too much olive and gold uniform on the elevator girls; too many clerks, counters, complications. The male guests seemed (God forgive him for thinking so) unnecessarily large, stout, broad-beamed, blond, crop-haired, clean-shaven, Nordic. There was innocent flamboyance about everything. Perhaps he was alarmed about it because he is too much like that himself—though he always insists that his very soul (if you can get at it) is dark and sombre, of the Celtic fringe. Those people who are all mixed up with paradoxical contrasts are always odd fish. Or perhaps he was feeling low and broody as he always is (I've watched him) when he knows he must presently face the impossible ordeal of public talk. For if he tries to blurt out the sort of things that keep his mind happy, people conclude (indignantly) that he's mad; if he tries to be politely agreeable they damn him as a trifler. But it's hard, he told me rather grimly, to tell secrets in a loud voice.

But about that hotel: I hope I have him right: he gave me the impression that he loved it, and only feared that some day the management might get the idea that something was wrong and try to change it. It can't be changed, he cried; it *mustn't* be changed. It is what it is and no fooling. It's a monument; and you know what a monument is; a reminder.

Since Old Quercus was so happy in that hotel I'll leave him there. I want to speak of something different. I visited the prison where O. Henry once lived.

It's in the heart of a big town. Outside, from the front, it looks at a casual glance almost like a pleasant old-fashioned factory. You don't see, at first, the watch-tower and the grim side walls. What do they manufacture in such places? Penitence? You need not expect here any final word on the matter. Men have worried themselves about it for many centuries, and have made some progress. Perhaps the old sentimentalism about punishment—"It hurts me more than it does you"—is so. Perhaps it hurts society more than the offender.

The first thing you see in the entrance is a sign: POPULATION TODAY: *White* 2872, *Colored* 1418, *Yellow* 2. One's first thought was, yesterday the total was 2 more. Two men had gone to the chair the night before. Of that total, 4292, only 49 are Jewish. That struck me as interesting. When a man goes to the pen only three things are important. They are lettered on a little board on his cell beneath his name. His number, his religion, and does he use tobacco. QUERCUS, 515907, P, T, would mean he's a Protestant and smokes.

In the main entrance there are barred fences, one within another. They are beautifully gilded, but they are bars no less. Even the nozzles for tear-gas, unobtrusively located in the side walls and pointing toward the door to the prison yard, are gilded.

The Warden's office is pleasant and friendly; something very institutional about the chairs; paintings and ornamental screens done by prisoners. One of these an illuminated broadside of IF— Kipling's name not mentioned. Many prisoners take to literature, the Warden's kindly daughter told us; one has made $7000 selling stories to pulp-magazines. But plagiarism is frequent.

The Warden is a conscientious man in a hard job. He does not sentimentalize it. He lent me a photograph never published before, of O. Henry when he entered the prison. He did so with some reluctance, wishing to be sure that no one's feelings would be hurt if it were printed. I assured him that every lover of O. Henry thought of his prison sentence, probably unmerited, and heroically borne, as the greatest triumph of a great life. But the officers have little opportunity for gentle musing. They know, or remember, the job is thankless and dangerous. There are guns in the Warden's desk.

In the yard, that bright autumn morning, were squads of men, in gray uniform, marching to and fro, in quick lockstep shuffle. Keep them moving, keep the squads separate, seemed to be the idea. In the center of the great open space is a statue of Omphale which puzzles everyone. Omphale, it appears, was the queen whom Hercules served and for whom he acted as handmaid. Does this symbolize the supremacy of reason over brute force? The men, marching by, scan visitors curiously. The visitor does not, if he is sensitive, return the gaze too closely. After all, he wonders, their mistakes may not have been much worse than mine.

But you don't sentimentalize.

The prison hospital, the same where O. Henry worked as night-clerk in the pharmacy, is a relief. The prescription room, now partitioned off from the ward itself, is sunny and professional. Perhaps many of those drug-bottles are the same he knew. At the back is a shelf of books. One old volume caught my eye: could it be the same pharmacopeia in which Will Porter is thought to have taken his pseudonym from the name of a French druggist? It was Cooper's *History of Surgery,* published I think in the 1840's. I glanced through it: in the back, written in pencil, were alternative spellings of several words—*decide, deside,* etc. But I don't think it was O. Henry's hand. And O. Henry was a good speller: you remember that Webster's dictionary was his favorite reading on the ranch in Texas.

The "ranges" as they call them—the great cell-blocks—were like vast bird-cages; towering tier on tier, four men to a cage. They were empty at that moment; the men were out for exercise. In the great mess hall there's a sign at each door: EAT SLOWLY, CHEW YOUR FOOD.—There's plenty of time. About 600 are there for life.

It does no harm for the easy reader of detective stories to have a glimpse of the other side.

"EFFENDI"

(FRANK NELSON DOUBLEDAY, 1862–1934)

"EFFENDI" (the nickname was Kipling's coinage, suggested, of course, by the initials) suited him perfectly. It had the quality of affectionate intimacy, but no one was likely to use it prematurely; and one did not forget that the word is a title of respect. All, whether editorial cubs or the most irreverent ink-stained printer in the pressroom, loved him for his humor, his easy masterful way, but respected him also with a little something of awe. The good old monosyllable *big* is the word that comes first to mind. He really was an effendi. In his office at Garden City there used to be a photograph of him taken in the burnous of an Arab chief. How well he looked the part: the tall, athletic figure, the bronzed face with its fine eagle nose, the brilliant eyes. It was always a thrill for us youngsters when we saw him coming into the office with his long swinging stride. One was instantly aware of power. The sound of the bindery machines on the floor below seemed to move with steadier rhythm; everything began to co-ordinate a little faster, a little smoother. People began going in and out of the big room in the corner, and there was an exciting feeling that things were doing. If I could just give you an impression of the strong, unhurried and yet unstoppable way he used to come down the aisle you would get some notion of the man. He seemed to gather speed and force (but never mere *hurry*) as he got near that corner room. He always came in as though some idea was urgent and motive in his mind, something he wanted to do promptly. I used to think what a grand experience it would be to serve as his secretary for a while, to get some idea of his extraordinary gift of easy, calm achievement, his genius for human relations. He was himself a writer of much humorous charm. There was once a little book called *A Plain American in England,* published as by "Charles T. Whitefield," which even many of his own staff did not know was by him. It was delightful, dwelling upon phases of Anglo-American comedy which always amused him. He, no less than his partner, Walter Page, was one of the most valuable ambassadors of friendship the two nations have ever had. His insistence on his own plainness, rusticity, was very characteristic of so subtle a negotiator.

It was touching to see, among the flowers at his funeral the other day, a large floral replica of a book —from one of the departments at the Country Life Press, I expect. There was a good simple symbolism about that, like the old workmen or warriors who were buried with their tools and weapons beside them. It was an afternoon of brilliant sunshine and snow, and after the service at the church it occurred to some of us to go over and look at the sun-dial in the garden at the Press. Snow was crusted deep over it, but we rubbed it away; the bronze facsimiles of the old printers' marks were bright and clear. How surprised Aldus of Mantua would have been to find his own dolphin and anchor reprinted in that Long Island garden. And those of us who in one way or another had worked for Effendi and loved him couldn't help feeling that what would please him most would be for us to get back to town and sell some books. His passionate enthusiasm for the job never failed even in the long years of illness. George Seiffert remembers how, long ago, he was hustling to catch a train back to the city after the weekly conference at the Press. Effendi met him in the aisle. "Selling any books, George?" George, caught unawares, and modestly embarrassed, took refuge in jocularity. "Once in a while," he said bashfully, and hastened on. Effendi called him back. "Try all the while," he said.

Not only for his enthusiasm, for his organizing genius, but for his delicious humor The Boys loved him. There was a peculiar tenderness in the relation during these last years when the man we had known so strong, so unshakable, was broken down with long illness. Even then he would drive over to the Press every day; when he could no longer get out of the car members of the staff would go out to drive with him; his passion for every business detail never left him. During long drives he enjoyed dictating reminiscences of the various humors and crises of publishing. I wish I had available at this moment a copy of those *Indiscreet Recollections,* as he called them—a book printed in only a few copies for his immediate family. That, I remember telling him, was the true *Parnassus on Wheels,* for it was composed entirely in his famous Packard—which, he thriftily liked to remark, had run over 140,000 miles. Shrewd sense about money matters was strong in him as in all great men of affairs. He never forgot, in telling the story of the time when he and Sam McClure, a pair of young publishers, were offered the management of the famous Harper business, that the excited McClure interrupted him in the middle of a telephone call to Philadelphia which cost 90 cents.

Anecdotes of Effendi would be innumerable wherever publishers, booksellers or writers get together. Some of those anecdotes would concern famous names, for he had walked with greatness of many kinds. We used to think secretly, we young zealots of his renown, that in any company anywhere Effendi would be at once recognizable as extraordinary; and indeed it was so. Men of every sort had always recognized him as someone to tie to. He had hardly started his own business when President McKinley wanted him to print a book of his speeches—a fine way to lose money, and Effendi was shrewd enough to evade it. John D. Rockefeller told him his life story during games of golf. Andrew Carnegie advised him about his savings. Frank Norris read manuscripts for him. Rudyard Kipling wrote *Just-So* stories for Effendi's youngsters. (Doubleday had slept on a couch in Kipling's sitting-room at the Grenoble Hotel when Kipling was desperately ill in New York, so that he might not be disturbed.) A Prime Minister of Great Britain has testified to the lasting impression a meeting with Effendi made on him. Even while sitting in the chair at an Imperial Conference, he confessed, he found his thoughts wandering to a recollection of Frank Doubleday. But I am thinking now of the love and admiration he inspired in those who worked closest to him and who saw him in the full gusto of his power. He had also a delicious skill in pricking bubbles that needed bursting. I remember once, long ago, going in (after secret indignant brooding) to tell him that I really thought a raise in salary was disgracefully overdue. I had fermented the matter in private (it was very serious to me) until I was probably a bit incoherent, but he listened patiently. When there was an opportunity he asked how much I was getting. I told him. "Yes," he said blandly, "there must be something wrong if you haven't made yourself worth more than that." He must have passed on a good word, for a raise came through the next day, but the double significance of his comment remained memorable.

In his private office there was always a framed notice to the effect that a man can get a lot of good work done if he doesn't worry about who gets the credit for it. Lyman Stowe, another of his alumni, is reminded by this of a time when Effendi himself brought up some idea at the weekly editorial meeting. Everyone except Stowe was opposed to the suggestion. After the meeting Effendi called him in. "Stowe," he said, "you seemed to be the only one who thought there might be a glimmering of sense in that scheme. Suppose you wait about six weeks and then bring it up again as your own idea. Maybe then we can put it over."

There was an office episode Effendi enjoyed recalling, one which I often think of when I find myself buried rather deep in papers. A young man of whom Effendi was very fond, son of one of his North Shore neighbors, had a minor post in the Manufacturing Department which involved checking a great many orders, estimates, job schedules, etc. It so happened that the shortest path to Effendi's own office led past Billy P's desk, and Mr Doubleday was always annoyed by the enormous mass of papers there. The Effendi was a great believer in cleaning up one's desk before going home, and finally he mentioned the matter. He did it in his usual oblique way: he took Billy into the private office, pointed to his own desk, which was clear of all debris, and remarked that that was what a desk should look like. But Billy, a young man of thoughtful disposition, always liked to rationalize everything with a little argument. "Yes, Mr Doubleday," he said, "but you forget the volume of work that passes over *my* desk." Effendi used to continue the story by insisting that one evening, coming by after Billy had gone home, he swept off all the floating papers, deposited them in a drawer in his own room, and waited to see what would happen. He used to affirm that everything went on just the same and Billy never knew the difference. This, however, I do not quite believe.

Effendi always had his own singularly humorous way of going after what he wanted. When it didn't work he was just as much amused as when it did. I've been told of the time when he wished to dismiss a private secretary without having to tell him so in so many words. He dictated a letter to the man himself suggesting the advisability of his resignation. The victim took it down without comment, but replied with another letter, duly sent through the mail, insisting on his merits and the desirability of his remaining. I believe he left eventually; but Effendi always enjoyed audacity that had some warrant of ability behind it.

An old incident dating from his days at Scribner's was very typical of his ingenious stratagems. When he was the young manager of *Scribner's Magazine* he was disturbed by a series of articles on philosophy by William James which the editor gave first position in the magazine every month. Doubleday thought them too heavy for the lead-off position; he was fighting hard, as always, for large distribution, and hankered for some more popular feature. His protests did not seem to have any effect, so one day he cut out a particularly solid paragraph of Professor James's text and pasted it in his hat. He began leaving his hat around where he thought Mr Scribner would see it. Perhaps Mr Scribner did see it, but with good old-fashioned gentility believed that what another man carries inside his hat is his own affair. But finally, as they were going out to lunch one day and the inside of the hat was carefully exposed to Mr Scribner's view, he could restrain himself no longer.

"Doubleday," he said, "what on earth have you got in your hat?"

This was the young manager's moment of triumph. "I'll show you," he said, and held out the passage from Professor James. "That's the kind of thing you expect me to sell on the front page of *Scribner's* every month." Mr Scribner read carefully some passage or other on the Validity of Conscience or the Ontology of Being, and admitted that perhaps it was not good editorial strategy.

Effendi was really the first of a new era in book publishing—which he visualized foremost as a business, not merely as a dignified literary avocation. He realized, perhaps more clearly than any other man, that the possibilities of book distribution have hardly been scratched. He developed the Mail Order and Subscription phases of the business to remarkable dimensions. Against much opposition and advice he moved his business 20 miles out into the country to secure space and attractive working conditions; he repeated the same brilliantly successful experiment when he became majority owner of the famous Heinemann imprint in England. He was inexhaustible in fertile schemes for larger distribution. The idea that publishing should be essentially an intelligently conducted commerce, not a form of æsthetic bohemianism, appealed strongly to his authors. He was, I think, the first publisher anywhere to submit to his authors royalty statements checked and substantiated by outside accountants. He developed a successful chain of his own bookstores as laboratories of selling. He was frequently under fire from the Trade for his experiments in new directions, but I think he firmly believed that every form of book distribution is ultimately a repercussion of benefit. No man was ever more enthusiastic in his heart for fine things; he dreamed night and day of a List which would be the greatest ever put together. When a group of de luxe French binders found the going too hard in New York he moved them bodily out to Garden City to do special jobs of beauty. Years ago, before the name of Joseph Conrad was known to more than a few critics, he was contributing a monthly stipend to keep Conrad writing—and this long before any of Conrad's books were under his own imprint. It was his young enthusiasm that first got all Stevenson's books together under the Scribner name. On his own list, to speak only of the greatest, there were three for whom his service can never be forgotten—Kipling, O. Henry, and Conrad. Those are his classics.

And now, as he would say when talk began to run overlong, let's get back to work.

P.S. I was late with this copy and was hastily reading it over as I came downtown in the subway. I looked up and saw a girl carrying a book—a book that has Effendi's name on its back and which would never have been written but for him. And that, I thought to myself, is the publisher's real epitaph. Many thousands, to whom his name may mean little, yet carry it round with them. It seemed symbolic of the endless way in which our trade, though small in figures, interweaves human lives and can even move the globe itself. It was that "dynamite and wildcats" (a phrase of his own) which he felt in the publishing business, and in which he took more manly joy than any man I have known.

HUNTING MARK'S REMAINDERS

"I WAS having a good enough time seeing them hunt for my remainders" said Huck Finn on Jackson's Island, while the ferryboat went cruising to and fro—filled with people and firing cannon, "trying to make my carcass come to the top."

Very likely Mark himself would recall that scene if he could hear all the literary critics, this month of his centennial, booming away. The carcass won't come up by solemn gunfire as to whether Mark was really a tragic frustrated figure; whether he was Huck himself, the bad boy locked in and disciplined and forbidden to curse or smoke; whether he was a pessimist, or a clown, or a raging radical seduced by shekels. Huck himself lies behind the log, "powerful lazy and comfortable." Mark Twain was, in the deepest meaning of the word, a humorist; and the one quality that so few of his commentators (I except the admirable Leacock) have brought to bear upon his work is a sense of humor. Dreadful as it seems to have to say it (to a generation confident of its own ultimacy) William Dean Howells—writing *My Mark Twain* in the immediate sorrow of his friend's death—dealt with Mark in more deeply observant ken than most critics since. "A humorist," said Howells as long ago as 1901, "in whom the sense of the droll is never parted from the sense of the dreadful."

Every detonation of the boatload of critics is an honest charge, well rammed and loudly exploded;

but so far as I can see these blasts of blank do not bring up the carcass. For Mark, like every great artist, was the creature of a thousand moods; every man in his humor. He was the loaf of bread plugged with quicksilver (these were the humble witchcraft of the body-seekers). Of the great creators it is usually best to know nothing but their work. To *Huckleberry Finn* one can pay the highest tribute one ever pays to any book: I wish to gosh I'd never read it so I could have it all before me. To be a boy again reading it that unforgettable first time—and very likely missing many of its subtlest touches. And then I am reminded of an extraordinary statement in Van Wyck Brooks's truly brilliant *Ordeal of Mark Twain,* a book which set the fashion in Mark Twain criticism for some 15 years; a book of flashing insight and of noble spirit, but which did as much harm as only a brilliant book can do. "Who does not see in the extraordinary number of books about boys and boyhood written by American authors" (said Mr Brooks) "the surest sign of arrested moral development." That is what I mean by approaching the work of a humorist without a sense of humor. And the famous comic passage about the "solitary oesophagus," not a very good joke I grant, Mr Brooks bitterly instanced to prove that the tendency of Mark's humor was "to degrade beauty." Mr Lewis Mumford, more aggrieved still, brooded over a fatuous message that Mark wrote for Walt Whitman's 70th birthday (certainly a silly letter, probably hounded out of him by some committee) and found it evidence of Mark's "fundamental barbarism."

The damned human race, as Mark called us, never shows its invincible stupidity more plainly than in its extraordinary querulity about its great benefactors

—instead of simply enjoying their gifts. Obviously Mark Twain's humor was freakish and often crude; his speeches, as they exist in print, the merest occasional guff; his philosophic and religious notions, which he innocently supposed so rending, are childishly banal; the long-annunciated notebooks and secret writings do not seem to contain any very startling revelations. They are not only posthumous but posthumorous. He was "spoiled by civilization," says one biographer; he was "frustrated by life" say others. But what the deuce? Being spoiled and frustrated, and yet getting in a few good licks here and there, is the first premise of existence. Pure spirit is spoiled and frustrated by the mere fact of having to be incarnated at all. Chesterton once wrote a delicious piece about those frantic liberators who are always wanting to release something or other from the very condition of its being. If you free a tiger from the humiliation of wearing stripes, said G. K. C., it is no longer a tiger; if you beg a triangle to burst from the bondage of living in three sides it perishes lamentably as a triangle. Civilization may have currycombed Mark a bit, but also it gave him the impetus to be something more than an Artemus Ward. It spoiled Bret Harte too, but Harte wrote some pretty grand tales. My sympathy is all with those wise and peaceable folks who all these years have been reading and enjoying *Tom Sawyer* and *Huck Finn* (the other books are fast fading out) quite unaware that they are supposed to be Freudian testimony. Huck and Nigger Jim go drifting down Endless River, and behind all the learned argument I hear their voices. "It warn't often that we laughed—only a little kind of a low chuckle." And I occasionally recall what everyone else seems to have forgotten, the Author's Notice:—

"Persons attempting to find a motive in this narrative will be prosecuted; persons attempting to find a moral in it will be banished; persons attempting to find a plot in it will be shot."

It has been encouraging to observe the general sanity, one might say the general decency, of the homage brought out by this hundredth birthday. As in the case of Anatole France (the two, so different, show interesting parallels) the depression is over. Young doctrinaires will always, every so often, crowd aboard ferryboats to shoot cannon. It does no lasting damage, often much good. The air has been cleared of some hypocrisies and false idolatries; now, until some new theory of literary ontology becomes modish, they will let him alone to be the multiple entertainment which was his destiny. There was good reason why Mark Twain shot up to apotheosis and then, in the recent era of horsewind and general deflatus, had to suffer such horrid expounding. He fitted perfectly into a Great American Legend (we've seen it lately in Will Rogers). That is, that a man risen from rough and tumble pioneer circumstances can make merry at Kings and Emperors, outwit philosophers and scholars, hobnob with financiers and generals, take apart foreign languages and cultures and show how funny they are, know more about Shakespeare than people who have spent their lives studying him, and more about religion than the Archbishop of Canterbury. To the American mass, the largest articulate mythopoeic group, this doctrine is wafer, wine and hassocks. When these extraordinary lustres are found (as they can only be) upon a man of enormous talent, charm, and courage, it is likely that he will be publicized more for what is preposterously outside his true compass than for his essential gift. Not unnaturally his publishers and zealots seek to keep alive the whole mass of his work, including scraps, shavings, and jetsam. The cycle inevitably rotates to a damnation for what he actually did best. There were times, in the past decade, when it seemed as though some of the highbrow critics must have handled that rattlesnake skin that brought bad luck to Huck and Jim.

But—like Jim—Mark Twain had a hairy breast which was bound to bring him luck in the end. If you ever had any doubts, try *Huck Finn* again. There never was writing more perfectly adapted to its purpose. If you have been told that Mark always attempted "to degrade beauty" note the exquisite little pictures of the great river, always kept within the range of what a boy would notice. "There was freckled places on the ground where the light sifted down through the leaves, and the freckled places swapped about a little, showing there was a little breeze up there." You will not miss the slashing dexter impressionism of some rapid passages: Huck's fright at the strange campfire—"it made me feel like a person had cut one of my breaths in two and I only got half, and the short half too." Or when the raft is run down by a steamboat; or dawn on the river and the sounds across the wide water. That galoot seen chopping on a raft far across the stream, the axe flashing in the sunlight, the *k'chunk* not arriving until the blade glitters up for the following stroke—there he goes, chopping away for as long as print holds magic. And every vine-hung cove and creek with its willows and cottonwoods where they hid raft or canoe is dear to memory; you'll gaze in search of them, as I did, the first time you cross that stream. No one who has ever crossed Mississippi can be unhappy about American literature.

It would be silly, or impertinent, to point out the things you'll notice. You'll find plenty of flaws: occasional japes of the lecture-platform sort; and flashes of anger where Mark forgets Huck in his passion to describe something he hates—the attempted lynching of Colonel Sherburn, for instance; or the sardonic descriptions of Arkansaw rustics. (If Dickens had done this how sore everyone would have been.) Mark Twain shows himself always of the great breed, the Shakespeare-Cervantes-Voltaire blood, in his hatred and contempt of the mob.

Of the most famous incidents I say nothing: they are got by heart in most readers. To me one of the finest touches in the whole yarn is when Huck and Jim find a wooden leg in the floating house. "We couldn't find the other one, though we hunted all around." They assumed of course that wooden legs, like real ones, come in pairs.

Too many critics, thinking about Mark Twain, have hunted for a wooden leg that never was there.

In all the recent palaver I've seen no mention of one of the happiest things ever written about Mark Twain. It comes from the man who, of all our present writers, has the spirit most akin to his; who also was raised close to the great river; and it's in a book that Mark would have loved to write, though he wouldn't have printed it. It's called *Chapters for the Orthodox,* by Don Marquis. God, interviewed by a reporter, happens to let out that Mark Twain has a river of his own in Heaven. I'm quoting from Mr Marquis:—

"It's an immense river, thousands of miles long—millions of miles long, in fact, when Mark wants it that long; and he has steamboat races on it all the time. You never saw such a spectacle as one of Mark's steamboat races, with Mark on the deck of the winning ship, archangels, saints and devils lined up on the banks of the river shouting and cheering, the boats belching fire and smoke, and Mark making the welkin ring with profanity."

"Profanity?" The reporter was a little surprised.

"Listen," said Jehovah, "and get me right. Of course, I have an objection to ordinary profanity. It's common and vulgar and undignified. It is, in a way, and if I ever wanted to take the matter up officially, an affront to *me*. But Mark's profanity! It's different! It's a gorgeous lyric. Just to listen to it is a liberal education. When I found that a lot of angels and saints were going down to the bank of the river to listen to it, I was a little doubtful at first of its effect on them.

"Mark ran his river, with one of his most exciting races going on, right through the middle of Hell one time, and Satan turned blue with envy and admiration. He said that for pure *style* and interest it laid over anything he could invent. He came and begged me to let him have Mark and his river for a while. I put it up to Mark, and he was all for going. But he didn't go, in the end."

"Why not?"

"His wife and William Dean Howells wouldn't let him," said Jehovah. "They said it would look bad . . . people wouldn't understand . . ."

COLLEGE HIGHWAY

I WAS WONDERING what to do about the floor in the Knothole: whether to scrub, paint, stain it, or what. My neighbor Fontaine Fox made a wise remark. "Walk about on it a while first," he said, "to give it character."

The same thought occurred to me when having a look at the new colleges at Yale, where architects have gone whoopsdearie in Gothic. It will be fifty years at least before any slow-minded observer should venture an opinion. The new Yale needs a lot of walking on to give it character. It's magnificent, but what is it? By Oxford out of the Belfry of Bruges? New England has been thrown overboard. The effect is not as depressing as that endless acreage of synthetic Georgian at Harvard, but it does begin to weigh on the mind after a few hours. I wonder what four years of architectural second-hand do to a young mind? Certainly some of the fine old Puritan elms look astonished shut into such high-church quadrangles. With extraordinary sense of relief, catharsis, one goes to look at the little houses north of the Green: the Pierpont House, the Graduates' Club, the Tory Tavern.

In the interior court of the great Sterling Library some youths were palely loitering with geometry books; I suppose awaiting an entrance examination. Near them was an inscription that my faded Latin finds a bit flabby to construe. NON CALAMI STILI AUT PENNAE SUFFRAGIO SED MIRA PATRONARUM FORMARUMQUE CONCOR-

DIA PROPORTIONE ET MODULO. *Modulus,* which I take to mean restraint, is hardly the exact word to describe the hilarities of those architects. Yet some of the things theoretically deplorable—such as Davenport College's mixture of Gothic and Georgian—are, in actuality, rather amusing.

The new colleges at Yale are certainly something to be seen; and then kept quiet about. Any comment on them now is a lifetime premature. But my heart grieves for any young Yalensian who gets a Rhodes Scholarship and has to go on for three more years of real Gothic after four of replica. His taste will be permanently distracted.

Mr Santayana, in his novel, was shrewd to have his young hero flee both Harvard and Yale and go first to an up-country college (Williams, in fact). When, I'm wondering, did our two greatest universities (which began as such sturdy places) develop their passion for imitation?

There is a rather solemn announcement in stone at the entrance to the Sterling Library (which is, I must be frank, a place of stupefying magnificence). *A Library is a Summons to Scholarship,* it says; they have wisely planted creeper which will soon occlude this naïveté. But there was an exquisite coolness and peace in the air that September morning. I thought with affectionate curiosity of the class of 1939, about to begin its ardors and endurances. May they have what has lately been promised the world of commerce, a Breathing Spell. Which is what college ought to be. They won't find much of it afterward, unless they are singularly agile and obstinate.

We arrived in New Haven at midnight, after a longish drive by moonlight along my favorite grievance, U. S. Number 1. Across the street from the

Hotel Taft is a small café with quite the authentic college-town flavor. It has a list of 64 cocktails and mixed drinks to stimulate education. These are advertised under glass on the tables; very grievous to contemplate at breakfast time the next morning. A tactful innkeeper would not mention them at least until noon.

Northward from New Haven is a road called the College Highway, toward Mount Holyoke, Northampton and Amherst. Connecticut is always a beautiful State; at the moment suffering a little from tercentenary selfconsciousness. Such pleasant towns as Farmington do not really need to placard every elderly house with its date. In an outdoor box at the Farmington Bookshop I found for 10 cents the first volume of *Derringforth,* a novel by the late Frank A. Munsey. I have always wondered whether this is as grievous a book as I like to suppose. The preface, dated September 1, 1897, states that *"When should a girl marry?* is the theme of this story." It admonishes young women to remember that "freshness, sweetness, innocence, faith and enthusiasm stand for the highest possibilities of happiness." What happens in volume 2 I shall probably never know; I found volume 1 soggy.

South Hadley, our next pause on the College Highway, knows more about young women than Frank Munsey was likely to. 306 freshmen were registering at Mount Holyoke that day and a large addition to the college library is just being completed. Mount Holyoke has a delightful combination inn and bookshop and we found Miss Phillips, the manager, looking forward to a busy season. The Bookshop Inn is now celebrating a tenth anniversary, and the college itself, so pleasantly secluded on its hilltop, will soon mark its hundredth. It struck us as amusing to find Mount Holyoke and Amherst divided by a stream called Bachelor Brook.

Of all Mary Lyon's pupils at the Female Seminary (as it was then called) the one who most interested us was now close in spirit. Once before, several years ago, we drove through Amherst, fleeing from Fourth of July celebrations, and forgot to look for Emily Dickinson's house. This time we found it, but had no thought to intrude. Those who love Emily do not speak easily of her, but one wanted to divine the feeling of that house and garden. To find it exactly as one would have hoped was fortune indeed—one of "the soul's superior instants." By happy chance and the kindness of Madame Bianchi and Mr Hampson we were able to see—almost, one could say, to recognize—pictures and furniture that Emily loved. The quiet lawn behind high hedges is much as she knew it. Beside her brother's house, next door, is the most exquisite silvery old barn, sagging a bit, shingled with colors of cobweb. As you come upon it suddenly, among the trees, it seems the ghost of a barn rather than actual timbers. It looks as soft as a scarf that Emily herself might have worn, cool evenings in that garden. A fragile spinster among barns; a symbol of the poet's own heart. I suppose its delicacy came upon it in the fifty years since she died, but it could never have grown so beautiful and shy unless she loved it. If my mind goes back to search for meanings, I find more of them in that lichen-colored shed than in pinnacles by wholesale at New Haven. Both have their place, of course. As she once said, "To multiply the harbors does not reduce the sea." But I am a connoisseur of barns; this one of Emily's

"THE GHOST OF A BARN"
Emily Dickinson's Barn-in-Law, Amherst, Mass.

thrills me as did the School of Philosophy at Concord.

"I fear for the rectitude of the barn," Emily wrote; referring I suppose to the stable behind her own home; the occasion was when the coachman was in liquor. But it would apply now to her brother's gently faltering coach-house. I think it was because we loved the barn at sight that Madame Bianchi, Emily's niece, was so gracious to us.

"Twilight was touching Amherst with his yellow glove"; we had to go. Long ago we promised some children a visit to the Toytown Tavern at Winchendon. But one thing and another kept us from it until those children are nearly grown up. We expected a kind of gigantic nursery, with toys and Mother Goose decorations and gauds appropriate to extreme youth. And so it is; which made it all the odder to find most of the guests distinctly elderly. One of our ageing progeny, whose tastes are violently adult, remarked bitterly, "How can I sleep in a room with little rabbits running all over the wallpaper?" What amused me most was an outhouse called The Pirates' Grill, with a sign on the door: *Ring Bell for Pirate Captain.*

OHIO STEAMBOAT

IF YOU THOUGHT the sternwheelers were only a romantic and picturesque relic of ancient days, a few hours on the levee at Cincinnati will change your notion. The steamboat *Chris Greene* was loading for her evening run to Louisville. Apparently the Ohio River brings down freight as it does its occasional floods, in big plenty. Already, several hours before sailing time, she was loaded end to end. There was more than she could possibly carry, even with Mr Bondurant, the Mate—known as Uncle Bud, and profoundly respected by the black stevedores—supervising storage. The word *stevedore,* by the way, is interesting: it is the Spanish version of *constipator,* a packer-tight. Which is what they were doing in *Chris Greene's* tween-decks. Some of the cargo would have to wait until next day. Specially notable the extraordinary number of cases of glass lamp-chimneys. There are plenty of kerosene lamps still burning down the Ohio River country.

I wish there had been a chance to see Mr Mate driving his crew at the time of peak load. Though gentle and soft of speech he has the look of an Ohio River Dante, and there is something in his deep competent eye that puts immediate omen on a colored rouster.

The *Chris Greene* is only nine years old; her hull is of steel, but in general style and shape she conforms to the traditional plan of those oldtimers of the Currier and Ives prints. "All they need to travel on," in the old saying, "is a heavy fall of dew." To the eye of a deep-water man they are certainly an astonishment, and undoubtedly have overland blood in them for I noticed that the steamboat men use railroad terms such as "hauling" and "riding." But I must tread softly here, for the steamboaters are older than the railroaders, and properly proud of their own lingo and tradition. As Roy Barkhau of the Greene Line office told me, "The old river packets are what really built up the country, the railroads' propaganda to the contrary. Did you know it's possible to go by steamboat from Pittsburgh to the Yellowstone? In the early days the boats ran regularly from St Louis to points in Montana." The Greene Line has been on the Ohio for fifty years; in the engine room they showed me that some of *Chris Greene's* cylinder castings, still in full service, were salvaged from a previous vessel and dated from the 80's. I liked the air of Southern ease which not even heavy traffic can dispel—the chief's wicker armchair and rack of magazine reading; the skipper's big airy stateroom with its own tiny verandah; the high upholstered bench in the pilot house for visiting pilots. I hope that a visiting commodore is allowed to ride there sometimes, for I have just received a commission as complimentary Commodore on the staff of Governor Ruby Laffoon. Kentucky Colonels are fairly numerous, but a Kentucky Commodore!—Even the fireman off duty has his alcove of repose, a gaily decorated hutch (known as the Coon Pen) aft of the engine room.

Captain Volney White, nicknamed "Stogie," who has been with the Greene Line since he left high school, did Three Hours for Lunch Club honors in the white main corridor—which, with its woodwork scrimshaw, looks rather like a tunnel in a cocoanut cake. It was an impromptu occasion, and only, as the skipper needlessly apologized, a "port-lunch," but what then must be the luxury of the passengers—who get stateroom, dinner and breakfast all for $3.75. Bean soup, corn-beef and cabbage, and "wheelhouse pudding," (a kind of tapioca, I think) with admirable coffee. The Captain spoke of other steamboat dishes—*jambolai,* a Creole side-dish of rice, tomatoes and peppers; and *stern-wheel duck,* a kind of hash served for the rousters. He showed us photographs of the races, a few years ago, between the *Chris Greene,* her sister *Tom Greene,* and a rival packet the *Betsy Ann. Betsy Ann* is the better known in the East, as her owner wrote a delightful book about her (*The Log of the Betsy Ann*) but I believe that in the racing *Tom* and *Chris* nosed ahead. They have a pair of gilded antlers as trophy, to prove it.

Sitting in the high chairs of the pilot house, in the pleasant drowse caused by such a meal, it required Spartan resolution not to accept the invitation of friendly Chris Greene himself (General Manager of the Line; the boats are named for him and his brother, the President) to ride down to Louisville. The visitors tried to persuade John Kidd, the bookseller, to get that night's literary dinner transferred to the boat. What more perfect setting for a cultural jamboree: a moonlit spring evening, the *Chris Greene* kicking her way downstream along the curly border between Kentucky and Indiana. The big "pitmans" (connecting rods) would slosh the old wooden millwheel round and round in a hammering gargle of spray; even muddy water would be silver under a Kentucky moon. I could imagine all the layers of delicious smells—down below, coal and engines and cargo savors of tobacco, packing cases, coffee and

STEAMBOAT "CHRIS GREENE," OHIO RIVER

groceries. On the saloon deck, aromas of dinner and fresh varnish and clean blankets. Up on the texas, in a cool spring breeze, the gust of the new Blue Grass. And, as they say in their folder, "Always a new picture round the bend." *Chris Greene* has her literary association, too. At the purser's office is a framed photostat of a Pilot's Certificate which is precious to all steamboat men. It asserts that the holder was "a suitable and safe person to be intrusted with the power and duties of Pilot of Steam Boats on the Mississippi River to and from St Louis to New Orleans." It is dated April 9, 1859, and the name of the pilot was Samuel Clemens.

Duty won, as it usually does; we went ashore to observe our honorable and well-mannered obligations. But I wonder what Louisville looks like? I suggested to Captain White as slogan for his company a phrase familiar to the Grand Central zone—*Follow the Greene Line.*

What are the spiritual marks of the Middle West, I often wonder? In my own superficial observation I have always considered the barn-side blazon CHEW MAIL POUCH as one identification of that great empire; as the codfish signs are the emblem of New England. I wish the proprietors of MAIL POUCH would tell me the actual spread of their legend. But even dearer to me are the little roan pigs one sees in spring scampering across the fields of Ohio and Indiana. I have heard rumors of a Federal massacre, or at least a limitation *in gremio,* among these gay and humorous creatures. No one who plays Herod among these innocents can lightly be pardoned. But to the open-hearted observer the Middle West is always a land of surprises—as every land should be.

On the road from Cincinnati to Dayton one passes through Lebanon, Ohio, where we are startled to find an old hotel once visited by Dickens. And Dayton itself is an astonishment. There should be a great municipal chime or carillon there, somehow symbolizing and integrating the merry tinkle of nationwide cash-registers. Great bells of mighty timbre, cast of the same metal used for the sharp tingle of the familiar machine; it would be a pleasant symbol of reviving circulation. Dayton is a delicious town to encounter; its wide streets, trackless trolleys, its Masonic Temple and Art Institute (perfect in acoustics) above the Miami River. There is no less thrill in meeting the Miami, the Wabash, the Tippecanoe, than in the first glimpse of Avon or Arno. (I've never seen the Arno, but let it stand.) And if you want to know what perfect hotel service can be, try the Van Cleve in Dayton—almost too perfect for an humble traveller, as they earnestly offer so many kinds of help, solace and service, one gets confused.—There is such a thing as hotels being too solicitous: in the various Statlers, I've noticed, if you go to bed without locking your door the night watchman comes round and wakes you explaining that you might be disturbed by someone.—But I quite realize that running a hotel is an impossible problem. The only solution, perhaps, would be to ask each arriving guest to classify himself: is he one of those who want to be Serviced, or is he the kind who desires complete anonymity and seclusion.

On the road from Dayton to Indianapolis it is a pleasant surprise to encounter Greenfield (Indiana), "Riley's Home Town"—and there's the Old Swimmin' Hole, in a well preserved little park.

O. W. FIRKINS

TWO of the most exciting periods for a young reader of American journalism were the years 1914–18 or thereabouts when O. W. Firkins was writing reviews of current poetry for the *Nation* and the old *Evening Post,* and 1919–21 when he was doing drama for the *Weekly Review.* With many opacities to apologize for there is one observation in which I take pride. As long ago as 1918 I said in print that Mr Firkins was one of the three critics in America whose praise was most worth having—and most difficult to obtain. I have seen no reason since for changing that opinion.

Oscar Firkins, most of whose career was in service of the English Department at the University of Minnesota, died in 1932. Shy, frail, sad, myopic almost to blindness, but with an extraordinary acuteness of the inward eye, he was one of those characters that keep a university true to its function. The sort of person often called eccentric, by which one means that the center is pitched not upon convention but upon some intuitive plumb. The conventional center is too often a dead center. Now the University of Minnesota Press is honoring itself, and delighting thousands of Firkins's former students, by publishing his letters and papers. *Selected Essays,* including the remarkable "Man: A Character Sketch" and other keen observations on literature, drama, and religion, appeared some months ago. It is now followed by *Memoirs and Letters.* These two volumes would be fortunate baggage for any vacation which hopes to rise above the dull tidewater level of the mind.

Firkins's sister, in her preface to the *Memoirs and Letters,* tells us that unavoidable excisions in the correspondence (including "caustic remarks about persons still living") may tend to leave an apparent emphasis on urbanity, geniality, which was no dominant trait in O. W. F. "There was in his nature a rigor, a tenacity of opinion and purpose which admitted no compromise. . . . His habitual mood was one of sadness and depression." In a world where there are so many damned genials, clowns, and meliorists, how appetizing that is. A vibration of singular honesty moves in his comments. Asked to attend a reunion of old classmates he replies, with perfect courtesy and definiteness, No, because he does not wish to. Called upon for a letter of commendation for an instructor whose work is mediocre, he remarks that "—— is a faithful, well-meaning fellow with the merits of a good dog." Yet with what careful patience and insight he defends the plodding virtues of students to whom he thinks the university has been unfair. Hypersensitive himself (he was deeply hurt when the *Atlantic Monthly* accidentally returned a MS of his with only the formal rejection slip), he knew how to safeguard the feelings of those who were worth consideration. Incidentally the little exchange of letters between Firkins and the *Atlantic,* with Mr Ellery Sedgwick's tactful regrets for an office error that must sometimes happen everywhere, is a charming episode that honors both sides. You will divine in the letters those recurrences of nervous melancholia that restricted Firkins from certain phases of human mirth and companionship, and perhaps limited his sympathies. This is compensated by an extraordinary astuteness, a most delicate and witty awareness of intellectual integrity. He can be devastating enough toward what he disesteems. Of a fashionable metropolitan humorist he says, "By the time the last of his reeking witticisms had been received my ear felt like a cuspidor." When asked about his frequent attendance at an orthodox church he replied that he was studying the cleric "as a curiosity." Of a thesis offered for a master's degree, apparently based on some discussion of sex in literature, he wrote:

> I do not think a naïveté so egregious is entitled to the ratification of a master's diploma from an institution which stands for self-discipline rather than for unchecked impulse, and which prefers a modicum of good sense even in its graduate students.

After the performance of an undergraduate play which he considered in evil taste he wrote to the college daily:

> The jubilation of the animal in his power to reproduce himself, however natural and biologically right, is not fit cement for an audience in an institution which a commonwealth has dedicated to the mind. . . . Our dramatists are cooks whom it is vain to scold or hector; but there is one act that impresses the most head-strong and tempestuous of cooks —the leaving of the viands untouched upon the table.

Another letter to the same paper, in February 1916 when the university faculty was said to be unanimous for greater military "preparedness," shows his instinct for protesting mass emotionalism:

> If a nation loved peace well enough to put itself at a practical disadvantage for the sake of peace, that fact would com-

mand the attention, and eventually the faith and veneration of the world.

The so-called unanimity of the faculty on this topic is not, I think, of any overpowering significance. The truth is that agreement on such matters loses force in the exact measure of its completeness. Had only three-fourths, or better still, only two-thirds of the respondents concurred, the fraction would have been weightier than the total. Division is the proof of independence and when men who would normally divide on religion, on politics, on morals, manifest in a special field a consent that reaches or approaches totality, the fact points to docility or imitation. When all the wheat-stems in a field bend southward, it does not mean an organic predisposition on the part of each stem to a southerly inclination; it means merely that the wind is in the north.

There is not space here to give you more than a crude suggestion of the independent mind, the flashing felicity of phrase, the humor both light and sombre to be found in the work of this man who said that ink is the least nutritious of fluids and that his mood was contentment *within* despair. His comments on European travel, on hotel life in New York, are as exciting to me as any novel. Some thrillingly ponderable brevities from his lecture notes are included. "Keats's muse is a siren but his art is a vestal. That is the irresistible combination." There are some things so deeply and temperamentally said that to quote them outside the comprehension of context would do them wrong. Who but a man steeped in professorship would have written, of a loss infinitely near and dear, "It is sad to have to use the subjunctive mood and the pluperfect tense of one whose personality has so long been part of the present indicative." Yet that austere and proud spirit was never overborne by the mere pedantry and equipment of scholarship. He wrote once:

> I sometimes wish that every envelope and impediment were swept away, that teacher and pupil could meet in some genial climate in a bare plain under the open sky, without an appropriation, without a building, without an appliance, without a committee, without a program, without a ceremony: then, teacher and taught could look straight into each other's faces, and the manhood, the mettle, of both could be tested.

COLUMBIAN EXPOSITION

THIS has been a very idle day in the Knothole, with rain on the roof and a fire breathing in the chimney. The only achievement I can point to is having bought, for $2.98 at the local hardware store, an electric clock that fascinates me. Perhaps it was a mistake to buy one with a second-hand, which goes round and round with smooth insistence. But there is no malice, nor unrelenting symbolism in it; for the little leaflet says "If started backward, this clock will run backward at exactly the same speed as forward." Some day I shall try it.

"It takes 10,368,000 impulses of the alternating current," the leaflet says, "to advance this clock 24 hours." I often feel rather like that myself. "Where power interruptions are frequent enough to be annoying," it advises me to buy a more complicated kind of clock.

This afternoon, as regards cerebral dynamics, the current was very alternating and power only fitful. But finally, after tinkering with various notions I settled down to enjoy the new Columbia Encyclopedia, a grand book in one solidly made and excellently printed volume of 1950 pages. As much as Dr Clarke F. Ansley (the editor) and his staff of compilers, the printers too deserve congratulation. It was done by R. R. Donnelley & Sons of Chicago, whose work (through the whole gamut from telephone directories to volumes de luxe) has always been notable.

Dr Ansley says, in his brief and modest preface, "The traditional rule for preparing a reference work is, Find the right woman and do what she says." He pays courteous tribute to the assistant editor, Elizabeth J. Sherwood, and many others, both women and men, who have helped in this important work during a number of years.

Not simply to plunge at random into such wide and deep waters of information I thought I would amuse myself by taking a recent expedition of my own and corroborate or fortify some of its details by reference to the Encyclopedia. Italics are quotations.

It was Labor Day. (*Inaugurated by the Knights of Labor in 1882 and in 1894 Congress voted it a legal holiday.*) I went to town (*pop. 6,930,466*) in the late afternoon by the Long Island Railroad. (*Long Island, 118 mi. long and 12 to 20 mi. wide . . . with an area of 1,682 sq. mi., it is the home of 4,103,638 people . . . its location insures it a fine climate.* At this point I think of looking to see if there is an article on Mortgages, but refrain.) Perhaps owing to the difference between Eastern Standard and Daylight Saving Time (*Farmers have opposed Daylight Saving. Farming is adjusted to a natural rhythm that is not affected by make-believe. Cows do not yield their milk before they have secreted it; hay-making is disastrous if done before the dew is gone*) I did not catch at Grand Central the train I thought to. In fact there was no train to the Berkshires (*like the Lake Country of England have long been a resort of nature lovers*) until next morning. Meditating what to do I went to Liggett's drug store and found some Thoreau on the 49 cent counter. (*He extolled the right of man to withdraw from civilization and the conventions of society.*) Then to the peaceful old Murray Hill Hotel for a drink. (*Cocktail, a mixed drink having a basis of gin, whisky, rum, or brandy, combined with bitters and flavoring materials . . . served, with wafers or canapés, before a meal as an appetizer.*)

I can see that it's not possible fully to document my brief holiday by the encyclopedia. To give the complete historic or sociological, even the sentimental or jurisprudent, background of any human adventure would require more space (perhaps even more effrontery) than Pareto. Take the case of Murray Hill. That would set me thinking of Mr Robert Cortes Holliday, who used that name as pseudonym in many rambling essays while editor of *The Bookman* some years ago. I don't find him in the book; nor do I find Robert Murray who gave the hill its name. It was Mrs Murray, I think, who delayed the British officers with tea and cakes at her farmhouse on Murray Hill while Washington made his escape from what is now the shopping region of Lord and Taylor's. I do find Lindley Murray, the grammarian (*He was a Quaker and lived quietly in Islip, Long Island, during the Revolution*) of whom I have somewhere read that it was his farm, "Belle Vue," on the East River, that became the site of Bellevue Hospital. A first edition of his famous *English Grammar* (1818) would be an interesting item for collectors. That sets me off looking up McGuffey; Columbia says his Readers had sales estimated at 122 million copies (*Their influence in shaping the American mind of the mid-19th century can scarcely be exaggerated*).

I decided that I could reach my destination as quickly by taking train to Albany, spending the night there, and asking some friends to drive me to Copake Falls in the morning. (*Albany, pop. 127,412*

. . . . the seat of several academies, a State Teachers College (1844) . . . . the second oldest town in the United States.) I hope Albany won't ever let anything happen to those lovely little old wooden houses along a wide street on top of the hill, in the general neighborhood of State College. At the State College Co-op bookshop I found another book to beguile the journey. Jules Verne's *Michael Strogoff*. For some unknown reason Albany is always a rich pocket for the hunter of Jules Vernes. There is also a tempting little back room of secundiana at the Mistletoe Bookshop (*The American Indians chewed mistletoe to relieve toothache*) which I did not have time to examine properly. At the Mistletoe Bookshop I found a pamphlet reprint of a little known poem by Robert Frost, *The Gold Hesperidee,* which I think has not been included in his books. 200 copies were printed by the Bibliophile Press, Cortland, N. Y. (*pop. 15,043, S. of Syracuse, on the Tioughnioga River in a dairying region famous for its Holstein cattle.*)

My bookseller friends were kind enough to lay aside work and drive me down to my destination. They pointed out the Governor's Mansion (*Lehman, Herbert Henry, b. New York City 1878, grad. Williams College, 1899*). We passed through Rensselaer (*railroad shops, and manufactures of felt, dyes, leather, oilcloth, and shirts . . . . at Fort Cralo, near by, Yankee Doodle was written by Dr Shackburg, a surgeon in the British army*). Presently we passed a lovely village from which has come better poetry than Yankee Doodle—Austerlitz, the home of Miss Millay (*The curious blending of Elizabethan words and rhythm with modern words and ideas gives her work a charming originality.*)—

This is rather an odd comment: I don't offhand remember any special Elizabethan tinge in Miss Millay's prosody; I must think it over.

Here, I'm sorry to say, I got completely sidetracked. Looking up the entry about Millay started me into a search for other writers, or special topics interesting to myself. As one of their Honorary Night Watchmen the Columbia University Press won't take amiss my offering a few modest suggestions; which are made not at all in a spirit of reproach. In the first issue of any work that tries to box the whole compass of current information there are bound to be accidental omissions. Even in the small field where I can pretend familiarity I found very few. My great pleasure in finding an excellent note on Logan Pearsall Smith was offset by seeing no entry for the late C. E. Montague (of the Manchester *Guardian*). Among American writers I must really insist on the inclusion of T. A. Daly and Columbia's own Simeon Strunsky. The entry on Joseph Conrad is in error in implying that *The Rover* and *Suspense* are two titles for the same book. They are two different stories; *The Rover* was published complete; *Suspense* was left unfinished at Conrad's death.—The note on Peru comes too close to implying that Sanchez Cerro is still President. The President since 1933 has been General Oscar Benavides. Incidentally, the cathedral in Lima is not "gray stone" but adobe of a tawny yellow which shines beautifully burnt-orange in a clear sunset; Limeños refer to it affectionately as "the biggest mud building in the world."

You can guess from this sudden and merely prefatory bushwhacking into a great book how good a companion it makes. The test of an encyclopedia is not casual picnic but long and useful resort. That test I think the Columbia is going to fulfil. I foresee a lot of fun to be had in examining its phonetic decisions. Valuable clues to national idiosyncrasies may perhaps be had—I observe that it says Newark, England, is pronounced Nū'ŭrk but Newark, New Jersey, is Nōō'ärk". And apparently Newark, Delaware, is different from both the others.

Speaking of towns, the Night Watchman pleads that Roslyn, L. I., be listed in the next edition. It more than fulfills the requirement of 1000 population, and deserves mention as the former home of William Cullen Bryant.

"* * * UNIQUE"

BOOKS of genuine rarity and condition still remain among the most solid investments. The Caliph A. Edward Newton remarked the other day "I paid $60,000 for an immaculate First Folio, selling a block of —— —— in order that I might pay for it promptly. The present value of the —— —— I sold is now less than $5000. Query: what does my First Folio stand me?"

And in spite of international broils it's going to be an exciting winter in the Going-Going-Gone business. Last week I happened to be upstairs in a big auction gallery while a sale was going on elsewhere in the building. I didn't even know about the sale: I was looking at some unusual finds that had lately arrived and were being catalogued for a future occasion. The working quarters of an auction house are as alert and responsive as backstage in a theatre; and suddenly among all those bins of ticketed "lots" the word ran round "Fifteen Seventy Five for The Whale." Which meant that Melville's book—an earlier version of *Moby Dick*—had just brought the remarkable price of $1575. Cataloguers laid down their scholarly collations and lit a cigarette to consider this. It sounded like the old era of Jerome Kern.

I may as well explain that my purpose in being there was to have a glimpse of a very odd item—"attractive" would perhaps be the austere cataloguer's technical word for it—connected with our old friend Sir Kenelm Digby. I haven't bothered you about Sir Kenelm for a long time, but you needn't suppose I've forgotten him. Here, beautifully written out by some professional scribe but with numerous corrections in Sir Kenelm's own hand, is a vellum folio containing the letters he wrote to his children, his relatives and intimates, after the death of his wife, the Lady Venetia. And the notably interesting fact is that the amanuensis was evidently the same copyist who engrossed the famous *Private Memoirs* (not published until 1827). I remember once expressing some puzzlement as to whether Sir Kenelm really did write those memoirs himself. Perhaps I shall have to reconsider that: Mr E. W. Bligh in his delightful book *Sir Kenelm Digby and His Venetia* (London, 1932; I think it has not appeared over here) seems to have no doubt of the authenticity of the memoirs. And odd as they are, K. D. was fantastic enough to make anything possible.

The big vellum letter-book now locked up on 57th Street waiting to take its turn in some forthcoming sale should particularly interest the library at Harvard. For it is the best rebuttal yet to hand of the unpleasant rumor that Sir Kenelm's "Viper Wine for the Complection" caused Venetia's death. Here, in his own innermost vein, are moving and lengthy essays on his lady's virtues. The first letter, "To my three sonnes Kenelme, John & George," an attempt to fix upon the "tender and slippery memories of childhood the character of their mother," is no less than 68 folio pages. The whole series, written in K.D.'s period of grieving retirement at Gresham College immediately after Venetia's death (1633), has a convincing eloquence of sincerity. A bit longwinded I admit, but Sir Kenelm could be longwinded about anything. The "solemn assembly" at Montpellier which listened to his Discourse of the Sympathetic Powder may well have been solemn before he had finished. Yet those who slept missed some excellent anecdotes.

But why, I hear someone asking, should Harvard be interested? Because Sir Kenelm was one of the earliest benefactors of the Harvard Library. The ancient theological books which he sent them were destroyed in a fire (1764 or 1765?); and oddly enough the same happened to books he gave to Oxford—an example, Mr Bligh suggests, of his doctrine of Sympathy. He also gave 50 oak trees to the Bodleian Library, and it would be pleasant to think that they still form part of those ancient shelves and alcoves. Do any records still exist at Harvard of Sir Kenelm's gift—which we know of only by a hearsay allusion in the works of pious Richard Baxter.[1] At

[1]Mr Theodore F. M. Newton, of the Harvard faculty, very kindly put me right on this matter. He says:—

"This gift is very much more than a matter of 'hearsay' or pleasant 'legend,' and is mentioned not only in Baxter but in Cotton Mather's 'Marginalia' and John Dunton's 'Life.' The books were fairly stuffy (at least, for modern readers) and consisted mainly of works of fathers of the church. Although fire in 1764 destroyed them, a record exists as follows:

Catalogus Librorum ex donis (word clipped out) Equitis Dni Kenelmi Dighby Ano Dni 1655

Biblia sacra cum glossa ordinaria sex tomis comprehensa
Opera Gregorii Nazianzeni graeco-lat. duobus tomis in fol.
Justini Martyris Opera Graecae
Origenis Opera
Conciliorum tomi duo in fol.
Hermes Trismegistus cum comentariis Rosselii in fol.
Ludovici Blosii opera
Venerab. Bedae tomi 2
Johan Damasceni Opera Graeco-Lat.
Anthonii Possevini bibliotheca
Alvarez tom 3
Rob Belli tomi duo

any rate the legend is a pleasant one, and some friend of the great Widener Library should see to it that this unedited curiosity from the seventeenth century reaches its most appropriate destination. It well deserves the annotation that sympathetic cataloguers sometimes employ: "* * * UNIQUE."

As for Mr Bligh, a Digbyolater like ourself, he will certainly wish to visit this country to see the manuscript. His book is written in the gayest and most fetching humor; he quite sees the comic side of laborious pursuit of so quicksilver a creature, and yet —as happens to all devotees of Sir Kenelm—he ends by loving him. He quotes letters that were never in print before; K.D.'s anecdote about the naïveté of St Francis deserves reprint but I don't quite dare. . . . Best of all I like Bligh's admission that he and three friends met at an inn (the famous Spread Eagle at Thame) to drink to the memory of Venetia. There's plenty of testimony that (in the modern jargon) she had what it takes. As Master Shallow used to say (in the most humane piece of writing in our language, *King Henry the Fourth*) "She was then a bona-roba. Doth she hold her own well?"

I think she does.

Epitome Annalium Baconii
Oecumenii Opera in tom 2 bus
Harphii Theologia Mystica in 4°
Joh. Cassiani opera in 8°
Cypriani opa in manibus

"There were 29 books in all and valued at £60—no small gift in those penny-pinching days. John Harvard donated only 320 volumes."

AN INDISCRETION

LOVERS of Thomas Hardy still remember with pleasure an article which appeared in the New York *Times* shortly after Hardy's death in 1928. It informed the American public that "according to Sir Edmund Goose" (*sic*) Hardy's first novel, after being rejected by two publishers, had been burned by the author.

Professor Carl J. Weber, of Colby College, reminds us of this agreeable gaffe; and indeed Sir Edmund Gosse was anserine to believe that so careful a hoarder of MS as Hardy had destroyed his firstling. Professor Weber, in a little book now published by the Johns Hopkins Press,[1] brings forward satisfying evidence that the gist of Hardy's maiden effort has been lying unrecognized all these years in the *New Quarterly Magazine* for July 1878. Only three copies of this magazine have been discovered by Professor Weber in this country: one in the Library of Congress, one in the Brooklyn Public Library, one in the possession of Mr Paul Lemperly of Lakewood, Ohio, whose name is well known to collectors. But there must be plenty more of them, and I advise the cherishers of old magazines to rummage their bins.

It was the sharp-eyed Mr Lemperly who collated the story *An Indiscretion in the Life of an Heiress* in the *New Quarterly* with a letter written to Hardy

[1]*AN INDISCRETION IN THE LIFE OF AN HEIRESS. By Thomas Hardy. Hardy's "Lost Novel," now first printed in America and Edited with Introduction and Notes by Carl J. Weber. Baltimore: The Johns Hopkins Press.* 1935. $2.

by Alexander Macmillan in 1868. Macmillan pointed out the soft spots in a novel, *The Poor Man and the Lady,* which the young architect had submitted. Mr Lemperly was convinced that the *Indiscretion* was simply a revision of the earlier novel and started Professor Weber on the trail. The conclusions reached by the latter seem convincing enough. The thrifty young Hardy carved up his rejected MS, which had been (and very justly) deprecated not only by Macmillan but by John Morley and George Meredith. Bits of it, Weber thinks, Hardy put into *Desperate Remedies* and *Under the Greenwood Tree.* When in '78 he moved from Dorset to London he rewrote and condensed the rest and sold it to the magazine in the form of a novelette. We may well be grateful to Carl Weber for disinterring it, for it is deliciously preposterous. The ironical title, and an occasional phrase of brooding power, show the genuine gristle of Hardy; but mostly it has the savor of tripe. It can be read with encouragement by any editor or struggling writer; supreme evidence of how lamely a great hand may begin its career.

The heiress, whose indiscretion was a very mild one, is Geraldine Allenville, only child of a Wessex squire, "a hard featured man of five-and-forty." The story opens (and very charmingly) at evening service in Tollamore Church—probably Stinsford, where Hardy's heart is now buried. The young schoolmaster, in charge of the village children in the gallery, is gazing down at a solitary young lady in the squire's pew below—"and a very sweet lady was she." Occasionally she even returns his gaze. This is Geraldine, only seveteen, but seemingly (from her conversation) mature beyond her years.

A few days earlier the schoolmaster (Egbert Mayne, age 20) has rescued her from walking heedlessly into the belting of a steam threshing machine. She thanks him impulsively—"almost, indeed, with imprudent warmth"—and he, regardless of their difference in social grade, promptly falls in love with her. This difference of station, which is the burden of the whole story, might not seem to us to have been so serious: Egbert's father had been a painter of some talent who had settled in the country and married a farmer's daughter. But the early-Victorian abyss between the squire and the village must have been a real one, and perhaps painful to Hardy himself in youth. We must accept the assumptions of the tale as naïvely as we would a Boucicault melodrama. Geraldine herself, moved by mischief or curiosity, finds excuse—in her position as local châtelaine—to make a visit of inspection to the school. Poor Egbert is entranced by her beauty, which the young novelist describes with deep feeling, even to "the elegant contrivances of her attire."

But of course we require complication, and it is at hand. Old Farmer Broadford, Egbert's grandfather with whom he lives, is to be put out of his tenant farm by the hard featured squire. The old gaffer is ill with anxiety; Egbert hangs about the squire's grounds in the hope of interceding. He walks, reading a book, through a shrubbery near the mansion; there he sees Geraldine "robed in fur and standing at ease outside an open French casement." Naturally she asks what he is reading; it is *Childe Harold's Pilgrimage,* "a poem which at that date had never been surpassed in congeniality to the minds of young persons in the full fever of virulent love." (A delightful essay could be written on the various books which in different epochs have been judged suitable to touch off a sentimental rapprochement.) At any rate she expresses her interest in books, and he has a chance to plead for his grandfather. She averts the eviction, and he is all the more her slave.

As in the *Aeneid,* or in *Troilus and Criseyde,* it's a rainstorm that starts the trouble. Geraldine comes again to visit the school; a downpour starts, and detains her; after the children have gone the young dominie suddenly kisses her. He feels that he has committed a crime. And on top of his remorse, word comes that the grandfather is to be turned out after all. Desperately he waits again to see her; to apologize and renew the appeal. He is so eloquent that she weeps, and forgives him, but the "dressing bell" at the big house calls her away. Shortly afterward Gaffer Broadford, who has never been himself since the threat of eviction, falls from a corn-stack, is badly injured, and dies. This tragedy, moving Geraldine with a sense of guilt, brings them together again. Her innocent mind had not realized that she was "on the verge of committing the most horrible social sin—that of loving beneath her." Egbert decides that his only course must be to go to London, to become rich and famous. Then he can honorably propose. In the admirable scene of the parting Hardy shows some of the searching humor which was truly his. Of Egbert's early rising in the sadness of departure, "Few things will take away a man's confidence in an impulsive scheme more than being called up by candlelight upon a chilly morning to commence working it out." And Geraldine, encouraging him: "You will come back some day a wondrous man of the world, talking of vast Schemes, radical Errors, and saying such words as the 'Backbone of

Society,' the 'Tendency of Modern Thought,' and other things like that."

Just for a moment, at that point, I quite fell for Geraldine myself.

Five years elapse. Egbert "had progressed from newspaper work to criticism, from criticism to independent composition, from the latter to the publication of a book which nobody ever heard of, and from this to the production of a work of really sterling merit, which appeared anonymously." Since his one aim was to make a name for himself, it is odd that he published it anonymously—except that Hardy's plot demands it. But Geraldine has been ordered by her father not to write to her swain, and he has heard nothing of her for two years. Then, walking along Piccadilly, he sees her drive by in the family landau. He is greatly agitated. He loiters about the Allenville town-house in Chevron Square and hears her playing airs from the *Messiah*. He knows that a gala performance of that oratorio is to be given shortly, and anticipates that she may be there. He buys a seat close to those reserved in the name of Allenville—and in the emotional thunders of the Hallelujah chorus they see each other again and grasp hands. He asks her to meet him at her front door at midnight; certainly a very unlikely appointment; and when he goes there he finds a snobbish letter pushed under the door for him. Escaped from the influence of music, she has reconsidered. The difference between them is too great, she says. "I have become complicated, exclusive, and practised. If I could accept your addresses without an entire loss of position . . ."

Well, Egbert is upset. Instead of saying to hell with her, he walks the suburbs all night. The next day at the club he reads the papers, which contain not only the revelation of his authorship of the much praised book but also an announcement of Geraldine's engagement to Lord Bretton.—And immediately afterward arrives a letter from her (how did she know his address?) congratulating him on having written the book—and saying that her marriage announcement is premature.

By this time you will have guessed that (in spite of many fine and moving passages) our young author's interest is in satirizing a social fetich, not in writing a credible or lifelike story. From here he proceeds rapidly down the slope of bathos. Egbert makes yet another attempt to see Geraldine; but she is evasive, says they'll be glad to have him to dinner some time, "now that you're famous"; but that's all. He feels "in rather an ailing state" and goes back to the country. The little church at Tollamore is being decorated with flowers for a wedding; and of course he learns it is to be hers. He encounters her alone in the church on the eve of the wedding; and (thank goodness) highhats her briskly. She blurts out that she doesn't really love Lord Bretton. And then, while Egbert lies grim and sleepless in a neighboring village early the next morning, Geraldine turns up in the garden calling for him.

He hurries off on horseback to get a marriage license; they are secretly married at once; and have three honeymoon days at Melport—which we know in later stories as Budmouth. But a newspaper item about "The Tollamore Elopement" makes Geraldine think she had better go back to ask her father's forgiveness. She leaves the rising author in the summerhouse while she enters the mansion. He waits and waits, anxiously. Then a servant appears and brings him in. Geraldine has burst a blood vessel with excitement when she saw her father, and is dying.

She dies.

Rarely has a more engaging fragment of a great writer's prentice work come to hand; rarely have both the strength and weakness of a noble talent been so vividly prefigured. We are grateful to Professor Weber for this Indiscretion in the Life of a Novelist.

STYLE

Thomas Hardy and I first met at a club in Piccadilly where he had asked me to lunch. It is a club where they afterward adjourn to the smoking room and talk for a breathless hour or two about style. Hardy's small contribution made no mark, but I thought, "How interesting it is that the only man among you who does not know all about style and a good deal more, is the only man among you who has got style."

—Sir James Barrie, at a dinner of the Society of Authors, as reported in the New York *Times,* Nov. 29, 1928.

AS BARRIE'S anecdote implies, those most likely to talk about it are least likely to have it. Style in writing corresponds to intonation in speaking. It may be harsh; shrill; nasal; affected; a soft Southern timbre, or a cockney vivacity. It is as personal as clothes or complexion. It can be controlled and educated, but beneath control it must partly remain instinctive, unconscious, and organic. As in clothes so in literature it is most admirable when least obtruded. Its very plainness implies high cost; the cost of thinking and study.

The word means the pen itself. Thence, the individual's way of using the pen. There are many different ways. When language, spacing, cadence, punctuation, are skilfully adapted to the intended purpose, the result may give extreme pleasure.

In school and college we hear a great deal about literary "style," and rarely think of it again. The word has come to have a disagreeable, self-conscious, or snobbish taint. That is a pity, for it suggests important realities. Remember that the word means an instrument: one of those omnibus tools that can be put to a thousand uses.

There is, in the absolute, no such thing as good style or bad style. The question is, does it accomplish the intention. The intentions, involving human moods and characters, are innumerably diverse. Ford Madox Ford once said that good writing exhibits a constant succession of small surprises. This was a shrewd comment, but also there may be a constant succession of fulfilled expectations. But these trickeries are dangerous. What specially stultifies or stiffens a writer's method is constantly writing for the same audience. Boredom, regularity, laziness, fatigue, instantly show themselves. Style becomes stunt; a mannerism; an "act."

Where I sit now there is an open window near the table. If the wind is northwest it flutters the papers and is a nuisance. If I close the window, the room becomes stuffy. But for concentration sometimes the window must be shut. It would have a good sentimental sound if I were to say we must keep the window open—the window into Reality—while we are writing, even if it blows our papers around. It's a temptation to say just that, which would have a hearty masculine ring; but it wouldn't be so. Genuine writing—as distinct from blather—cannot always be done in a strong draught of reality. Writing is an art; an illusion. "A prepared selected illusion of reality," or words to such effect, was the phrase Walter de la Mare once used in a lecture at the Town Hall. Style is the enzyme in the literary system; the digestive chemical that makes chunks of tough reality soluble. Lowell said it well, in his verses on Dr Holmes—

> *Master alike in speech and song*
> *Of Fame's great antiseptic—style.*[1]

Some kinds of writing that you perhaps thought very offhand were prepared and selected with sharp care. Some of Ring Lardner's stories, for instance. Or, as examples of "prepared selected illusion" consider the advertisements of New York department stores; or circulars proposing to vend First Mortgage Bonds. These are masterpieces of condensed selection. Equal art, with purer motive, are the Notices to Mariners which Joseph Conrad praised as the finest writing he knew. I once asked a ship-master to copy out for me the *Admiralty Sailing Directions for Sable Island*, a good example of statement on which life or death may depend:

> . . . When seen from the north, from a distance of 8 to 10 miles, the Island presents the appearance of a long ridge of sandhills some of which are very white. From the south, the range of white sand appears more continuous, and very low towards West point. On a nearer approach many of the sand-hills are seen to have been partly removed by the waves, so as to have formed steep cliffs next to the sea. In other parts they are covered by grass, and defended by a broad beach, which, however, cannot be reached without passing over ridges of sand covered with only a few feet of water. These ridges, which are parallel to the shore at distances not exceeding 4 cables, form heavy breakers, and are dangerous to pass in boats when there is any sea running . . .

This is the Robinson Crusoe style; there is none better—for its purpose.

Sensitiveness in these matters cannot be taught;

[1]Viz.—antiseptic against the corruption of time.

we can only grope and guess. The distinctions are subtle. In London some years ago, when beer was served under strict licensing restrictions, I was amused by one regulation. If you went to a pub for an after-theatre supper you couldn't have beer unless you ordered a "meal." I suggested sardines on toast. That was not a meal. I tried jam omelet. That also was not considered serious enough. But a Welsh rabbit, said the waiter, was a meal within the meaning of the Act, and made beer legal. Evidently there had to be something the gastric juice must elaborate. (I chose the unusual verb *elaborate* there, because I assume the reader of these notes to be in a mood to relish accurate words. I should have preferred *work on;* but that closes the sentence on a weak tone. I had written *really elaborate,* and dropped the adverb because it clumsily duplicates the EAL sound. So pleasantly intricate are the considerings of sound and sense.)

The distinction between style and stunt is as delicate, as absurd, and yet as full of meaning, as that supper-table dilemma.

There are no rules. Let us remember that language is a living element and we can't learn all about it in textbooks. It is employed with many different purposes. Every time we instinctively vary our accent or choice of words to suit the recipient (whether reader or listener) we show our awareness of style as a reality. A telephone conversation, a dictated letter, a newspaper story, a book review, all differ utterly in tone and tact. When in search of meanings it is often helpful to take the suggestions of familiar common phrase. To "do the thing in style" is to do it in a way that is suitable to the mood of the occasion.

The minims of a really subtle style are a delicious secret between the author and the fit reader. That is reading that becomes ecstasy. Every student of Shakespeare has gloated over tricks of assonance and colliteration of which he imagines himself sole discoverer. The bombast opening of "Richard III," *Now is the winter of our discontent,* etc., have I not often thought that the play on the consonants D and S, varied first with B, then with M, then with MB, was put there for my joy alone? Or "Hamlet," Act I, Scene 4—*The King doth wake tonight:* with pursing lips one follows the KW changing to WS, the WS to SR and DR and TR. Trivial but happy examples! For any writer of real virtu plays a myriad tricks that he expects none but his own kin to notice—concealed satirics and burlesques, implied significances, buried allusions, broken or suspended rhythms, omissions of the obvious. In some kinds of writing the measure of art is how much can he convey without quite saying it. The sum total of what he did not need to write is the mutual triumph of writer and reader. This is the esthetic form of Squaring the Circle. I read once that the reading room of the Public Library is a famous place for trafficking forbidden drugs: buyer and seller, taking adjoining seats, can pass the stuff unnoticed under cover of pretended study. The dangerous drug of complete understanding also passes, in thrilling privacy, between book and reader. Our best joy in it is, it can rarely be made general or vulgarized by publicity. Something essential in ourselves floods out to meet it, helps to create it. Shakespeare, I say to myself, would never have written such delicious vulgarities unless he knew that someone as coarse as myself would come along who could understand them.

All this has not necessarily much to do with what we call "good" writing. Style is idiosyncrasy; it may be very annoying. Conrad, certainly a very great writer, often erred widely from the meridian of strict English. But his style, his quiddity, was unmistakable. Style is bad when it gives the wrong impression. There was a big advertisement in the newspapers the other day about a certain tobacco. "Old man Wellman," it said, "knew how to make pipe tobacco. —— is packed in a sensible, soft foil pouch and it keeps the tobacco just like it left the factory." Old man Wellman, we say to ourselves, didn't know how to write English; but his error doesn't in the least invalidate the ad. In fact, the more people notice the error, the more —— tobacco is fixed in their minds. But when a department store advertises "Our engineers have improved this lighter to such an extent that it will now light 500 cigarettes, instead of only 3 or 4," the stenographer's slip becomes painful. What was meant was "3 or 4 hundred."

The arts of writing are first acquired by imitation, as Stevenson insisted in a famous passage. Many of us in my generation began by aping Stevenson himself; in my own case I followed that by some educative paraphrase of Belloc, Don Marquis, and Simeon Strunsky. Each will find by chance or intuition the model that best pleases him. H. M. Tomlinson has admitted that he bred himself on Thoreau. C. E. Montague—whose "A Writer's Notes on His Trade" is one of the few textbooks worth reading in this matter—was packed and primed with Shakespeare. Wherever his prose bursts open it shows the glint of Shakespeare underneath. It doesn't matter so much from whom you borrow if you pay it back, eventually, with earnings of your own.

I hope I have said enough to suggest some private thinking. Underneath the printed page, unconcealable from the skilled observer, is the quality, the personal coefficient, that reveals the performer himself. We come back inevitably to the old saying "Le style, c'est l'homme." It is the blood pressure of the mind.

TRANSLATIONS FROM THE CHINESE

GUAVA JELLY

AT MEALS in airplanes
They serve guava jelly,
So tensile and viscous
That even if the ship
Does one of her swoons
It won't fall off the knife.

O little *chinoiseries*
May you also cling
To the knife-blade of Now:
Adhesive enough
That the flying reader
May spread relishing thought
On his own slice of life.

CONSTRAINT

Why, said the Old Mandarin,
Does one wear evening dress to make speeches?
I am suspicious of the kind of thoughts people think
When they are all dressed up.
Besides, he added, my formal robes
Are now much too tight.

NUCIFER

Why is it, pondered the old statesman,
Strolling the grounds of the State Capitol
In Columbus,
That government buildings are always
The haunt of squirrels?

DIABETES

In books, as in life,
An excess of sugar
Does not promote
Longevity.

CALLING ALL CARS

A white miscellaneous bitch, otherwise lovable,
Chases every car that comes by
With shrill suspicion and fracas
And has led into this detestable habit
All the other dogs of the region
Including many of more homogeneous lineage
Than herself.
Convinced by her that cars are hostile
One of them will presently prove it conclusively.

I shudder to watch them all
Asymptoting the wheels of the garbage truck
And see no wisdom whatever
To be drawn from my anxiety—
Save this: it's comforting to know

It isn't only human beings
Who run with joy to learn bad habits.

Ethics also have their inertia:
The aristocrat always apes the mongrel.

NO COACHING

I went to the theatre
With the author of the successful play.
He insisted on explaining everything.
Told me what to watch,
The details of direction,
The errors of the property man,
The foibles of the star.
He anticipated all my surprises
And ruined the evening.
Never again!—and mark you
The greatest Author of all
Made no such mistake.

AN INTERVIEW

Disregarding the Mandarin's mumblings
The reporter dashed off an interview
In which he fed into the visitor's mouth
The reporter's own favorite notions.

Excellent notions, no doubt, grieved the old sage,
Only they don't happen to be mine.
But, he added resignedly,
This remains the oldest
Labor-saving device of journalism.

Even Moses did exactly the same
When he went for an interview on Mount Sinai.

HEGELIAN ANTITHESIS

When, as a child, I noticed
That coal and ice were always sold
By the same merchant
I first suspected
The irremediable duplicity of the world.

EXCEPTIS EXCIPIENDIS

Partner, sidekick, pal, old friend of mine
(Cried Chancellor Mu Kow,
Benign with Burgundy and cheese soufflé)
I trust you everything: life, fortune, fair repute. . . .
But I noticed the swift anguish
With which he retrieved, when he dropped it,
His little red book of Telephone Numbers.

MANDARIN ON THE AIR

I

In a pellucid calm of summer sunset
The Old Mandarin sat idling in his bamboo grove.
Putting up his chin, like a cat,
To be stroked by silence
He thought of all the hullabaloo
Passing unapprehended through the air around him.

He was astonished to consider:
In his autonomous ears and nostrils
In the private basin of his brain
Orchestras jostled unheard,
Commercials teemed in his belly;
Orators inspissated the bag of his lungs,
Syllables thridded his lumbars,
His entrails were embryo with palaver,
Electric with spores of speech.

Oh circumambient air
Wherein we live and are,
They should choose with care
Words that go so far.

II

When I first went on the air, many years ago
(Reflected the Old Monologue)
Radio was still primitive.
When a thunderstorm came along
Broadcasting was suspended
Until the kilocycles abated
And the amplitudes quit howling.
In those days they said I used words too long and heavy
For the stripling ether.

But now the air has grown up
And can carry almost anything.
Think of the political and economic brainstorms
That have rumbled through space:
Yet as I look outdoors
It seems still pure, transparent, unblemished,—
Even unresentful.

SCIENTIST ORDERS HIS TOMB

I like to think of Van Ceulen
The methodical Dutch mathematician
Who ordered to be carved on his tomb in Leyden
The value of Pi
To 35 places of decimals
(As far as he had reckoned it.)

Implying, presumably,
The Endless Incommensurables
Life and Death.

DISCRETION

The Old Mandarin
Was taken for a week-end motor trip.
He was much impressed
By Adirondack gorges and chasms.
He said, "They remind me
Of Van Raalte's advertisement
For ladies' summer bifurcations—
So sheer they can't be photographed."

SWANKER TO WINDWARD

We rode 800 chromo miles
(At a cost of only $10 for oil and gas)
In a little car that never faltered,
Drummed her faithful rhythm
Through sun and shade and storm.

The old philosopher began to brood.
"Is it possible that your young hotskulls
Poop off at modern industry?
Nux vomica and library paste!
Where is the writer, artist, economic orgiast,
Who does his job as well and truly
As that unswanking anonymity
The motor engineer?"

TRAVEL NOTE

Put me back on the road again,
Cried the wanderlusting mage:
On damnable U. S. 1, the premier road of North-
america,
Arterial highway poisoned with big blood count.
The frenzy of that swarming traffic,
Trucks, busses, dog-stands, gas pumps, Shore Din-
ners,
The horrors of New Rochelle, Portchester, Green-
wich, Mianus,
Cos Cob, Stamford, Darien, Norwalk,
Endured because I know I will soon turn off
On lovely U. S. 7.
Put me back on the road again,
Let's itinerate!

ONCE IN A BLUE NOON

Hot summer noon
In the train yards at Long Island City
Rails gleam dark blue

Like parallels of yonder,
Samples of horizon.

ROSE IS A ROSE

We speak of aphids and rose-lice
(Said the Old Mandarin,
Reluctantly spraying arsenate of lead on the bushes)
As if they were merely contingent parasites,
Entities alien and separate
From the plant itself.
But actually, as life is encountered
In a world of approximation and asymptote,
They are a function of the rose,
A necessary part of its phenomenon:
As integral to its completeness
As Error to the heart of man.

The aphis, for roses,
Is part of the plan,
And Sin presupposes
Existence of Man.

ANOTHER VERSION

The question curst
And sure to baffle
Is, which came first
In the endless raffle?
The cotton boll
Or the hungry weevil?
The human soul
Or the itch of Evil?

ROYAT (PUY–DE–DÔME)

It is characteristic of humanity
Observed the travel agent
That every summer come renewed inquiries
For the name of the town in France
Which is said to have a climate so bracing
That a season spent there caused a Bishop
To bite a Barmaid in the neck.

REQUISITION

I saw crates of bees
Unloaded from a train Upstate
To fertilize fruit orchards.
No one has enough bees in his own bonnet
To pollinate the flowers of his mind.

Import me a few hives of strange notions—
Mine are too sluggish.

COLD TURKEY

Once upon a time, said the Old Mandarin,
Political speeches were limited
To a few thousand simpletons in a hall
Exhilarated by crowd contagion.

But now, sitting at home in cool judgement
Yourself can hear on the radio
Their poverty of intellect,
Their richness of mispronunciation.

I am actually embarrassed for them
Hearing their crisscross of stale quotation,
Their comic argument,
Their gobboon catchwords.

O candidates, be advised:
People are listening.

WHOSE EAR IS BORED

I smile as I hear them reproach each other
For not living up to platforms and pledges,
As though anyone (but the Other Party)
Ever took a political platform seriously.
The very word means platitude, showmanship, artifice.

Even Jehovah, fortunately,
Never lived up to his savage platform
Communicated on Mount Sinai
And warned old Moses to look out
For "the servant whose ear is bored"
(See Exodus, XXI.)

A platform (like a pulpit) is something to talk on.
Nobody lives there.

REFUTED

Gossip said of Lady Curlynostril,
She drinks too much.
But when she invited me
To take wine in her boudoir
I noticed her corkscrew was rusty.

CEILING ZERO

The ceiling of your Thinking-Room, O. M.,
Bulges with crack and sag—
It will soon come down on your head.

Aye, said the Old Mandarin:
My ambitious daughter, Lady Quicksilver,
Does tap-dancing in the chamber above
Whenever she feels a small private merriment
Or gets good marks
In her lessons.
If she wins her Imperial Scholarship
I shall be whelmed in plaster.

So does each new generation
Saltarello on the ceiling
Of its apprehensive and dubitating sires
But I rejoice they have something
To dance about.

FEBRUARY FILLDYKE

Snow is beautiful
But there can be too much of it
And the ancient Chinese poets
Who praised it in crystal verses
Never had to drive a car
On icy roads.
But still, enduringly romantic
I maintain that snow
Makes brick steps wonderfully pink
When you sweep them.

SUGGESTION FOR LADIES

The sign in the subway said: *Be considerate,*
Cover Up Your Sneeze;
But changed by the pencil of some kidder it
Substituted *Knees.*

DENOUEMENT

By old stage superstition
The tag or curtain line of the play
Is never spoken at rehearsal.
There may be some analogy there
That applies to ourselves.

TOO LATE

Certainly, cried the book agent,
You must have these four volumes
Of the world's greatest Encyclopedia of Sex
3000 pages in a wooden box
And bound in gold and scarlet.

The autumn colors? said the Old Mandarin.
No, I don't like your symbolism:
I'm too close to a wooden box myself.
It's too late for me
To learn about these things
From books.

And once again, he added, I implore
Your solemnly annotating sexologists

(Who may have lost much joy
By being too laboratory about it)
To make up their minds
How to spell Krafft-Ebing
Which not even the eminent Santayana
Can get right.

NATIONAL EMBLEM

If there were no such thing
As a can-opener
Most of us
Would starve to death.

A CHILD READING

Oh happy miracle of childhood reading—
Andrew Lang's Red, Green and Yellow Fairy Tales,
Gulliver, the Arabian Nights, Edward Lear,
Louisa Alcott, E. Nesbit, *At the Back of the North Wind,*
Hans Andersen, *Chatterbox, Saint Nicholas,*
Mayne Reid, Uncle Remus, The Jungle Books—
Even poor old Oliver Optic and G. A. Henty—

Why is it that now I never find that unconscious oblivion
Except in Detective Stories?

WARNING

But the children I most admire
Are like everyone else:

They enjoy best
The books that were not
Too obviously
Intended for them.

Perhaps everything
Deliberately written for a special audience
Is second-rate.

LIFE AND LETTERS

He woke at 4 A. M.
And said to himself,
"It's unwritable."
The Unwritable replied:
No, only unwritten.

PUBLICITY MAKES PEACE

The Camera is the great pacifier.
In the rotogravure sections
The Great American Bulk first learned
That a Soviet commissar
Looks quite human.

SET BACK

O terraced perpendiculars!
See, said the happy architect
Expounding a new group of metropolitan miracles,
The triumph of modern design
Is the set back.

Yea verily, murmured the Merchant Prince
It set me back
About a hundred million.

WINDSHIELD WIPERS

In Los Angeles, the panhandlers
Rush up to your car
When it is halted at a crossing.
They wipe the windshield clean
And hope for a tip.

In the world of intellect,
That is exactly
What philosophers do.

ONLY A TREE

The redwood tree
Is the most majestic of living things
But the little dog
Who trotted with us down the canyon
Knew that, after all,
It was only a tree
And available as such.

DEPLORABLE

Deplorable indeed, observed the oriental cynic,
That what one wishes forgotten
Is always longest remembered;
And he read again, with ill-bred amusement,

The story of Abu Hasan
In the *Arabian Nights.*

ANTHROPOMORPHIC

Even Jehovah
After Moses had got the Commandments
Committed to stone
Probably thought:
I always forget the things
I really intended to say.

A FRAGMENT

In due season we are granted
The artists we require
And they [are granted]
The emotions they need.

VOLTAIRE

Voltaire, an admirer of the Quakers,
Said that if it were not for sea-sickness
He would come to live
In Pennsylvania.

Pennsylvania
Would have been very much shocked
If he had.

"ENGLAND, THEIR ENGLAND"

Everyone has his own point of view,
And the whole history of England

Is summed up in the famous headline
Of the London *Times*:—
TERRIBLE GALE IN THE CHANNEL
CONTINENT ISOLATED

A RAY OF SUNSHINE

Sociologist need not gloom
About Machine Civilization.
Man still personalizes
His great engines.
See the huge red truck delivering groceries
At the branch of the A & P—
On a gilded crossbar
In front of the radiator
Is painted the monster's pet name,
BUDDY.

Man is still an instinctive poet.

EMPEROR ON AN ISLAND

I choose my games of solitaire
(Said the Old Mandarin)
For the oddity of their names
And their eschatological suggestions.
Best I like *Napoleon at St Helena,*
"Supposedly," says Paul Kearney,[1]
"Invented for Bonaparte
During his days of exile."
Is not every mind
Napoleon at St Helena?

[1]See Kearney: *Fifty Games of Solitaire.*

BLUE JEANS

"Each observation," said the scientist
(Jeans, in sombre vein,)
"Destroys the bit of the universe observed."
True. Life proceeds by continuous extinction.
Coming and Going are born twins,
And Consciousness is an embrace of opposites
That cancel and expire.
As the novelist once said
With singular wisdom:
If I had two friends called Food and Hunger
I'd never introduce them
To each other.

ODIOUS COMPARISON

An editor was flattered to receive
An invitation to lecture
In a distant city.
"We could not pay more than $100,"
Wrote the Committee,
"If it were Shakespeare himself."

But my overhead, brooded the editor,
Is much bigger than Shakespeare's.

CHANGE OF FACE

I sometimes remember
The late-drowsing gentleman in pyjamas
Who put his head out of a window

STREAMLINES

At the Hotel Webster
When he heard fire-engines on 45th Street.
Idly curious he surveyed the scene
Until he became aware
That the blaze was in the flue of the Harvard Club
Against the wall of his own room.

When he realized
That the affair might concern *him*
How his face changed.

SPIDER BOY

One midnight, lying on the couch,
I saw a spider, with patient skill
Hoisting a succulent beetle
(Much bigger than himself)
Up to the underside of a chair.
He lashed it with silken rigging
Then paused to consider.

There is much thoughtful booty
That I also have made fast
With gossamer block and tackle
But would not dream of printing.
Ink is a poison for truth.

THE DIFFERENCE

I shall never know the hope and obsession
Of the man who chants *Love's Old Sweet Song*
Underneath the apartment windows

While I am trying to work.
There is only one possible explanation
For his perseverance.
It must sound very different
To him.

COMIC STRIP

When the Old Mandarin
Was taken to a Burlesk Show
At first he was a trifle scandalized,
But he soon got the idea
And whenever a lady came up the runway
In billowy raiment
He learned to look for
The snappers on her gown
And could accurately foretell
Just how and where she would begin
To remove it.

But after a long evening
Of that sort of thing
He began to mutter,
"Almost persuadest thou me
To become a vegetarian."

CHECKED IN

During the floods in New England
I saw a news-photograph
Of a lady in a rowboat
Registering at the desk
Of the Hotel Bond in Hartford.

And I thought, O punctual parable
Of the meaning of literature:
Man, in his leaking punt of civilization
Adrift on the swollen stream of Hitherhence,
But striving, in his moment,
To sign his name in the book.

TRADE SURVEY

"NIGHT CAP and sandwiches in the Elizabethan Smoking Room" said the steamship company's folder. Colatine and Old Quercus were enjoying the night cap, but Q. was shamed (after so excellent a dinner a few hours before) to call for his usual bed-time victual. It would not have been tactful: for Colatine, the Sales Manager, this was the Bicarb Hour. Indeed they are the oddest of travelling companions: one has to eat himself to rest with platters of eggs and sausage; the other reaches his necessary nescience by starvation and soda.

As he evaporated, towards 3 A. M., it occurred to subconscious Q. that the ship was exceptionally quiet. Dimly, faintly, like thoughts of Eternity or next year's Income Tax, he heard a great far away Gabriel sending his soul through the invisible. But he paid no heed. His is a confiding heart. Before turning in he had thoroughly conned the geography of the ship; the route to the nearest lifeboat; the two lifebelts under Colatine's bed; then dismissed all doubt. This time, he had thought, we'll go to Boston by boat; get a night's sleep beyond the possibility of railroads; be at the old Parker House by breakfast time. Fog was something that had not occurred to him. So it was a shock when Colatine seized his foot and shook him awake at 8 A. M. "Well, Penurious," said the publisher, "we're anchored outside the Canal and it looks like we'll be here all day."

Except that Quercus missed a handsome professional engagement that afternoon, the first in a long career of chrysostom that he has ever failed, it would be hard to imagine a pleasanter day. After a hasty eruption of radio messages the passengers all settled down to enjoy their unexpected vacation. There was horse-racing in the main companion, dancing in the stern lounge, excellent Complimentary Luncheon served by the company, and capacity business at the bar. "7½ times round the promenade deck makes a mile," says the folder, and Colatine and Quercus made several such, always amused by a sort of New England precision in the sign over a doorway, CREW'S ACCESS. The *Acadia* is a natty ship, built at Newport News and designed by Theodore E. Ferris. She is not an excursion steamer but a genuine liner (403 feet long, 61 feet beam) with bulkhead construction in excess of the International Convention requirements. Whatever momentary inconvenience it caused we heartily approved the master's caution in not attempting to proceed in fog. And we swiped a little blue glass stirring rod from the smokeroom as an affectionate souvenir.

Except for 7½s round the deck, and visits to the Elizabethan Room and the Radio office, the two Trade Surveyors spent the day reading. So they had no occasion to test the advice of a humorous young daughter who had remarked "There 'll be beautiful women and dancing on that boat, won't there?" To which Old Q. observed cautiously "Even if there are, Mr Colatine and I won't know them." "Don't you worry a bit," she suggested. "Go right up to them and say Hi, Toots!" Admittedly there were anxieties in late afternoon as we crept delicately toward Boston Harbor. For Q. had a date to speak at the State House at 7.30, in the very hub and axle of New England, the absolute center of the codfish ball. This indeed Penurious did not wish to miss; nor to have to send any more radios at 21 cents a word. We docked at 7.10, and made it.

Time abbreviated thus, Quercus lost several pleasures he had counted on. Particularly he wanted to visit Lauriat's new quarters. That famous bookstore has moved down to Franklin Street, where it will have opportunity to encourage trade of a more leisurely and connoisseuring sort than on crowded Washington. Colatine, himself an alumnus of Lauriat's, went there and returned with enthusiastic report; also with his vowels gently flattened by the unconscious return of his old Boston accent which is rarely audible in New York. Visits to the Paakeh House always do that to him. Meanwhile I had the delight of a call on Edwin Edgett, veteran literary editor of the *Transcript* and one of my earliest friends and tutors in the profession of journalism. It was good to find him young and alert as ever in the narrow crannied office where for so many years he has compiled shrewd and generous judgment on books. It was equally a pleasure to note the ancient wire-rope elevator in the *Transcript* building still at working service. It is the only one I know of still in existence; Mr Edgett calculates that if all the ups that have been handed along that wire cable were added together the old cage would be at least half way to the Moon.

Another renewal of an old friendship was a salute to Joe Jennings, the anchor and capstan of the Old Corner Bookstore, where he has been for 52 years—since he was a boy of 16. Is it Boston's famous diligence in literature that keeps her book-men young? Neither Joe Jennings nor Edwin Edgett seems to have shed a hair since Quercus first knew them 22 years ago. And in the adjoining room the steadfast tradition of the trade was being carried on, where Colatine (in the role of Saint George) was locked in struggle with Joe Jennings's buyer, whose name happens to be Arthur Dragon. If Colatine were again to refer to the psalter, for a rueful description of Mr Dragon, he would probably borrow the rubric *Adhaesit pavimento,* he keeps his feet on the ground.

Quercus's own quotation for the present time would come a little later in the same psalm (119th) —*Appropinquet deprecatio*—which might be translated by the book trade as *Price-Cutting Ahead.*

The Survey also had a chance to visit booksellers known previously only by pleasant hearsay: the Personal Book Shop at 95 St James Avenue, opposite the enormous John Hancock Life Insurance Building. It is as small, intimate and alluring as its neighbor is vast and formal, and I think that John Hancock himself, whose name has become synonym for personal penmanship, would be more likely to loiter in the bookshop than in the citadel of premonition. And in Wellesley there was the famous Hathaway House which has done so much to collaborate in that college's love and support of the Muses. Miss Geraldine Gordon, manager of the shop, has given the front room, her most valuable selling space, entirely to the poets. This shop alone has kept many a versifier's work in print. The poets' readings held every year at Wellesley, on a fund perpetuated in memory of Katharine Lee Bates, have been a constant flow of influence upon the young devotees. One who had almost forgotten having been a poet, and supposed that everyone else had forgotten it too, was gratefully moved and thrilled to be summoned to that platform. In Wellesley at least Don Marquis's saying is not so: that publishing a volume of verse is like dropping a rose-leaf down the Grand Canyon and waiting for the echo.

All my life I'd been hearing about the Boston and Albany route, but never had occasion to travel it before. It begins by passing under the Massachusetts Avenue bridge where I am pleased by the tablet in memory of Edward Everett Ginsberg, whose combination of names is a sociological palimpsest. Miss Louella D. Everett, who is Public Friend Number 1 for all quotation hunters, has her workroom near there and happened to be looking down the street some years ago while the actual dedication of the tablet was taking place, with flags, music, and oratory. It so happens that under the Massachusetts Avenue bridge is a favorite loitering place for locomotives, which pause just there and exhale fumes. From her vantage in a high window Miss Everett could see a lounging B. & A. monster gently nearing the arch, all ready to vent surplus of combustion. Her heart ached for the celebrants, but there was nothing she could do. She still remembers their dismay, and blackened faces, as gas and smoke strangled them in the midst of the pious exercises.

NOTES ON A YELLOW PAD

I

September

THIS is yellow weather. Sunlight outside looks the same color as this yellow pad; the fire on the low hearth behind me is the orange of this pencil. Under the bellies of my dachshund firedogs it deepens to tangerine, or a clear pink embershine for which I have no word. (Good. I approve things that are not "like" other things, only describable as themselves.)

I'm thinking of something a poet said, while he was still a poet—

"Extenuate these hours so wide and thin
You'll almost see Eternity shine through."

How might one take this yellow weather and stretch, or fold, or crumple it to thin (or thicken?) that dim color into full gold? But you can't make Time longer except by thinking more thoughts. I turned the clock back to Standard this morning: supposedly therefore I had an extra Hour; which gave me so large a sense of leisure I wasted at least two in a dumb idling amazement. The conies who thought they had Ringside Seats for a recent prizefight found themselves parasangs away.—"I saw Eternity the other night" (said Vaughan) "like a great ring." But it offers no Ringside Seats.

What, then, am I thinking? Why does a line from

Kipling come to mind: "Enthrones on shrieking circumstance the Sacredly Absurd." Prizefights: I think of radio, symbolized for me by a little bottle of cherry-colored syrup, *Citri Cerose Wyeth.* All summer long I had to talk on the air every Friday night; and as Friday is always a day of huge palaver in the office, towards evening I would take a slug of this thick sweet lubricant which seemed to avert nervous anxieties of the throat. So that phial on my desk became emblem of a whole paregoric philosophy. (You don't have to soften or sweeten or saponify the glottis before talking to yourself.) I shall think with kindness of that secret drug, the color of a Vermont maple tree in October.

Is it the lingering effect of that anesthetic, is it the perlustration of this same lion-skin weather? I find myself in a mood of lentil soup, of genuine pococurante. It won't last, but here in the Knothole I find it delicious. I *really* don't care who wins football games, or what the *Herald Tribune* says in its editorials, or whether Mr Hemingway believes that a Florida hurricane is a plot on the part of the government. If you can be indifferent passionately enough it almost has the virtue of a positive creed. There is here an old armchair which is still known as Donny's Chair as it was never used except by an ancient sheepdog curled up for good some years ago. He was a great gentleman, a considerable philosopher; I've been hoping that by sitting in his chair perhaps I might inherit some of his quality; though I doubt it. His majestic self-control in the realm of manners: once by accident he was shut up in the house all day (from breakfast to midnight) without possible egress: yet he would have burst an entrail rather than defile his host's affairs. I can still see his

Socratic shaggy face peering agonized through a glass door when I arrived to release him; when it opened he could not even stay for wags-and-licks but almost knocked me down in his rush for the nearest easement. The Relief of Lucknow was not more dramatic. This was stupidity, perhaps, but stupidity on a high note. His prime temperament was the alternation of violent excitement, desire for battle and argument, defense of imaginary sheep against hordes of (equally imaginary) wolves, with prostrations of supreme passivity when he lay for hours in glorious exhaustion. He may have, must have led, unknown to me, a secret emotional life more intense than we could have guessed. At any rate in eight or nine years together I learned toward him not mere affection, which is easy and soft, but intellectual respect. Even when almost blind and toothless he retained his dignity; his views of life, if I could have heard them, I should attend as I would Mr Santayana's. Indeed, in their indestructible innocence of life's meaner phases, both were thinkers of the same kind.

Without moving from this chair there are plenty of things not to get steamed up about. I look through the magazine called *Fortune* and find a chap advertising himself as "Annuity Counselor to Persons of Consequence." This might be embarrassing: how does one know whether one is a consequential person?

I'm wondering just what was the nudge behind these notions? I think I can identify it as a letter from V. B. enclosing a remarkable passage he found in the London *New Statesman* ten years ago. It was in one of the articles by "Affable Hawk"—which was a pen-name of Desmond MacCarthy, wasn't it? Anyhow V. B. suggests it for reprinting, and I agree. We are quoting, then, from the *New Statesman* of August 8, 1925:—

What have I really felt? What are men and women really like? What do they really feel? Wherein really lay the charm and significance of that object, that place, that person, for me, the exquisiteness or the horror of that moment? What sort of stuff is our life made of? If I take a strip called a day, an hour, can it be called happy, miserable, good, bad—anything? How much of it was merely liked, as though mechanically? Yet if I put it under the microscope, how complicated its texture seems? What delicate things there were in a morning's boredom, what excruciating ones in my delight! And those emotions which snatch me out of myself? Love? What is really happening to me when I "love"? Am I in pain or is this happiness? When the pain stops, do I still "love"? In what way do I care for someone else? Have my feelings any relation to the object? Do I ever really see her or him, or only my own feelings? Is it all imagination and desire? Imagination? Why was I so disappointed at that moment? Why did that other event fill me with such secret and complete satisfaction? Why have I ceased to care about what a moment ago seemed so immensely desirable? Why does my soul ache for a past, spent perhaps in longing for the present? Are others possessed by the same egotism, which snatches at what must disappoint, clutches at what it would rather let go? Is the reality always a cheat? Is it only distance which lends enchantment to the view? What do I really care about? *What?* Art? God? Man? Myself?

In a literary work of art these questions, and a hundred more, find an answer, though they are not necessarily asked in it. But on the pertinacity with which the artist has put them to himself depends the clearness and depth of his vision; and if he can only reach down to what he has really felt, that vision will carry with it an imposing authority for others, posses a kind of unity which, though philosophically it is no pledge of truth, is nevertheless capable of giving satisfaction to the mind and the esthetic sense which piecemeal observation of truths never can. Such a work is, too, a substitute for that intimacy of communion which life seldom allows. He who asks of art a purpose beyond itself forgets that to respond to it is an escape from human loneliness, the only one except religion possible to man.

II

Now it is evening; as black outside as it was yellow before; several odd things have happened since the paragraphs above. I was given a chance to read *The Eve of St Agnes* aloud to two young women of 15 who had been assigned the poem for school work. Delightful to see how their unspoiled apprehensions seized upon its loveliness, noted its humor, fell fresh and happy under its sovereign spell. They agreed that it would make a grand movie, and I think they noted (though without comment) how Keats's fine taste passed rapidly over the danger-points of the narrative where a celluloid director would be tempted to linger with crude emphasis. Their immediate comment was that they'd like to dramatize it for their school play at Christmas. Indeed I hope they will!—And then this evening, a night suddenly windy and chill and apt for verses, a young poet from Pittsburgh found his way here in the dark and exclaimed that he owed me Three Dollars. I had quite forgotten them: it was true that six or seven years ago, when he was possessed with frenzy to start a bookshop, he had written begging a loan. Everyone else he wrote to had the sense or kindness to turn down his project; but I, a natural numbskull, had saddled him with a loan too small to be any use yet large enough to bother his good conscience.—His poetry is not as good as Keats's, nor like to be, but of course I begged him to let the small contribution stay on deposit. I'm glad to have it in such Live Storage.

Then, rummaging some old letters, I found one of a year ago, from a stranger in England who had seen (in a book written a good many years past) an allusion to another poet—who also died at Keats's age of 26. Poets whom you might think forgotten have sudden surprising ways of coming back to the instant. Here is the letter:—

You mentioned Francis Ledwidge, well I can tell you that brought back memories. We were pals in the Royal Inniskilling Fusiliers.

It's strange all the war books that have been written, and by poets too, I have never seen Ledwidge mentioned. You will probably guess that I am not a literary bloke, for we never discussed poetry, my fault of course, but Francis introduced me to rum punch one terrible cold night near the Serbian frontier. I was only nineteen then (Dec. 1915) and wouldn't touch anything, but he made me drink some, it certainly warmed me up for the night.

If ever anyone looked a poet it was Ledwidge, his hair used to be of unsoldierly length, and he was the one and only person I've ever seen with "burning" eyes. He made no attempt to be popular in the battalion, he was red-hot Sinn Fein and he didn't care who knew it. I believe it was Lord Dunsany who got him to enlist. Lord D was our company officer, the fellows could spin some yarns about Dunsany who was *very* unorthodox as an officer. My last memory of Ledwidge was when we had to retreat on Salonika from Serbia, and how I remember that long swinging stride of his, anyway before we reached Salonika he took sick, before going into the ambulance he calmly sold his waterproof cape to a French cavalry officer for forty drachmas, gave me a wave and away, later I heard he was killed in France.

WM. FITZGERALD

Sheerness, Kent, England

After all, poetry and rum punch are essentially the same.

A SAMPLE OF BRAN

The Knothole, January.

IT'S an exquisite morning; in the exact sense of that bonny participle a cull of mornings; sought out, chosen, attained. As the French would think it, recherché. A morning, surely, for candor. The oil stove has been filled and burns a tulip-shaped blue flame; the fire lit in the chimney. Old seasoned splits of oak burn talkatively, crackle their last argument as they go up the flue, and scent the room with a faint peppery smell. Almost a whole oak tree has gone up the chimney since last August. It was a grand old tree, killed several years ago by lightning; its sawn stump is over 36 inches diameter. At a guess I suppose it had a life of 80 years in a region of strong competition. Fair enough, for tree or man. First laid out in the hearse-shaped woodpile (I myself disposed its limbs in decent catafalque) now I like to think of it going aloft the chimney in yellow apotheosis. Sifted into the clear in wefts of blue reek, somewhere an idea of it, whole and tremulous, hovers impalpable. Perhaps only in my own mind; Plato would know more about this than I. But I see perfectly that Tree of Fire, passed through the dark chimney of change (death is an ugly word) and now become imagination and weather.

When I came out to the Knothole this morning I found that some wandering bagman, supposing (as occasional foreigners do) my cabin to be a minuscule residence, had tucked a sample of his goods in the latch of the door. *Kellogg's Bran for Constipation,* it said. I took this as a reproach, deserved; not physical but mental. For I have long been costive in spirit; indolent, sloven and slug; as Stevenson once said in some letter "dumb, dowie, and damnable." This is partly the general distemper of the time, to which even journalists are sensitive; and partly an introverse bashfulness which too often inhibits the well-mannered from betraying their own private hilarities. Let's have no more of it. North America, laid out in vast platitudes for the express flourish of comedy, presents now so vast a spectacle of intellectual prostration that it must enchant the gods. It is meat and drink to me to see a clown, said someone. Politically we are well fed. I don't know which is funnier: the Republicans moaning because F. D. R. has access to the air; or the things said by F. D. R. when he gets it. What is more entertaining than to see the grave economists and sociologers toiling at the pumps, attempting to suck up the ocean through the centerboard slot. We have spoken before of the ancient story of the city slicker, taken sailing for the first time. He looked down the centerboard trunk and exclaimed in horror that the boat was filling. So they set him to pump it out. The water in the centerboard of government is human nature and no fantastics of theory will syphon it out. No imaginable plan of economy will prevent people with a sense of humor having more fun than those without it; or people of diligence earning more money. The old stenographers' abracadabra is universally true. The quick brown fox jumps over the lazy dog.

Which is not to say that one is out of sympathy with reasonable attempts to control and mortify the difficult animal man. Forget not yet, as Sir Thomas Wyatt sang, the tried intent:—

> *Forget not yet the great assays,*
> *The cruel wrong, the scornful ways,*
> *The painful patience in delays,*
> *Forget not yet.*

Notable experiments of all kinds through some thousands of years, are not forgotten. And as I think it probable (perhaps even desirable) that the present administration will be re-elected I warn them affectionately against radioing themselves out of office. The smart thing to do would be to let the Republicans have as much air as they crave. Nothing will show them up quicker.

Only one political document I have seen this winter seemed to me to have some sense of reality. It has already been praised by the astute *New Yorker.* It was the *Letter to the Electors of Oxford University,* written by Mr A. P. Herbert whose witty and humane books are well known. Mr Herbert, candidate for the House of Commons at the British election November 1935, addressed an appeal to his constituency which was straightforward, humorous, and based on the considerations that actually move men in the business of living. He was elected. I can think of no greater service anyone could do here than to reprint this bold and genial paper for the meditation of our own legislators. The problems it discusses are to some extent different from ours, but the spirit in which Mr Herbert approaches them is one that all legislatures need.

Probably the basic problem of economics, which no politician is likely to mention, is the fact that there are too many people in the world. It may be—speaking in a perfectly heartless cosmic perspective—a sound instinct that causes so many to bump themselves off in all sorts of recklessness; because evidently a good many of us are economically *de trop*. I should regard the birth-rate curves in the various nations as a state paper of high importance; and I have a hunch that if one were to read old discredited Malthus one would find in him a lot of stark sense.

But I started to escape from grievous topics; from the cheap amusement of kidding statesmen and wiseacres, most of whom are probably more conscientious than I would be in their place. I know a young Velvet Brown who found she had been gypped by some racing tout for whose horse-gambling letter she imprudently subscribed. Sir, she wrote, "I am writing you a letter of askance." The phrase is genius, even a bookie might be riven by it. But it was not my intention here to write a Letter of Askance. I began only to reproach myself for having vented a lot of dull copy that gave no idea at all of what a good time I often have. Surely the artist (of any sort) is tolerable in a world of harried people only on condition he has a good time—and communicates it. To enjoy an excitement and not tell anyone about it is a serious offense. Too often I have sat down to write in a mood of duty or drudgery. Not that I felt that way in my heart, but somehow I found myself growing self-conscious about my small pleasures, or thinking them too simple, silly, or selfish for print. I was wrong, and the package of Kellogg's bran can symbolize as aperient.

Vindica te tibi old Sir Kenelm scrawled as motto in his books. My only vindication can be truthful report of what I find thrilling; an endless curiosity, rising sometimes to almost lunatic intensity, in the small change of existence. This pellucid forenoon, while I waited impatiently for the room to grow warm enough for writing, I was almost in an ecstasy of detail. To come out here three or four mornings a week, split kindling, light fires, sweep floor, go to the hardware for kerosene, to the post office for mail, is my idea of (there is no better phrase) good clean fun. Perhaps while I am at the p. o. the faithful old 9.30 train comes in. Delightful to stand and watch it rumble away and I not aboard. The engine has a queer hunched-up look, roundshouldered with fidelity. I have commuted over twenty years on Long Island trains and know them well. When they are tardy we remind ourselves it is the railroad's Philadelphia blood. So many of the cars have little tablets on them stating that they are the property of some bank in Philly. The 9.30 A. M. is a train completely mysterious. It is too late for business men, too early for hussifs. Its passengers are, I think, those agile duplex people who run with the hare and hunt with the hounds, eat their cake and have it, and live between the millstones. Some of them, I suspect, are jurors and attorneys on their way to the county court at Mineola. That train is never uncomfortably crowded and even the conductor knows that it is a vehicle of no social prestige and is grateful to all who come aboard. He would be hurt if he saw me standing at the depot, deliberately not going. I would not for anything have him know that sometimes I play him truant and take the electric thing (a vehicle of no sensibility at all; a mere tram) from Manhasset.

Surrounded by such delights, whether in town or country, one should write for pleasure; not as a chore. I have no serious envy of those who go South for the winter, escaping the laborious charms of winter. I was remembering just now the languid gold of mornings in Hawaii, that Garden of Eden air, that dulce and tepid softness. Marvellous; but like Duke senior I look upon my winter landscape: "I would not change it." Here, as I sweep snow from the path, is Muggins the Magnificent (a Scottish terrier) snouting in each shovelful, until he wears a frosty chinbeard like a nerve specialist. To hear a child playing a harp in the next room is as good as living in a MS by Chaucer. I smile to myself as I write that, remembering a gentle young reviewer (who lives under a low ceiling of economists' catchwords) reproached me for not having "sociological contemporaneity." But Chaucer, bless his old heart, is probably less old fashioned than Karl Marx. And I am equally thrilled by the sunlight I shall see tomorrow morning where it glazes in silver fire on the edge of the Empire State Building. Caught just on the desired oblique it dazzles that rigid perpendicular with burning curves, clear out of plumb. A suggestion for dogmatists.

There's an extraordinary little paragraph at the very end of Franz Kafka's posthumous book *The Great Wall of China* (London, 1933) :—

"You do not need to leave your room. Remain sitting at your table and listen. Do not even listen, simply wait. Do not even wait, be quite still and solitary. The world will freely offer itself to you to be unmasked, it has no choice, it will roll in ecstasy at your feet."

"BARABBAS"[1]

AMONG the obscure New York hotels to which, for reasons of my own, I have sometimes made sentimental pilgrimage, is the Aberdeen on 32nd Street. It was an occasional overnight refuge for Grub Street Runners when I first had a publishing job. In those days there were a number of publishing offices on 32nd Street. I wonder if anyone else remembers a little chophouse on that street called the Blossom Heath Inn? It was almost next door to Doubleday's office at 11 West, and often—with a Pink Slip cashed by Angie Murphy (now as then Doubleday's admired exchequeress in the New York office)—promising authors were well gruntled there at lunch time. Surely the great success of Ken Roberts's fine historical novels on Doubleday's list really dates from an all-afternoon lunch at the Blossom Heath twenty years back. Dear old Guy Holt, who died a year ago, would remember those lunches. There was a brand of cigar obtainable there, called *Nabocklish;* the name sounds Gaelic, I have no notion what it means, but it became a kind of password among us; it had a sort of carefree sound and became an ejaculation suggesting "We should worry." Among the young writers who were entertained there were two who happened later to write two very different books with the same title. One, a novel now known to all the world; the other, earlier by several years, a little book of agreeable verses. Both were called *Main Street.* It was disturbing to learn, after cajoling Miss

[1]*CHRONICLES OF BARABBAS,* 1884–1934, *by George H. Doran. New York: Harcourt, Brace & Co.,* 1935. $3.50.

Murphy to O. K. the pink slip for Editorial Expense, that these two authors belonged to a rival house. Joyce Kilmer was faithful to George Doran; and Sinclair Lewis was at that moment Doran's literary scout.

But what I am leading toward are not my own small recollections but those of a much livelier fellow. I mentioned the old Aberdeen Hotel because George Doran once lived there to be handy to his office at number 15. It was from the Aberdeen that he looked down and saw his office building on fire—just after he had providentially paid a premium for $10,000 extra insurance. It was there too, I think, that the most important accident of his whole publishing career took place. It was in 1908, soon after Mr Doran had started his own business. Mrs Doran, ordered by the doctor to take a few days' complete rest, needed some books to read. Among those sent up for her by G. H. D. was Arnold Bennett's *Old Wives' Tale,* newly out in England. After a day's reading she telephoned her husband and begged him to cable for the American rights. He did so, and 1000 sheets were ordered. It is pleasant to hear that it was the enthusiastic selling of young Fred Melcher, then a clerk at Lauriat's in Boston, which exhausted the first importation and started the book moving. Not only for Bennett's own books, and the intimate friendship that ensued, but also for the succession of brilliant young writers who came to Doran at Bennett's suggestion, this was a turning point in the publisher's career.

George's book is one which will have very great interest for all who are concerned or curious about our little world of publishing. Memoirs of publishers are always exciting because there is no other career that brings a man so intimately and frequently in touch with egregious people; and on terms of immediate social freedom. George tells a delightful anecdote of sprightly little Buffy (Elizabeth) Cobb, Irvin's daughter, when the Dorans arrived as strangers to live next door to the Cobbs in a well-mortgaged Suburban-on-Hudson. "They must be nice people," said Buffy, who had been watching the new neighbors' kitchen premises; "they have such nice garbage." Even the garbage of the publishing business, if you'll condone the phrase, is attractive. Combining the charm of the arts with all the hilarity and headache of commerce, in a trade of great social influence, it is a business of compelling allure. It is overcrowded, and it breaks hearts, but those who know it would exchange for no other.

And George's book is George himself. To tell you the truth I had no idea he would be so good a writer. Except for an occasional overuse of the word "precious" or for the description of Mary Roberts Rinehart's smile I would not edit away any of his vivacious zeal. The homage to Mrs Rinehart is well-deserved—not only for their affectionate personal relation as grandparents of the same child, but because she was at that moment autographing innumerable books for customers at Marshall Field's. And George is not only a sentimentalist but also an intensely alert business man. This book, which describes 50 years of adventure in the book trade, has the same quality of infectious impulsive charm, high spirits, mixed Irish emotionalism and mischief, together with something hard and canny at bottom, which we have always relished in G. H. D. I find a parable of sadness in the book reaching us just at the time that the *Mauretania,* which George loved and travelled in so often, sails to be broken up.

And George himself was not unlike the *Mauretania*—a handsome craft on a smart schedule, making a quick turn-around and carrying important passengers.

The pleasantest phase of this excellent book is its spirit of youthfulness, its sympathy with the younger generation in publishing. There was always a touch of gallantry, swank, panache, in G. H. D. When he carried a cane he swung it and went along the street as if he were going somewhere. Young authors were fascinated by him at sight. When beautiful and powerful booksellers came to town, his handsome car was at their disposal. In his own office I rather guess he might be a pretty exacting taskmaster. I remember that poor Ivan Somerville, his manufacturing man, used to look pretty haggard sometimes. He made a very bad mistake (he admits it handsomely) in not understanding Gene Saxton who is one of the real editorial geniuses of our time. I hope all this doesn't sound like epitaph; but George speaks with such honest candor in his book that he invites his friend to talk blunt shop. On the final and fantastic error of the Doubleday merger he touches only lightly. It was an error of the first magnitude on both sides. George thought he was safeguarding the future of his young men. Doubledays' thought they were securing the remarkable literary prescience which had marked the Doran imprint. But the publishing business is (on its creative side) an intensely individualized affair. Like the theatre it revolves on hunch and temperament. It's all very well to draw up stock agreements, but personalities, diverse ambitions and methods, don't merge so easily. The long illness of Frank Doubleday, and then the era of declining business, helped to complicate matters. The union was entered into in good faith on both sides. It didn't work. In the detached perspective of the outsider its most important result was the founding of one of the ablest and most successful of younger houses, Farrar & Rinehart. I keep, as a rather pathetic souvenir, one of the special copies of Tarkington's *Claire Ambler,* bound in white bridal vellum, issued in 1928 as a consummation of the marriage. "This first volume over the new imprint," it says, "has been autographed by the author and the publishers." In 1930 George fled to the embrace of the Iron Maiden, Mr Hearst—where he became a "notable prisoner." That, by the way, is St Matthew's description of Barabbas. The line "Now Barabbas was a robber," which Lord Byron jocularly altered to "was a publisher," occurs in St John, XVIII, 40. George, as an old Bible salesman, should have checked this.

It's odd that a man who was himself a brilliant salesman says nothing in this book of his own sales boys who helped him build up so remarkable a business. It grew from $200,000 in 1908 to 2½ millions in 1927. I wish there were space to suggest the whole story, which he tells with most infectious good humor, and with many vivid little character sketches of his authors and associates. It begins in the familiar way: the ambitious boy of 14 who sees the sign SMART BOY WANTED. That was in Toronto, where G. H. D. was born of North of Ireland Presbyterians in 1869. He just escaped being christened, for his mother, George Oliver Doran, which would have given him embarrassing initials. After early experience in a Tract Depositary he joined an evangelistic publisher in Chicago, "the predatory Fleming H. Revell." Nothing in this book is more agreeable than George's deliciously ironic and yet fair-minded description of the humors (and occasional hypocrisies) of evangelical publishing. As a boy of 15 in Toronto he had met old Matthew Hodder of the famous English firm Hodder & Stoughton. Twenty years later he became the official representative of H. & S. in America, and their publications were the nucleus of his list. His description of old Hodder, and his brilliant grandson the lamented Ernest Hodder-Williams, is rich in mirth and affection. Dulac's edition of the *Rubaiyat* horrified old Mr Hodder until he learned it was earning £800 a year profit. The early connection with pietistic publishing helped to tinge the Doran list for many years, and sometimes was a source of humorous incongruity—as when G. H. D. was reproached for bringing out, almost simultaneously, Moffatt's New Testament and *The Green Hat*.

The chronicles of this very lovable Barabbas are full of good stories. His first capture outside the devotional field was Roswell Field's *Bondage of Ballinger*. He became an American citizen; heard Bryan give the Cross of Gold speech. Like all publishers he has errors of judgment to look back on. Ralph Connor was Revell's big fiction seller, but G. H. D. agreed with his employer to turn down Harold Bell Wright and also Sheldon's *In His Steps*—showing that even then our young editor had germs of admirable literary taste. His valiant attempt to find a public for Mary Webb was an example. There is refreshing candor in some of his confessions: that he never understood why all the excitement about *Revolt in the Desert;* that Marie Corelli's pique (because he did not mention her name in an interview) caused her to cancel her contract and saved him $20,000 in promised advances; that he was always incapable of appreciating really great poetry. (He is evidently at a loss to know how to comment on Elinor Wylie, the greatest poet on his list.)

I have given you no notion of the richness of anecdote and comment in this valuable book. George's lively blend of British and American temperaments makes him a unique officer of liaison between the two countries.

Similarly his paradoxical mixture of sacred and profane makes him the most enchanting of companions. Vivid and frank as his chronicle is, he has been more discreet than you might suppose. I think of many things he might have told; some of them were generous kindnesses done by him to people in trouble. He says that the book he would best like to have written is *Of Human Bondage,* which tells much of himself. Ambitious, highstrung, sensitive, sometimes a bit of a snob, a multiple soul. It is impossible to believe that he will not again have his suite at the Savoy and throw the most intelligent frolics in the publishing business. Blessings, George, from a friend and beneficiary of long standing! If some of the copies of *Barabbas* look a little worn in the shops it will be because the booksellers themselves have been reading them.

BRIEFCASE

ONCE I wrote, years ago, about Chipmunks in the Wall (or perhaps they were mice); how I listened to them frolicking behind my bookshelves; scraping, scuffling, nibbling; freaking my silence with a lace of sound. But I didn't know exactly what they'd been at until I began carrying out a lot of books to the Knothole.

Exactly behind the ten foot shelvage of my books about Shakespeare they'd been busiest. There I found a collection of dry cherrystones, each one drilled hollow with clean-bored indenture. They had taken many more bites than one. I thought kindly of their secret labors, their patient gritting edacity. It wasn't even Will himself they were after; it was their own Little Kernel Stories . . . and I thought of all the Shakespeare Scholars, gnawing away.

* * *

I noticed in a London bookseller's catalogue that a first edition of Dr Johnson's *The Prince of Abissynia* (Edmund Gosse's copy) is offered for sale at £40. The tale was not known as *Rasselas* until after Johnson's death. The only thing worth knowing that has come to me from reading many sorry dispatches from Africa is that the name Rasselas should probably be written Ras Selas; apparently Ras is an Ethiopian prefix of honor. Ras Selas evidently means something not unlike Prince Selassie.

There's a passage in *The Prince of Abissynia*

(1759) that has almost a painful timeliness. It's in the famous chapter on the art of flying:—

> "If all men were virtuous," returned the artist, "I should with great alacrity teach them all to fly. But what would be the security of the good, if the bad could at pleasure invade them from the sky? Against an army sailing through the clouds, neither walls, nor mountains, nor seas, could afford any security. A flight of northern savages might hover in the wind, and light at once, with irresistible violence, upon the capital of a fruitful region, that was rolling under them. Even this valley, the retreat of princes, the abode of happiness, might be violated."

* * *

I have often suggested Coleridge's birthday (Oct. 21) as a date to be observed. Suggestions for those disposed to any private meditations on S. T. C.:— the gorgeously humorous anecdote of Coleridge's father told by De Quincey in *Reminiscences of the Lake Poets*. The superb essay by Hazlitt, *My First Acquaintance with Poets;* describing how young Hazlitt (then aged 19) rose before daylight and walked ten miles in January mud to hear Coleridge preach. Also how he walked with Coleridge on the road toward Shrewsbury, and imagined that the pine-woods leaned over to listen to Coleridge as he trudged and talked. Later Hazlitt went over to Nether Stowey to visit, and Coleridge took him to Alfoxton where Wordsworth was living.—But I shall not recapitulate Hazlitt's account; not to have read it in youth, or reread it in caducity, is to have missed one of the purest pleasures.—Alfoxton is now a hotel; I like to wonder whether the visitor there can identify the "old room with blue hangings" where Hazlitt slept and heard the stags at dawn in the adjoining park. I should like to know exactly what it is that stags do; they "bell," don't they?—On a long day's tramp with Coleridge they passed through Dunster, "as pure and ideal," H. says, as any landscape in paintings. In honor of their expedition I keep a photo of thatched cottages in Dunster and I dare say the actual road they hiked. That same road had taken them through Watchet, the port from which the Ancient Mariner sailed.

And—speaking of roads—our secret celebration of Coleridge's birthday might well include some reading in Professor Lowes's *The Road to Xanadu*. Perhaps the formula for Ginger Beer which Professor Lowes found in Coleridge's notebook (*R. to X.* p. 22) deserves some share in the proceedings. This remarkable book (I have often intended to say) need not be considered merely as a study of Coleridge; it is of even larger interest than that; by observing the behavior of S. T. C.'s mind one learns more of one's own; and it is a grand essay in defence of desultory and unsystematic reading. You'll be interested to look up (p. 404) Professor Lowes's account of his own dream of Xanadu; and how also a day-dream was cut off by the telephone; which plays in our time the role of the Person from Porlock.

"Eager and divinely gifted spirit with piteously trailing wings," is Lowes's conclusion about S. T. C. —"the Artificer, for a few bright moments, of shapes touched with something as near magic as we mortals reach." As I went outdoors just now to look at the night I saw that the moon was full and clean; the same moon, I was pleased to think, that S. T. C. had seen over the Quantock Hills; the same light that glittered so strangely in the tearful eyes of baby Hartley. It was so bright that it even cast a shadow on the sun-dial—telling clear meridian by some quite alien reckoning. Was that not exactly Coleridge himself, I wondered: reckoning hours by moonlight on a dial marked for sun.

BROTHER-IN-INK OF THE FIRST FOLIO

There doesn't happen to be a First Folio Shakespeare around the office, so I can't compare it with the volume before me. But I reproduce the title-page of the latter because it was printed by the publisher of the First Folio, and in the same year. It is now in the collection of W. S. H.

William Jaggard, who printed *The Theater of Honour and Knighthood,* died in that same year, 1623; so that on the title-page of the First Folio his name is succeeded by that of his son Isaak Jaggard (and a partner, Ed. Blount). But "W. Jaggard" still stands in the colophon of the work as obviously the Folio had been long in the print shop, was very likely made up and put to press in sections. Sir Edmund Chambers (*William Shakespeare* I, 139) mentions a theory that work on the Folio began as far back as 1621 and was held up from time to time by other jobs that Jaggard (very reasonably) considered more urgent and profitable.[1]

[1]William Jaggard went blind about 1612; his son Isaak, then a boy of 18, began to help in the business. One is tempted to think that the printer's blindness might account for some of the oddities of the Folio. William did not live to see the publication of the book that made him immortal.

Tom Jaggard, another son, was a fellow-student of John Harvard at Emmanuel. I was interested to learn that William Jaggard's mother, after his father's death, married a man called Morley. I wish he might have been her first husband. See E. E. Willoughby: *A Printer of Shakespeare* (1935).

The pleasure of *The Theater of Honour and Knighthood* therefore is that it was unquestionably in Jaggard's composing room at the same time as the First Folio, and more than likely was printed with some of the same types and on identical paper-stock. A seventeenth century printer would scarcely have enough type on hand to set up two such large volumes entire, simultaneously? *The Theater* should be collated with a First Folio to see if some of the letters and ornaments are not common to both; and the watermarks of the paper.

A NATIVE EGGSHELL

November, 1932

A delightful lady came into the *Saturday Review* office with an old book carefully wrapped in tissue paper. It was found in a second-hand box in Atlanta (perhaps at Miller's famous bookstore?), and when Miss Catherine Miles saw the name written in it her heart leaped up.

It is a battered old copy of *A Textbook of Rhetoric* by Brainerd Kellogg, A.M., LL.D., published 1891. Inscribed in a bold young fist is *Don Marquis, Aug.* 29, 1893. In the usual schoolboy fashion the name is written several times, experimenting in various slopes and sizes; even in reversed looking-glass writing; and then, in a style slightly more mature, *D. Marquis, still alive Jan.* 20, 1899. (Bless his heart!)

Mr Marquis has told us that he left school at 15, so this must have been one of his final textbooks. (He probably parted with it when he was a newspaper man in Atlanta.) It contains the usual nota-

THE
THEATER
OF
HONOUR
AND
KNIGHT-HOOD.

OR
A Compendious Chronicle and Historie of the whole CHRISTIAN WORLD.

CONTAINING

The Originall of all Monarchies, Kingdomes, and Estates, with their Emperours, Kings, Princes, and Gouernours; Their *Beginnings, Continuance, and Successions,* to this present Time.

The First Institution of Armes, Emblazons, Kings, Heralds, and Pursuivants of Armes: With all the Ancient and Moderne Military Orders of Knight-hood in euery Kingdome. Of Duelloes or single Combates, with their Originall, Lawes, and Obseruations. Likewise of Iousts, Tourneyes, and Tournaments, and Orders belonging to them. Lastly of Funerall Pompe, for Emperours, Kings, Princes, and meaner Persons, with all the Rites and Ceremonies fitting for them.

Written in French, by ANDREW FAVINE, *Parisian:* and Aduocate in the High Court of Parliament.
M. DC. XX.

LONDON,
Printed by WILLIAM IAGGARD, dwelling in Barbican, and are there to be sold. 1623.

"BROTHER-IN-INK OF THE FIRST FOLIO"

tions *"To here"* marking assigned lessons, and casual scribbles indicating classroom conversation, such as *What did you say?* and *As I listen to the buzzing of the wheel within your head*—which sounds like the beginning of a poem, hastily broken off when the teacher came too close. Lesson 63 is specially marked; the Old Soak would be startled by this. The instruction is: "Bring in as many idioms of expression, without any taint of vulgarity upon them, as you have time to find." This is amusing in the case of a writer who has shown himself so deep and rare a master of the vulgate in its finest and richest, and also of simple moving piety.

The passages in Kellogg's *Rhetoric* that one might have expected to give Mr Marquis a premonitory prickle—Lesson 70, for instance, with its somewhat laborious analysis of Wit and Humor—show no signs of study. But on page 225 the boy Don showed a flash of his native quality. Dr Kellogg said: "The works of literature cannot be rightly read till we know under what circumstances they were written, what was the author's natural fitness for his task, and what were his limitations." This passage is severally pencilled, and in the margin speaks Young Illinois—*how damned idiotic!*

In Lesson 84, Matter for Further Study—how long a lesson 84 has proved to be for most of us—Dr Kellogg justly remarked that any attempt to eliminate the Latin element from our modern tongue and go back to Anglo-Saxon roots would be an "attempt to squeeze the full-grown fowl into its native eggshell." This amused his pupil. "Its *native* eggshell!" he writes. And as I look at this battered old *Rhetoric* from the schoolroom of Walnut, Bureau County, Illinois, I say to myself with affection and homage, a fragment of Don's native eggshell. And remind myself also, how little of literature can be learned from textbooks.

* * *

An ideal book for the library of an ocean liner is Jules Verne's *A Floating City,* a copy of which in the good old Scribner edition of our boyhood I was enchanted to find at Mr O'Malley's bookstore in New York. As many readers will vaguely remember, Verne describes an Atlantic crossing in 1867 in the famous *Great Eastern,* that grotesque paddle-wheeled leviathan with six masts and five "chimneys." Her length "exceeded 2 hectometers"; it was 680 feet—twice that of any other ship of her time. And we can learn plainly enough from Jules Verne's story that this maritime boarding-house, the marvel of her day, was unlucky, uncomfortable, and unsafe.

The chief joy of the book is in the grand old illustrations, of the *Great Eastern* herself and her passengers: whiskered men looking like mastiffs, and wearing either Scotch bonnets or straw hats with fluttering ribbons. Apparently that was before the days of deck-chairs; the ladies sat on campstools, the gentlemen in rocking chairs. There are some of Verne's favorite stock characters aboard: the American gambler, the Mormon missionary, the scientific and statistical ironist, the lady in distress; and when you see "a tall man with a look of profound duplicity" you know there's going to be trouble. There is indeed: it comes to a duel with swords on the top deck; and the villain is killed at just the right moment by a bolt of lightning.

I suppose we may assume that Jules Verne actually

visited America. His comments have the air of authentic experience, though there are odd slips here and there. Placing the "Tennessee cascades" at Rochester, N. Y., puzzles me a little—can it be Genesee? The translator makes his usual quota of errors, the sort of thing no publisher ever bothers to correct. Putting the poop at the bow of the ship is unexpected. There is some good-humored raillery at the expense of both Americans and British. But what M. Verne (if it is himself telling the story) most wished was to see the country of Fenimore Cooper. In his week's tour he stays at the Fifth Avenue Hotel, goes to the play "New York Streets" ("The Streets of New York," which, incidentally, Boucicault borrowed from a better one, "The Ragpicker of Paris"), takes the night boat to Albany and visits Niagara.

I enjoy his description of Long Island, "a great sandy bank enlivened with vegetation, covered with villas and pleasure-houses, the favorite resorts of the New Yorkists." As the *Great Eastern* nears harbor, "a group of spectators on Sandy Hook Point greeted us with a volley of hurras." And none of Jules Verne's stories about America ever omits some remarks on the New York *Herald,* which evidently made a great impression on him. You will remember that Gideon Spilett, of *The Mysterious Island,* was a *Herald* reporter. This time it was the Personals column in the *Herald* which startled him. He quotes:

"Mr X. begs the pretty Miss Z——, whom he met yesterday in Twenty-fifth Street omnibus, to come to him tomorrow, at his rooms, No. 17, St Nicholas Hotel; he wishes to speak of marriage with her."

There is much more social comment in the tales of Jules Verne than his boy readers realized.

* * *

The anonymous *Gourmet's Book of Food and Drink* (Macmillan) contains much fine manly stuff about the pleasures of the table and the bar; it is well worth adding to a selected shelf near the sideboard. What is quite unusual in a British work, it actually gives a respectable instruction for Mint Julep, without the heresy of pounding or crushing the mint—which is an abomination. The julep recipe given by "Gourmet" is that of Captain Marryat who is always supposed to have made the drink known in Britain. It is the Georgia formula, which equals cognac with peach brandy. This we do not personally approve; the blend of peach and mint flavors seems too dulcet or feminine.

It is well known among those who take juleps with due seriousness that Bourbon whiskey is the rear end, the transmission and the differential joint of the julep that travels far.

On the subject of Cheese, "Gourmet" is on firmer footing, and knows his stuff. He gives some valuable suggestions for travellers who want to sample the noble Stilton cheese in its own home. Stilton, he tells us, came originally from Melton Mowbray, but was made famous by the Bell Inn at Stilton. "The great sign of the Bell, in solid copper, still hangs from the wrought iron stays over the central door." Perhaps some travelling client who motors up the Great North Road will stop at Stilton (on his way to Peterborough Cathedral, perhaps, and after visiting the John Bunyan region at Bedford) and send us a photo.

Excellent fellow, "Gourmet" understands that the only way to eat really good Camembert is with a spoon; though he says that an artist friend of his has solved the problem by using a small trowel-shaped palette-knife.

I deplore his referring to the proud old *Mauretania* as a "boat." How many years must we wage war on this horrid error? "Boat" means small craft; lifeboats, tugboats, any sort of subaltern vessel. The *Mauretania* was a ship. To call the *Normandie* a "boat" (as we just managed to stop a radio announcer from doing the other day) would be like calling The White House a bungalow.

* * *

Speaking of the *Normandie,* F. C. H. and I were lucky enough to be aboard the *Alice M. Moran,* my favorite tugboat, when the great French liner came up New York Harbor on her second visit. No matter how many photos one has seen of her, to realize her extraordinary size and shapeliness you need to be on a small boat down close to water-level. The white V-shaped streamlined bulkhead above her focsle, intended to split wind-pressure, pleased me; it looked exactly like a snowdrift that has been carved prow-shape by a gale.

As a ship, anything of such dimensions seems to me fantastic excess; as a phenomenon she is thrilling to observe. (Will they find some way of abating the enormous quantity of smoke she exhales?) Captain Tony Huseby, master of the *Alice M. Moran,* was in charge of docking her, and had gone aboard at Quarantine. So Bill Banks was at *Alice's* wheel, and this time, instead of chasing under her stern we were promoted to the bow.

So you must imagine the picture: this enormous hull coming centrally up stream, beheld of all beholders; rather like Shakespeare arriving at a congress of English teachers. Every eye within gaze of the North River was attention. And the *Alice* far down below the steep flare of the *Normandie's* tall side. As we looked up, there was a cheerful little French boy leaning from a port, chanting to himself and evidently in proud spirits. We called to him, waving salute; but he was feeling too boyishly biggity to pay much heed to the lowly tugboat. A small spoof seemed in order. We put on (or tried to) a look of puzzled but interested curiosity, and shouted up:—

"Comment s'appelle le grand bateau?" (*Bateau* is to *vaisseau,* in French, as *boat* to *ship* in English.)

The lad was smart; he saw it was a jape, and smiled, without answering. But an excitable Frenchwoman at an adjoining port could not control herself. "Tell him, tell him," she ejaculated to the boy in rapid French, "he doesn't know the name of the ship."

Still the youngster grinned and forebore, but the lady was hooked. What, she thought—not to know the name of this magnificent vessel, this empress of longitudes, the world's hugest ship? She screeched out wildly:

"Mais c'est la Normandie, alors!"

We gazed up gratefully and took off our hats.

"Merci bien, Madame . . . voici *Alice M.*"

PRINTER IN THE SKY

I persuaded Richard Ellis, the distinguished printer of the Georgian Press, to fly with me to Buffalo where we were both due to attend the dedication of the beautiful Lockwood Memorial Library. It was Dick's first flight; he was a little apprehensive beforehand but I have never seen a man enjoy himself so much. It was an upper-case experience, he remarked. A great part of the way we skimmed above a billowy white ceiling, argentine tundras of cloud like polar wastes of snow; Dick said that even while printing some of his most de luxe books he had never so appreciated the beauty of White Space. He was specially pleased when he discovered the little ventilator gadgets. Turning one to admit a hissing jet of breeze he inhaled deeply and said "Real mountain air!"—And it was, for we were about 10,000 feet up.

Few have ever been rash enough to attempt any aesthetic description of the sensations of flying. They are not susceptible of easy testimony. My own first experience was in Hawaii; the glimpse of those islands and mountains as seen from the air was so exquisite I have never even attempted to spoil the vision with words. Also I remember the anxious eddies and vacua above some ravines and craters, where the plane dropped so sharply that I bruised my pate on the cabin roof; and a Japanese Lady, the only other passenger on that trip, who was so ill that she lay in a stupor on the floor.

Mr Ellis's novitiate was less dramatic perhaps but almost equally thrilling. From above we could see sylvestered New Jersey sprinkled with dogwood blossoms. The Delaware Water Gap, in late green and misty light, was a rugged crumple in the landscape. Then we hummed smoothly across snowy savannahs of cirrus, tumulated in soft curves and floes. (De Quincey's famous description of old Parson Coleridge's emerging shirt-tails, to which I have so often referred you in the *Reminiscences of the Lake Poets*, would be as near an account as any of that bulging wilderness of fleece.) On the far horizon sharper upwards of cloud caught the level sunshot like Alpine peaks. Sudden rifts and spreads of emptiness were blue as lakes of ice water.

Nearing Buffalo we dove down through the cloudbank and emerged into a sunset world. The green chequer of civilized earth is infinitely more orderly in pattern than the terrestrial mind supposes. Really now, with all his errors, man is a surprisingly neat animal from a distance—which is the best way of studying him. The vast general increase in sillyness, hysteria, uglification, which is so grimly apparent to anyone sitting close to a newspaper, recedes into long perspective. The Genesee River (if that was what it was) wriggles like a silver corrugation of intestines, but the little plots of man's estate are as regular as parcheesi. The sun, just falling into the slot of Lake Erie, stained the whole green billiard-cloth world with asymptotes of pink. The ends and corners of red barns glowed (thought the printer) like the initials on old vellum scripts. Admirable rubrication! Magnificent fore-edge painting! We were permeated, perlustrated, with gilded support. It shimmered on the great silver wings and fins of the big Douglas NC 14276. She was like a minnow in a golden stream. The air was so thick with sunset she seemed loth to come down. I wish they'd give those big passenger ships individual christening, because (it was Dick Ellis's suggestion, not mine) *Where the Blue Begins* would really be a grand name for a plane.

Agnes Nohava, stewardess of NC 14276, did much to make the printer's maiden flight a success. She explained everything to him, served the delicious "Complimentary meal aloft" (as the American Airlines timetable calls it) on a featherweight tray, and so won the hearts of her clients that they presented to her the actual first copy of Felix Riesenberg's new novel—appropriately called *The Left-Handed Passenger*—which they happened to have with them. Dick's ambition now is to do some actual printing in the air with a small hand-press. Why not, American Airlines?

It had been my hope that four gentlemen, all bound for the opening of the Lockwood Library, might have travelled together by plane; they were respectively a publisher, a printer, a bookseller and a writer. For, had there been a crash, it would have been so perfect an opportunity for the obituaries to isolate a pure culture of the *bacterium bibliophile.* And (it occurred to me while Dick Ellis was talking to the stewardess) to "isolate a culture" is exactly the function of a great library such as Mr Thomas B. Lockwood has given to the University of Buffalo. Not isolate in the crude sense of set apart, but to differentiate or make available. A biological culture (I read in the dictionary) is "a cultivation of micro-organisms in a prepared nutrient medium." And a prepared nutrient medium, of the most rich and comforting sort, is what Mr Lockwood has built and which his librarian, Mr Charles D. Abbott, is well fitted to cherish. The micro-organism of booklore is a more active germ than some sentimentalists suppose. Although it is one of the oldest and proudest subdivisions of the disease of thinking, it is the least snobbish: it accepts all genuine devotees on equal terms. And it is not concerned only with desiderated states, primary editions, or inlaid bindings. It must be shrewd to discern the tincture of genius even in the most unlikely format. I have small respect for the bibliophile who only raves about established excellences—such as Voltaire, let us say—and cannot recognize on the hodiernal woodpulp paper, the same spirit in Don Marquis or Westbrook Pegler. I was glad to observe that Mr Lockwood, though a Collector of the past with an upper case C, is also a spotter of merit in the humble shocker and the police romance.

I sometimes smile at myself—to forestall the grins of neighbors—when I go out to trim a bumpy piece of lawn with a pair of scissors. For, the grass plot being very imperfect, and sometimes made rank by hidden springs underground (like the grass plot of life itself), the dull old lawnmower does a very spotty job. Many leaves of grass—either too coarse or too flexible—are missed by the machine. So one takes the old office shears—the same that have compiled several volumes of essays—and has a delicious time hunting out and snipping down the grasses that still stand. Exactly such, on the lawns of literature, is the delight of the librarian and the scholar. In those realms of endless light, in the green savor of perpetual spring, he seeks the disregarded tuft that a mechanical mower did not catch. Occasionally he just sits on the grass and enjoys himself.

ESOTERICA VINIANA

Clients who have been taking up the study of wine in a humble and experimental way tell us that their chief difficulty, especially when dining with connoisseurs, is ignorance of the professional patter. This is quite true; those who esteem themselves gourmets have a jargon all their own. It is embarrassing, when given a wine your host evidently believes something rather special, not to know what to say about it. The Wine Steward of the Three Hours for Lunch Club has prepared the following list of appropriate comments which can be memorized by those who are at a loss when some knowing comment is desirable:

Of a modest Bordeaux (claret) it is ingenious to say, *A real Frenchman's claret: it makes you feel chez vous.* Or, *an amusing little wine! Does it travel?*

Of a wine you don't care for: never be so crass as to say you don't like it. Purse up the lips, gargle it round a little, corrugate the brows, cockle your nose, wait for the others to express themselves, and then ask to be allowed to smell the cork. This is always a social triumph.

Be careful about using the words *body* and *bouquet,* which anyone can learn from advertisements or catalogues. More impressive are *tone, ether, esprit;* or technical terms borrowed from other sciences—e. g., *frequency.* Of a fine cognac it is very knowledgeable to say *a very high frequency;* or, inhaling the vapors, *it throws a notable ether.* After drinking, look solemn while you count twenty, tap your chest gently with one finger, and say *a good clear echo.*

Of a genteel Barsac, *a bit virginal.* In the case of Chablis you are lost among connoisseurs unless you remember to allude to *the gun-flint savor.* Of a big riotous Burgundy—a Chambertin of a superb year, for instance—you must be wary. Play safe, using some famous French dictum such as *it opens out in the mouth like a peacock's tail.*

It is well to keep a memorandum of the Big Years of Bordeaux and Côte d'Or written out on a card in the pocket of your dinner coat. This can be consulted in the lavatory.

A useful phrase in emergencies is to ask *Is it shottled?* the insider's slang for *chateau-bottled.*

Of a medium vintage, which proves more palatable

than you expected, say *seemed a trifle shy at first, but it has temperament.*

Never commit yourself prematurely. If asked for an opinion after the first few sips, say *It has nice ankles. I'll tell you more presently.* Or, *a little languid but I daresay it has something up its sleeve.*

Don't hesitate to call for a piece of Bel Paese or Pont l'Eveque or Port de Salut, because the real enthusiast always insists that a wine has been clandestinely married to one of these cheeses.

Occasional quotations from the works of Berry, André Simon, Warner Allen and Professor Saintsbury are of crushing effect. Imply that other writers on wine are *arrivistes.*

Miscellaneous standard comments: *delightfully feminine; a bit too luscious; rather trivial, what?; a real Englishman's port; is this a good year for laying down?*

Never ask, of a cocktail, *Did this go round the Cape in a barrel?* And such remarks as *it tastes of the wood* are dangerous, they recall Prohibition days.

It is not necessary to have any technical dicta for champagne; no wine lover cares much for champagne.

A sure score is to insist that the waiter cut off *the whole* of the metal capsule on top of the bottle. The inexperienced waiter rarely does so.

THE UNMENTIONABLE

"Brilliant public rooms, concerts by fine artists, expert golf and bridge instruction, first-run talkies. . . ."

"Renowned meals and service, the luxury of spacious rooms, cheerful informality of sport and talk and gala parties. . . ."

"All outside rooms with private baths, the largest outdoor tiled swimming pool, dining room with a dome which opens to the sky, Beauty Salon and pre-release Talkies. . . ."

"All outside rooms, mechanically ventilated, celebrated service and cuisine, outdoor swimming pools, ballrooms, dance orchestras. . . ."

"Spaciousness and luxury and wonderful service, staff whose mother tongue is English. . . ."

"Smart surroundings, air-cooled dining rooms, outdoor verandah, swimming pools, consistently tempting cuisine. . . ."

"Pleasure-planned, enormous swimming pools, cocktail bars, dance-decks, richly appointed. . . ."

"Urbane ease, intriguing little shop, coiffeur, distinguished food and impeccable service, the master chef, largest and most luxurious. . . ."

These are exact quotations from the steamship advertising in one issue of a monthly magazine (*Fortune,* February 1935).

How about an occasional mention of lifeboats, safety devices, emergency discipline?

TWO SUPPRESSED HOLMES EPISODES

The number of allusions to Conan Doyle lately seems to me symptomatic of a widespread revival of interest in that admirable writer. A healthy sign, indeed; personally I confess a deliberated assurance that more intellectual vitamin, and even more sound bourgeois sociology, is to be found in Doyle than in a large number of Keyserlings and Spenglers. Good old Sir Arthur! is it not odd how poor a judge he was of his own work? He singled out as his favorites those obviously third-rate *Tales of Long Ago*, sentimental *gouache* (or do I mean goulash?) of Roman legionaries and Christian martyrs, etc. . . .

But to the point. If Mr Vincent Starrett or other Baker Street Irregulars wish the Sherlock Holmes codex to be complete they must look at two stories in which Holmes is not mentioned by name but where he is certainly present by allusion. The episodes were probably suppressed by Watson because Holmes guessed wrong both times. The stories are *The Lost Special* and *The Man With the Watches*, both mystery tales laid in railway trains; and Holmes's interest in railroad romance is of course familiar to all. In *The Lost Special*, dealing with the complete disappearance between Liverpool and Manchester of a special train on June 3, 1890, you will find Holmes referred to as "an amateur reasoner of some celebrity at that date." He wrote a letter to the London *Times* of July 3, 1890, in which the familiar Sherlockian principle was stated: "When the impossible has been eliminated the residuum, *however improbable*, must contain the truth."

In the case of *The Man With the Watches*, which "filled many columns of the daily press in the spring of the year 1892," again we learn that "a well-known criminal investigator" wrote at length to the *Daily Gazette* giving his own reconstruction of the mystery. The letter has all the internal evidences of Holmes's style, though not at his best reasoning power; but it is the more interesting because this was during the time when Holmes—supposed by Watson to be dead—was travelling in Tibet. Even at that distance this remarkable man kept in touch with outrages in

Britain. His special interest in this case was undoubtedly the fact that the persons involved were Americans. The number of American malefactors in Holmes's career has often been noted. Does not the typical Sherlockian touch appear in this remark about the unfortunate young man with the watches—"He was probably an American, and also probably a man of weak intellect."

You will find these two stories in the excellent omnibus volume *The Conan Doyle Stories* (John Murray, London, 1200 pp. for 7/6) which reprints all the doctor's short stories other than the Holmes episodes. Among the many mysteries associated with Doyle none is more odd than the enigma of no publisher having issued it here.

STUDIES ON BAKER STREET

The Speckled Band, the play about Sherlock Holmes written by Conan Doyle himself (the drama known as *Sherlock Holmes* was written by William Gillette) should be a Must item for the Baker Street Irregulars. (It is published by Samuel French, 25 West 45, and can be had for 75 cents in their paper-bound Acting Edition.) It offers many interesting speculations for the Holmesian researcher. In any imaginative reconstruction of the famous sitting room at 221 B Baker Street we must certainly take into account the diagram printed in this book showing the arrangement of the stage-setting. This was presumably plotted by Sir Arthur himself at the time of the first production (Adelphi Theatre, London, June 4, 1910). There are several surprises, notably that above the fireplace is indicated a large settee.

("6 ft. double-ended Chesterfield couch" says the Property Plot.) This is sad, for we had always liked to think of the two armchairs before the hearth, and did not Watson once say that Holmes always kept them so anticipating a visit from the Doctor? More serious still, in the long list of props and furnishings drawn up by Doyle for the sitting-room scene—with "amorous precision," we must suppose—there is no gasogene, no tantalus. And where is the work-table for chemical experiments?

Perhaps after Dr Watson left Baker Street the landlady, Mrs Hudson, became more actively supervisory in cleaning the room. I seem to detect her hand in the Property Plot where we are told that there are "four books" on the center table, "four books" on the occasional table in the window recess, and "four books bound in red" on the mantelpiece. That mechanical neatness of disposition was surely not Holmes. One of the volumes, of course, was Winwood Reade's *Martyrdom of Man*. What were the others? Clark Russell, undoubtedly; and if only it had been published in time, Dr Watson would have had Lyman Stowe's *Saints, Sinners, and Beechers*.

There is, I repeat, much material in the play of *The Speckled Band* for Mr Vincent Starrett, Mr Elmer Davis and other students. There are interesting inconsistencies between the cast of characters listed for the original production and the text of the play as printed. One character, a Mrs Soames, who had an "American stamped envelope and newspaper cutting" in the Property Plot, has vanished altogether. Who was Mrs Soames? Dr Grimesby Roylott of the story becomes Rylott in the play; his step-daughters Helen and Julia Stoner become Enid and Violet Stonor. Best of all, we observe that it was Dr

Rylott's old butler who was perhaps the first to utter a very contemporary phrase. Of the brutal doctor he ejaculates: "What a man! What a man!"

You will be excited to learn (at least I hope you will) that Dr Watson's fiancée, Miss Morstan, had red hair.

PHONETICS IN THE MIRROR

SOMEWHY I have confidence in any book about language written by a studious alien. Birthright usage of any tongue probably sets the user in habits of hearing and feeling which are congenitally limited. The most pleasing work on English which I have examined is Dr Otto Jespersen's *Essentials of English Grammar,* and Dr. Jespersen writes from Copenhagen. I wish he would tell us how he learned so much about our puzzling and faulty lingo; how did he first use it, under what instruction, and what were his impressions? Even his comments on American usages are more accurate than those of most British philologists. Has he been in this country? I always get an enormous pleasure in considering the bewildering differences of English and American speech. On Christmas Day, when representatives of various nations told us hullo by radio, an English child piped up "Merry Christmas to American boys and girls" and the enormous oddity, in my ear, of just that way of saying "boys and girls"—irreproducible in print—was enough to keep me grinning for the rest of the afternoon. And then, by chance, we went to an Edgar Wallace picture that same evening—something so terrible that it was enchanting—and heard more of that phonetic queerness. In a function so intimate as speech, variations are a chief source of human delight. In a bookshop on 47th Street there's a bookseller from North Carolina. . . .

But what I had in mind was, the publisher of Dr

Jespersen's book really ought to give away a small mirror with each copy. I had to take it home from the office, for I couldn't keep going out to the washroom to verify the phonetic passages. "In our rapid survey of the organs of speech," says Dr Jespersen, "we begin with the lips, because they are most easily accessible to immediate inspection, and then move gradually inwards." Thus it is that the washroom mirror becomes necessary:—

> By means of the tip of the tongue are formed first the three stops [t, d, n], then three fricatives as in *thin, then,* against the front teeth, and [r] against the gums, often with a distinctly "flapping" movement. . . . With the blade of the tongue (immediately behind the tip) are formed the two hissing fricatives [s, z] as in *seal, zeal,* characterized by a chink in the tongue through which a very thin stream of air passes. If the air-channel is made a trifle broader, and the tip of the tongue is turned a little farther back, we get the sounds as in *she, mission, vision.*
>
> The *soft palate* is movable, and is either raised so as to shut off the mouth from the cavity of the nose—then we have purely *oral* sounds—or else it may be lowered, in that case we have *nasal* sounds. . . . If the vocal chords (in the larynx, popularly called "Adam's apple") are brought together and made to vibrate, the result is a *voiced* sound. . . .
>
> Originally *r* was a full point-trill everywhere. In order to pronounce this trill the tip of the tongue is made thin and elastic, and then raised and made to move rapidly to and fro . . . the bulk of the tongue-muscle must be shifted backwards, sometimes accompanied with secondary trillings of the uvula. . . . *R* is now not trilled except in out-of-the-way parts of Scotland.

I was wondering what our old friend Captain Bone, a keen student of philology, would say about this, and practising a "secondary trilling of the uvula" with some success, when someone else came in to wash his hands. I pretended to be admiring the mass of the RCA building, which is very beautiful from our washroom in the dusk.

Dr Jespersen says in his preface, with excellent wisdom, "It has been my endeavor to represent English Grammar not as a set of stiff dogmatic precepts, according to which some things are correct and others absolutely wrong, but as something living and developing under continual fluctuations and undulations." And speaking of the continual necessity for condensation, he remarks:—

> Not only is the writer's art rightly said to consist largely in knowing what to leave in the inkstand, but in the most everyday remarks we suppress a great many things which it would be pedantic to say expressly. "Two third returns, Brighton," stands for something like: "Would you please sell me two third-class tickets from London to Brighton and back again, and I will pay you the usual fare for such tickets."

And as the Doctor says that, somehow there appears to me in a vision the long hall of the Gare de Lyon in Paris and myself inwardly formulating what I hoped would be an idiomatic request for the transportation I needed.—And as any variation from the expected may always be a source of humor, it is sometimes best for the foreigner (unless the train is leaving immediately) to expound his desires as best he can with complete and pedantic fullness. It often puts the ticket seller in an agreeable cackle, especially if you can do a secondary trill on the uvula.

A casual note such as this can give you no fair idea of the richness and interest of Dr Jespersen's treatise. He eases me (somewhat) of one old anxiety, a feeling that the expression *all of* a thing (which we all continually use) is indefensible. My notion was that *of* is necessarily a partitive, and therefore that one cannot have all *of* a thing. But he states conclusively that *of* is not always partitive but sometimes appositional, as for instance in *the City of Rome* (= the City which is Rome) or *that little wretch of a Rebecca* (= that little wretch who is Rebecca).

Dr Jespersen is interesting on such familiar anomalies as the cases of pronouns. "The natural tendency in English," he says, "has been towards a state in which the nominative of pronouns is used only where it is clearly the subject, and where this is shown by close proximity to a verb, while the objective is used everywhere else." He gives interesting examples—some of which cause pain:—

> "Oh!" she instantly replied, "*he* began it, not *me*."
> [Strachey: *Queen Victoria*]
>
> We've had our little differences, you and me.
> [Arnold Bennett]
>
> Another fellow, probably him who had remained below, came to the door.
> [R. L. Stevenson]

But the most interesting of these examples are the familiar exclamation "Dear me!" and such a sentence as "He saw it himself."

The same influence has been at work, Jespersen notes, in the interrogative pronoun *who;* but with opposite effect. Since the interrogative comes first, and usually followed closely by the verb, it has been generalized in the nominative case. "*Who* is now practically the only form used in colloquial speech," Jespersen says, and this has been so for at least three centuries. E.g., Shakespeare:—

> *Who didst thou leave to tend his Majesty?*
> *Pray you, who does the wolfe love?*

It would be pedantic, says our authority, to insist on "From whom is that letter" rather than the colloquial "Who is that letter from?" But he adds that grammarians have been so severe in blaming this anomaly "that now many people feel proud when they remember writing *whom* and even try to use that form in speech." In the matter of relative pronouns, *who* also tends to displace *whom*. He quotes a sentence from E. F. Benson:—"I met a man whom I thought was a lunatic," without stating pointedly whether he considers it wrong. To me, the error here is in misplacing the *was*. It should be either:—I met a man who was, I thought, a lunatic—or, I met a man whom I thought [to be] a lunatic.

But so are all of us [we all] if we brood too long on English grammar.

USAGE, U. S. A.[1]

IT IS GOOD to be reminded, and by so expert a student as Mr Horwill, of the almost innumerable divergences of meaning and usage between American English and English English. How few there are who can really talk both languages. Even Mr Horwill himself, who secretes a number of pleasant little anecdotes here and there in his dictionary, blundered occasionally. He tells us that in a hotel in Philadelphia he asked if this was the desk of the hotel clerk. No, said the young man, "This is the Hotel Lafayette." They had supposed him to be asking if this was the Hotel Clark.

Mr Horwill has come pretty close (an Americanism which he doesn't mention; the frequent use of *pretty* to mean *fairly* or *rather*) to breaking a good old tradition; that of the Englishman's inability to get the hang of the American language. I was looking forward to finding some grand howlers in this book, and I honorably confess my disappointment. I think that Mr Horwill sometimes generalizes a bit too hastily on the basis of casual examples or individual idiosyncrasies. And he has neglected some very savory and valuable examples of our current argot. But this is not a dictionary of American slang. It is a systematic and intelligent study, continued through the past thiry years, of the more important

[1]*A DICTIONARY OF MODERN AMERICAN USAGE.* By *H. W. Horwill. New York: Oxford University Press.* 1935. 360 pp. $3.25.

diversities in the two languages. There are innumerable stories of embarrassments incurred by travelers on both sides who have innocently said something that meant something quite different to the hearer. Mr Horwill's warning to the Englishman about the phrase *knocked up* is a fair example.

It would take more time, more thought, and more remembering than are available at this moment, fairly to analyze this valuable and entertaining book. I will simply set down some of the notions that occurred to me while going through it, in the hope of invoking other more accomplished amateurs of philology. The more one thinks about the subtle sea-change the English language has undergone in this country, the more one realizes that the differences are not mere chance but a happy illustration of temperamental discrepancy. Mr Horwill is shrewd enough to have noticed (what we ourselves do not always realize) that the American is a slower speaker than the Briton. Though slower speakers we tend to be more slovenly in syntax; which has its large advantages too. I don't always agree with Mr Horwill's findings: when he says, for instance, that "even educated writers and speakers" in the States treat *data* as a singular. The fact that Mr Haskin, Professor McCarthy and Colonel House so use it does not disprove (or surprise) me. There is more stark unconsciousness of grammar in this country than in any other; if some newspapers spell *carousal* when they mean *carrousel* that does not make it accepted American usage. They simply don't know any better. Mr Horwill says that the distinction between *lay* and *lie* "is not strictly observed in America." But that is true everywhere of beginners in the language. There are some grand examples in Joseph Conrad. See the story

Amy Foster: "He crept into one of these boxes and laid down there." In despair at the frequency of this solecism I once wrote a verse:—

> Lie *and* lay *offer slips to the pen*
> *That have bothered most excellent men:*
> *You may say that you lay*
> *In bed, yesterday;*
> *If you do it today, you're a hen.*

Set and *sit* are just as bad; I have on my desk a handsome colored postcard of the Capitol in Washington on which the printed legend begins: "The Capitol . . . one of the stateliest buildings in the world . . . sets on a height." But ignorance is terrestrial, ecumenical and always sublimely pleasing; it need not be nationalized. Mr Horwill is too gentle with the universal Americanism *all of* a thing; we all use it; but it is wrong. If *of* is a partitive then *all* annuls its meaning. When President T. R. wrote "All *of* the nations of the world" he was mistaken. So were Thomas Bailey Aldrich and Professor G. L. Kittredge, also quoted.

I guess that though Mr Horwill spent several years in this country, as a newspaper man, his acquaintance with American colloquialisms is more through the printed word than in actual hearing. This must account for several slips. I cannot believe that "the department of the municipality that is responsible for the care of the streets is commonly known as a *street-cleansing department.*" Nor is it a *trainsman* on the railroads. He quotes the phrase *fixing to* (which is Southern) as meaning *attempting* to. It is more likely to mean getting ready to. *Allow* ("he allowed that, while he wasn't a doctor, he had had to cover up a good many of the doctor's mistakes," etc.)

doesn't quite mean *assert* or *declare,* but something more like *admit.* I think the phrase is more often *keep tabs on* than *keep tab on.* He says that the word *handscrub* is used alternatively for *nailbrush,* which startles me; and that *slumber-robe* (which I have never encountered) is the equivalent of bathrobe. There is always a danger in accepting as general the weird or nifty coinages of the department store advertising. Which reminds me that he mentions our verb *to merchandise* with the comment that in England it is a noun only. But it was a good Shakespearean verb . . . see Sonnet 102. The retention of antique English usages that have since become obsolete in Britain is admittedly one of the pleasures of the American language.

Mr Horwill mentions so many savory Americanisms I'm sorry he doesn't go a little farther and include several others that are rapidly becoming familiar on the other side. To kick in, to pass the buck, get the breaks, it's an act, to kid, to rib, the pay-off, to belong (in the sense of being in the know, regular, one of the right people, etc.) are examples of phrases that might be included in the next edition.

He mentions many little oddities of our double usage. For instance the puzzlement of English readers when Edith Wharton mentioned a *dinner-pail.* The American passion for the preposition *on*—"sale *on* men's suspenders." The fact that in England they usually put the word River first: The River Thames, whereas we say the Hudson River. Our odd use of the word *shape*—"the banks are in better shape." Our continuance of the Shakespearean *deck* of cards, which has vanished in England. Our horrible phrase "in the neighborhood of" when we simply mean "about" ("in the neighborhood of $200,000").

Surely he is wrong when he says that the American sailboat is the equivalent of the English sailing vessel? A sailboat is only a small pleasure craft; a sailing vessel may be a full rigged ship. He mentions *bromide*, but not *Babbitt*. The use of Gentile as meaning non-Mormon is not general but mostly local to Utah. The word *brook* (small stream) which Professor George Herbert Palmer thought was "the most regrettable loss the English language has suffered in America," has not vanished as much as he supposed. The word *branch*, also for a small stream, is I think mostly Southern. And by the way I hope our author will refrain from giving any credence to Yankees who tell him that the phrase you-all is ever used in the vocative singular. It *always* implies the plural.

Anyone could find variant opinion or inadvertencies in a book of this scope on so fluid a topic. Mr Horwill deserves hearty congratulation on one of the very few successful essays on the American argot ever written by a foreigner. The fact that he realizes —as so few Englishmen ever do—that it is actually possible for a Briton to be a foreigner, is the reason for his success.

If I were going to England for the first time, or coming here ditto, I would jot down and carry in my pocket a paradigm of equivalent terms just for the fun of hearing them used. Mr Horwill reminds us of many of them and gives me all the fun of going —"abroad." For instance:—

U. S. A.	ENGLAND
derby	bowler
The Dipper	The Great Bear
druggist	chemist

U. S. A.	ENGLAND
elevator	lift
fender (car)	wing
floorwalker	shopwalker
freight train	goods train
grade crossing	level crossing
long distance call	trunk call
baggage	luggage
check room	left luggage office
mail	post
mucilage	gum
sick	ill
suspenders	braces
truck	lorry
radio	wireless
vest	waistcoat
undershirt	vest
shoe	boot
custom tailor	bespoke tailor
can	tin
candy	sweets
checkers	draughts
cane	stick
chicken	fowl
sidewalk	pavement
pitcher	jug
bathrobe	dressing gown
bug	insect
ticket agent	booking clerk
cracker	biscuit
fall	autumn
composition book	exercise book
clipping bureau	press cutting agency

But just writing them down isn't nearly as much fun as hearing them said—in that indescriptibly and chirpingly odd way that the English have of using their own language. It always seems to me sad that they can never know how deliciously amusing it sounds.

And I dare say they have fun too, over here. Mr Horwill describes the perplexity of the visitor whose first New York headline told him that some eminent politician had just Bolted His Ticket.

The perfect motto for this book would be that grand old saying of Montaigne: "I reject nothing which is current on the streets—for the man who would correct usage by grammar is a simpleton."

SOME THIN PAPER

ONE DAY in February 1819, Keats wrote one of his journal-letters to George and Georgiana Keats. It appeared that there was nothing very remarkable to report. He had been indoors with a sore throat. He had been visiting some friends. "Nothing worth speaking of happened. . . . I took down some thin paper and wrote on it a little poem called St Agnes's Eve."

It is not to be forgotten that with all his delicacy of emotional perception Keats was also a master of simple understatement. When, a year before his death, he suffered the hæmorrhage which he suspected was the beginning of the end, his only comment was, "This is unfortunate."

The Keats of legend, long abandoned by all genuine readers, was always refuted by the Letters. Perhaps all easy typifications are false. The modern Advertising Man is also falsified by legend. Mr Earle Weller, for instance, a busy expert in space and copy in San Francisco, has for years spent his off hours studying Keats. He has now published his remarkable *Autobiography of John Keats* (Stanford University Press). Basing his work on the final edition of Keats's Letters as collected by Maurice Forman, by a little tactful editing, omission of salutations and valedictions, a few transpositions of names and pronouns, he has put the letters and prose fragments of the poet together so that they become a continuous narrative. Though we may have been familiar with this material for years, it gains extraordinary power and cumulating intensity when read thus, as a story. Mr Weller prefaces Keats's own narrative with the famous account of the schoolboy days written by Charles Cowden Clarke (first published over here in the *Atlantic Monthly* in 1861). He concludes with Severn's terrible description of the Last Days in Rome.

Keats's Letters, as manly and moving a transcript of human character as our literature affords, justify all those who have groaned in secret at the inescapable horrors of writing for public print. If I could write it as for a private friend (one has so often thought) what freedom, what joy! No fit person should ever be allowed to grow old without having read Keats's Letters. They show, perhaps, not that poets (a word that has grown to have uncomfortable overtones) are different from other men, but that all men are to some extent poets. Keats at a prize-fight, a card-game, a dance, a music party, at the theatre, or drinking a little too much wine, is someone we can understand. Perhaps literature is never so great as when it seems to be what all have thought but not bothered to put down. Do we not love him better for a sparkle of young candor? "I did not feel very sorry at the idea of the women being a little profligate." He was sometimes alarmed at his own "horrid morbidity of temperament" (as I dare say most of us have been) but his sense of comedy was equally keen. Of the all too human perfume of a crowded gallery at the play, he remarked "though it was but a shilling still you had to pay through the nose."

I think nothing could have pleased Keats more than the fact that a hundred years and more after his death the youngest generation would be getting from his work their first great thrill in poetry. Perhaps no poet has done more to implant the germinal ecstasy in others. At any rate that was so in my own epoch, and I think it is still true. But Keats known only in his poems is not the whole Keats. We need to know the boy who was invited to a party to celebrate Shakespeare's birthday and said, "Shakespeare would stare to see me there!" When he went on a walking trip in Scotland he was thrilled by the Highland fling. He admired the boys and girls at their capers: "Some beautiful faces and one exquisite mouth. I never felt so near the glory of patriotism, the glory of making by any means a country happier. This is what I like better than scenery."

One of the treasures of Mr Weller's book is a miniature of Keats never published before. It was painted by Charles Hayter who was "esteemed for the correctness of his likenesses." Mr Weller tells us that the little painting (on ivory, in a gold frame; with a lock of Keats's hair in the back) was probably once owned by Leigh Hunt, and was "hidden for scores of years in a small art and antique shop in London." The frontispiece of the book shows its clear and delicate coloring. But all the portraits of Keats are too ethereal for my private taste. He was not just something graciously tinted on ivory. With all his fine sensitive intuition he was much more than a complex of emotional responses. There was a clear sardonic intelligence also; a sombre and acute observation. He knew there were many things more important than scenery. I wish there were a photograph to show the lines on his face. The man who disliked "the favour of the public" and lamented that the life of Jesus had been transmitted "by men interested in the pious frauds of religion" had learned very early to think for himself. "I have that in me which will bear the buffets of the world."

The Letters, no matter how long known and loved, gain new impact from this method of putting them together. They cannot be read without the most profound twinges, but they might make better men of us. They isolate the bacillus of poetry and show us what it looks like. They show the intense and furious grasp of actuality, of the details of Now, which is one symptom of the disease.

> The candles are burnt down and I am using the wax taper —which has a long snuff on it—the fire is at its last click— I am sitting with my back to it with one foot rather askew upon the rug and the other with the heel a little elevated from the carpet—I am writing this on the *Maid's Tragedy,* which I have read since tea with great pleasure. . . . It would be a great delight to know in what position Shakespeare sat when he began "To be or not to be"—such things become interesting from distance of time or place.

A casual salute he paid to a fellow-singer lingers in my mind. It was at the beginning of the last illness, when already he suspected that his dream of happiness was not to be fulfilled. "That thrush is a fine fellow. I hope he was fortunate in his choice this year."

"THE DISTINGUISHED THING"

THERE are many pleasures waiting for the reader of Edith Wharton's volume of reminiscences, *A Backward Glance*. I was prejudiced in favor of Mrs Wharton's delightful book from the very start, for I noticed that in her brief preface she quoted Madame Swetchine, an admirable writer of whom one rarely hears. I encountered Mme Swetchine's *Letters* years ago, doing some college reading in the history of the French Republic of '48, and I always experience a special pleasure in meeting anyone who has even heard of her. She (I refer still to Mme Swetchine) is one of those felicitously unfamous writers who have been divinely shielded from being read by the wrong people.—Incidentally Mrs Wharton's parents, during a trip to Europe in their early married days, saw the flight of old Louis Philippe across the Tuileries gardens.

And Edith Wharton herself—how easily she might never have been a writer at all. She was reared under handicap, as a member of the dress circle of New York's provincial and complacent little bourgeoisie sixty years ago. I had always been a trifle alarmed by repeated allusions in print to Mrs Wharton's background of social azure, so it was a relief to learn that it was nothing more serious than the Rhinelanders and Joneses (of West 23rd Street and Hell Gate). For one has never been able to be wholly solemn about the tradition of New York "society" unless by that term you mean such people as Irving, Bryant, Whitman, Melville, Poe. And, as Mrs

Wharton points out with most urbane humor, bohemians like those were scarcely recognized in the fashionable world of her youth. The worthies of that time, who were proud of not being in retail trade, all had "libraries" of calf-bound books regarded as "standard," but would be painfully agitated if called upon to meet an actual author. This, Mrs Wharton very shrewdly suggests, was not from any sense of snobbish superiority, but rather a genuine shyness or embarrassment—"an awe-struck dread of the intellectual effort that might be required." And what has been so much and so foolishly hallooed as New York "society" was probably only a swath of kind, simple, innocent and rather self-indulgent people; intensely timid and conventional at heart. If one pauses to reflect upon the dullness, architectural misery, parochial naïveté and self-satisfaction of New York in the 70's and 80's one must realize that our bewildering and pinnacled uncertainty of today has its merits.

I didn't mean to get into argument; merely to say that Mrs Wharton, with extraordinary patience and courage, overcame the most serious obstacles; obstacles perhaps more deadening to the soul than poverty or mean birth. The happy accident of living abroad several years as a child gave her a valuable disgust for the banality of New York's architecture; the somewhat prudish Anglophilia of her parents implanted a sensitive gust for English undefiled. In the American children's books of the day, her mother said, the children spoke bad English *without the author's knowing it.* (Which was perfectly true; it is not until much later that one learns bad English has its uses too.)

I can scarcely imagine the youngest generation,

hotfoot upon its own desperations, taking time to read Mrs Wharton's very wise and moving book; yet it might start some interesting thoughts if they did. Among many charming things her glimpses of Henry James are particularly interesting. We see Mrs Wharton as a young person, putting on a new hat and a pretty dress to meet the great Henry, but so appalled by her shyness that she could not speak —and the new hat was not even noticed. We see James suffering grotesquely from a heat wave in Lenox and finding his only relief in constant motoring: how one would have loved to see that party pausing in roadside shade to read Swinburne aloud while Mr James perspired. We hear James talking about "the Emmetry" (so he called "his vast and labyrinthine cousinship") and in lengthy soliloquy bringing them alive to a group of hearers on a summer evening. "They glimmered at us," Mrs Wharton says, "through a series of disconnected ejaculations, epithets, allusions, parenthetical rectifications and restatements . . . and then, suddenly, by some miracle of shifted lights and accumulated strokes, there they stood before us, sharp as an Ingres, dense as a Rembrandt."—Or James at Lamb House in Rye, welcoming his visitors at the front door; James's firm and risible belief that he knew best how to direct the chauffeur to find the destination yet always missing the way—and only succeeding to confuse the yokel whom he asked for direction. This is surely of excellent symbolic purport. James, under the stroke that killed him, in the very act of falling hearing a voice that seemed to say, "So here it is at last, the distinguished thing." Always terrified of death (and of much of living too) yet he could meet it with his own absolute word. There is a very distinguished thing to be found and honored in Mrs Wharton's book, I hope many will discover it.

Her descriptions of James's conversation—and humor—are exquisitely happy. Peter Dunne, she tells us, was perturbed by the Jacobite circumlocutions, and felt like saying "Just spit it right up in Poppa's hand," but—

> to James's intimates these elaborate hesitancies, far from being an obstacle, were like a cobweb bridge flung from his mind to theirs, an invisible passage over which one knew that silver-footed ironies, veiled jokes, tiptoed malices, were stealing to explode a huge laugh at one's feet. This moment of suspense, in which there was time to watch the forces of malice and merriment assembling over the mobile landscape of his face, was perhaps the rarest of all in the unique experience of a talk with Henry James.

And surely I shall long remember her description of James sitting by the moat at Bodiam Castle, watching the reflection of the towers and the hovering dragonflies. "For a long time no one spoke; then James turned to me and said solemnly: 'Summer afternoon—summer afternoon; to me those have always been the two most beautiful words in the English language.' "

NOTES ON WALT

THE annual memorandum about Walt Whitman never came more pleasantly apropos than on this warm morning, looking off into the glades of his own Paumanok. The air, sun-heavy and tree-sweet, is garbled with bird cries. (When a catbird takes up his squawk the thrushes desist their twisted rippling.) Across the open windows wings pass in flight, sudden as thought and alighting as unexpectedly.

If you have read Walt long and patiently, he smokes in the bowl of the mind as savory as an old briar pipe. He has made himself so much our own, by innumerable confidences, that even his *gaffes* are part of the fun. One makes the affectionate semi-humorous allowance that one does for any household eccentric. In *Democratic Vistas* one sees him struggling to express his thought in the same mild but determinate persistence that he wrestled with the hickory sapling by Timber Creek (see *Specimen Days,* Sept. 5, 1877). Though much of the *Vistas* was oddly and lamely said, yet how well worth saying. It always interests me to remember that while he was grieving himself (in the *Vistas* about 1870, in the '72 and '76 prefaces) whether America would ever show any real poetry, Emily Dickinson in Amherst was quietly writing it. He worried himself much because Tennyson's poems kept on referring to knights, lords, chivalry and courtly matters; yet his own poetry was not necessarily "democratic" because he mentioned so many artisans and trottoirs.

I wish we might have had Walt's opinion of Emily

Dickinson's poems—none of which were published until soon before his death. I wonder if he could have grasped their quality?

And just as he was at his saddest complaint about our sterility ("America has yet morally and artistically originated nothing," he wrote in *Vistas*) some of the "autochthonous" literature he craved was getting ready for him. At the very moment when he called for "two or three really original American poets (perhaps artists or lecturers) to mount the horizon like planets . . . they would give more compaction and more moral identity to these States than all its Constitutions"—at that very moment Bret Harte and Mark Twain were publishing, Uncle Remus was starting in Atlanta, and Will Porter was going from kilts to trousers. *Moby Dick,* which had been published before *Leaves of Grass,* Walt does not seem to have noticed at all, though one would have thought its huge symbolism much to his taste.

Those who may have thought Whitman only the indiscriminating ballyhooer of American bigness will find plenty of surprises in *Democratic Vistas.* Those meditations, put together during the years soon after the Civil War (and his own dismissal from a government clerkship for having published immoral poems) were in gloomy mood. "Society in these States," he wrote, "is canker'd, crude, superstitious and rotten. The moral conscience, the verteber to State and man seems entirely lacking . . . our New World democracy is, so far, an almost complete failure in its social aspects." No escaped journalist ever turned more savagely on his old profession. "Our current copious fields of print covering the United States as in certain regions of the sea those spreading, undulating masses of squid, through which the whale swimming, with head half out, feeds." And though he admits that he watches with fascination "the proud, crashing, ten-cylinder presses," the bulk of their product is trivial—"to amuse, to titillate, to pass away time. . . . Conversation is a mass of badinage. . . . Everywhere are pervading flippancy and vulgarity—everywhere the youth puny, impudent, foppish, prematurely ripe—everywhere an abnormal libidinousness, unhealthy forms, muddy complexions, the capacity for good motherhood deceasing or deceas'd, shallow notions of beauty, with a range of manners probably the meanest to be seen in the world."

These sour comments may well have annoyed—or amused—the upper crust of 1870; for what indeed, they probably retorted, did Walt know of the higher levels of breeding and manners? But his cry for a nobler race cannot be read without genuine emotion. He speaks of the "little ships" of the spirit that have come down miraculously over oceans of time and loss—"Some of these tiny ships we call Old and New Testament, Homer, Eschylus, Plato, Juvenal, &c. Precious minims! Dante, Angelo, rich Shakespeare, and such as German Kant and Hegel. . . . Ye powerful and resplendent ones! On your plane, and no less, must we mete and measure for today and here. I demand races of orbic bards, with unconditional uncompromising sway. Come forth, sweet democratic despots of the west!"

How to "break up the limitless fallows of humankind," to supply "a copious race of superb American men and women, cheerful, religious, ahead of any yet known," and how to get the desirable native philosophs and literatuses, is his earnest inquiry. He confesses himself perplexed, as he well may, but believes that somehow, through the interplay of mass-democracy with revitalized individualism, and through more generous religion, and through the emancipation of Woman, it can possibly be done. He is not much more specific than any political speechmaker, but he has a great hankering for a mysterious quality that he calls *aplomb*. As for the females of 1870, they were evidently in parlous case. We need a new literature, he thought, "to achieve the redemption of woman out of webs of silliness, millinery, and every kind of dyspeptic depletion, and thus insuring to the States a strong and sweet Female Race." And though one may smile at some of the extravagances of his litany, his prophecies of a more generous womanhood are among the clearest foresights of *Democratic Vistas*. I have always supposed that he felt the more free to deplore the stereotyped women of his time because his happiness in New Orleans had been with one of very different temperament, a creole.

But anyhow Walt never minded being smiled at. When he and Peter Doyle sat on Washington doorsteps, eating watermelon, more conventional passers-by often stared. "Never mind, Pete," he used to say, "they have the laugh but we have the melon."

There are many notes in *Specimen Days* which reveal Whitman's acuteness of observation. He speaks of a soldier he met one evening in Washington; they walked along the street together. "He was small and not very young, and a tough little fellow, as I judged in the evening light, catching glimpses by the lamps we passed." He tells how he could sit for hours at his lodging-house window studying every detail of the cavalry camp in the vacant lot opposite. There is even a touch of humor occasionally, as when the rumor was that the Union forces would have to retreat from Culpepper. "But I cast my eyes at the mud, which was then at its deepest and palmiest condition, and retired composedly to rest."

When, after the paralytic stroke, he fought for health in the woods at Timber Creek, the dark mood of *Democratic Vistas* left him. Now he had his feet on the elemental "Personalism" which had been, before, something to write about. The jotted descriptions of trees, sky, birds, and his own sense of rapport with earth, are as good outdoor reading as one ever finds. We see him hobbling about the grove, bathing in his marl-pit, moving his campchair from shade to sunlight, walking the open fields like an old Socrates, sitting on a stump to jot his notes, brooding among the clumps of mullein. In these surroundings, not tormenting his mind to plan the future of American destiny, he reached deep and sure into peace. How delightful when he confesses, in a sudden loneliness, that he is not quite sure whether he is happy or not—"so let me give myself the benefit of the doubt." And then, under that sky of bright October, he says one of his great things: "Hast Thou, pellucid, in Thy azure depths, medicine for case like mine?"

There is simple pathos in his particularity about the little gifts which were all he could bring to the wounded men in the hospitals. He describes them: the stamped envelopes, the petty cash (which he raised from contributors up North), the horehound candy, oranges, tobacco, horseradish, blackberry syrup, tea. He reads the Bible to the men and expounds doctrine ("I think I see my friends smiling at this confession, but I was never more in earnest in my life"). He plays with them "an amusing game called Twenty Questions," and writes their letters.

And not least significant is his note: "My habit was to prepare for starting out on one of those daily or nightly tours, by fortifying myself with previous rest, the bath, clean clothes, a good meal, and as cheerful an appearance as possible."

To those who are willing to read him with patience he comes again as he did to the wounded in the hospitals of the war. Among the fevers, confusions and despairs of modern living he comes not only with his horseradish, horehound and tobacco, but with the greater gift of his enormous manliness, his sanity and hope. He has "a horror of ceaseless talkers or smart people, and of being questioned." (A line he himself wrote into Dr Bucke's biography.) But when we get to know him we don't ask him too many questions. We enjoy him as he is; and often find that he has medicine for case like ours.

One of Walt's characteristics—perhaps a valuable one to any writer as long as it remains innocently unconscious—was his naif superlativism, his assured certainty that what happened to him or was seen by him was the greatest, most important, most significant anywhere. The actors and singers at the old Park and Bowery theatres were "as mighty mimes as ever trod the stage." The two old ladies he saw in Washington handing out bread and coffee to the troops retreating from Bull Run were "the first in the city for culture and charm." An American crowd "has the finest voices in the world." The mountains of Colorado "emanate a beauty, terror, power, more than Dante or Angelo ever knew." [All he means, really, is "than Walt ever knew."] The train that took him across the Plains had "a first-class locomotive." Pfaff, the old Broadway restaurateur, was "the best selecter of champagne in America." Then when he saw the cliffs of the Saguenay, the Rockies dropped out of sight. Of Capes Eternity and Trinity, "I doubt if any crack points, or hills, or historic places of note, or anything of the kind elsewhere in the world, outvies these objects."

It's great fun to go through *Specimen Days* ticking off these harmless hyperboles. Walt, after all, was not a far traveler. Once down the Mississippi to New Orleans, once out to the Rockies, once up to Ontario and Quebec, were his longest ranges. He reported geography from a Long Island or New Jersey point of view. And how much more meat we find in his descriptions of Timber Creek (near Camden) than in his most bravura passages about distant scenes.